The New Brazilian Mediascape

Reframing Media, Technology, and Culture in Latin/o America

THE NEW BRAZILIAN MEDIASCAPE

Television Production in the Digital Streaming Age

Eli Lee Carter

Héctor Fernández L'Hoeste and Juan Carlos Rodríguez,
Series Editors

University of Florida Press
Gainesville

Copyright 2020 by Eli Lee Carter
All rights reserved
Published in the United States of America

First cloth printing, 2020
First paperback printing, 2025

30 29 28 27 26 25   6 5 4 3 2 1

Library of Congress Cataloging-in-Publication Data
Names: Carter, Eli Lee, author.
Title: The new Brazilian mediascape : television production in the digital streaming age / Eli Lee Carter.
Description: Gainesville : University of Florida Press, 2020. | Series: Reframing media, technology, and culture in Latin/o America | Includes bibliographical references and index.
Identifiers: LCCN 2020001892 (print) | LCCN 2020001893 (ebook) | ISBN 9781683401834 (hardback) | ISBN 9781683402800 (pdf) | ISBN 9781683404613 (pbk.)
Subjects: LCSH: Television broadcasting—Brazil. | Digital television—Social aspects—Brazil. | Streaming video—Social aspects—Brazil.
Classification: LCC HE8700.9.B7 C37 2020 (print) | LCC HE8700.9.B7 (ebook) | DDC 384.550981—dc23
LC record available at https://lccn.loc.gov/2020001892
LC ebook record available at https://lccn.loc.gov/2020001893

| UF PRESS
UNIVERSITY
OF FLORIDA

University of Florida Press
2046 NE Waldo Road
Suite 2100
Gainesville, FL 32609
http://upress.ufl.edu

To Marge, Don, and Peg

Contents

List of Figures ix
Acknowledgments xi
Introduction: Brazil Reframed 1
1. The Pay-TV Law and the New Brazilian Mediascape 16
2. Pay-Television Welcomes Brazil 42
3. The New Frontier: Internet Fiction 66
4. Entering Television through the *Porta dos Fundos* 91
5. Blackness in the Post-2011 Mediascape 113
6. Globo *Plays* Series 137
   Conclusion 161
   Notes 167
   References 185
   Index 201

Figures

0.1. Average number of yearly hours produced of *telenovelas* and series, 1965–2008   9

1.1. Brazilian cinema, 1995–2004   20

1.2. Number of households with pay-television, 1993–2009   26

1.3. Qualified space channels (CEQs)   31

1.4. List of qualified space channels   31

1.5. Total number of certified hours of pay-TV content, 2008 and 2014   37

1.6. Total number of series produced for pay-TV, 2006–2017   37

1.7. Audiovisual Sector Fund (Fundo Setorial do Audiovisual)   39

1.8. Brazilian cinema, 2012–2015   39

Acknowledgments

As with the undertaking of any large and meaningful project, the completion of this book would not have been possible without the support of many people and institutions. Numerous research and writing trips to Brazil were funded by awards and grants from the University of Virginia (UVa) (Summer Stipend Awards and the AHSS/VPR), where I am fortunate to have wonderful colleagues. Among those at UVa and elsewhere, I am especially grateful to Hector Amaya, Daniel Chávez, Tom Klubock, Carlos Minchillo, Anne Garland Mahler, and Deborah Parker for their continued support. David Haberly deserves special recognition for his kindness, encouragement, and careful readings of multiple drafts of the book manuscript. I simply would not have completed this project without you, Dave. Thank you.

I would also like to recognize and thank the Reframing Media, Technology, and Culture in Latin/o America series editors, Professors Héctor Fernández L'Hoeste and Juan Carlos Rodríguez, and my editor at the University of Florida Press, Stephanye Hunter. As a team, they were behind the project from the very beginning, and their professionalism and dedication ensured a smooth, relatively painless process. A special thanks also goes to Randal Johnson and the anonymous readers for the helpful feedback, which has made the manuscript better than it otherwise would have been.

On a personal note, I want to thank my family and friends, both here in the United States and in Brazil. I cannot sufficiently express how much I appreciate, love, and respect you all. Last, thank you, Abbey. Your love, patience, and positivity provided me with the energy to keep going. I am lucky.

INTRODUCTION

Brazil Reframed

In 1989, during Brazil's first full-fledged presidential election[1] since the end of the military dictatorship's twenty-one-year reign, Fernando Collor de Mello (National Reconstruction Party, PRN), then Governor of Alagoas, faced off against Luiz Inácio Lula da Silva (Lula) of the leftist Workers' Party (PT). After Collor's weak performance during the second presidential debate, TV Globo[2] edited the proceedings to favor the governor. As Collor himself later admitted, he benefited from his relationship with TV Globo, Brazil's largest and most-watched broadcast network, and with its owner, Roberto Marinho, who was concerned that a Lula victory would usher in an era of Communism (Sereza, 2009).[3] When the dust had settled, the relatively little-known Collor, from a small, impoverished northeastern state, became Brazil's thirty-second president, defeating Lula by a mere 6 percent of the vote. Only months after taking office, President Collor faced numerous allegations of impropriety. On March 24, 1992, in an interview with *Veja*, a weekly magazine similar to *Newsweek*, Pedro Collor accused President Collor, his brother, of corruption. The following day, TV Globo reported the story in detail on its *Jornal Nacional*, the most-watched national news program in Brazil. Over the next six months, the network continuously featured the ever-evolving story, which reached its apex on September 29, 1992, when Collor became the first Brazilian president to be impeached and removed from office.

After numerous other attempts, in 2003 Lula finally broke through in his long-standing quest for the presidency, serving the first of two wildly successful terms. Toward the end of his second term, President

Lula tapped Dilma Rousseff, his chief of staff, to be the Workers' Party's 2010 presidential nominee. Despite questions surrounding her experience in high-level politics, Rousseff became Brazil's first female president. In 2014, President Rousseff ran for reelection against the politically seasoned and well-funded Aécio Neves, former governor of and senator from Minas Gerais. Rousseff eventually won reelection, though by the slimmest of margins (3%).

Less than a year into her second term, within the context of an economic downturn and the unfolding of Brazil's largest-ever corruption scandal, *Lava Jato* (Car Wash), President Rousseff was accused of breaking budgetary laws. As had occurred with President Collor nearly twenty-five years earlier, the House brought impeachment proceedings against Rousseff. Although she maintained her innocence, she was stripped of her duties in August of 2016. Though no longer in office, Rousseff made headlines in 2017 and 2018 for her critiques of two major players in the Brazilian mediascape.[4] In the first of the two, Rousseff called out TV Globo's coverage of the Car Wash corruption scandal. She contended that TV Globo was practicing *"jornalismo de guerra"* (journalism as warfare) as a "weapon against democracy," designed to manipulate "the opinion of the Brazilian people" (Brasil 247, 2017).[5]

In the second critique, President Rousseff turned her attention to the recent release of the first season of the Netflix original series, *O mecanismo (The Mechanism)*. Created by the award-winning and polemical filmmaker, José Padilha, *The Mechanism* offers an intricate, fictionalized account of the Car Wash corruption scheme. Disturbed by what she saw as the fabrication and dissemination of "fake news," on March 26, 2018, only days after the series was made available on the streaming service, President Rousseff published an open letter on her website, "Dilma: presidenta eleita do Brasil" (Dilma: Brazil's *Elected Female* President), whose title takes a shot at her impeachment. In the letter, Rousseff addressed her removal from office—which she refers to as a "coup"—and what she believed to be Padilha's dishonest portrayal of both the corruption scandal and the roles she and President Lula supposedly played in it:

> Under the guise of telling the story of the *Lava Jato* investigation in a series "based on real events," the director José Padilha distorts reality and spreads all sorts of lies to attack me and President Lula. The series, *The Mechanism* on Netflix, is underhanded and full of lies.

The director invents facts. He doesn't merely reproduce fake news. He has turned himself into a creator of fake news . . . In my case, the director uses the same character assassination techniques used by the Brazilian press, spreading lies in the TV series, some of which are so blatant that even the big national media companies haven't had the courage to even hint at them. (2018)

In support of President Rousseff's position, many Workers' Party members or sympathizers campaigned to boycott the streaming service. This led to the creation of #CancelaNetflix (#CancelNetflix) and #OMecanismoCausando (#TheMechanismStirringThingsUp), the latter of which quickly became the most commented topic on Twitter in Brazil. Around the same time, President Rousseff doubled down on her critique, taking aim not only at Padilha and his series but at Netflix itself, suggesting that the foreign streaming service, whether consciously or not, was undermining Brazilian politics. During a press conference, Rousseff admonished Netflix for taking part in what she referred to as political campaigning (Nogueira, 2018). President Rousseff also told reporters that she would act by contacting political leaders from other nations to warn them of Netflix's potentially transgressive and subversive behavior. As she saw it, the California-based streaming service had strayed too far from its own backyard, consciously or unconsciously doing even more damage to local politics than Brazil's most prominent national media outlets.

While Rousseff was taking a stand against TV Globo and Netflix, presidential hopefuls were on the campaign trail in search of votes. Among them was the ultraconservative Jair Bolsonaro. After serving for nearly thirty years as a congressman from Rio de Janeiro, the former army captain set his sights on the country's highest office. Inspired by Trump's success in the United States, Bolsonaro employed Twitter to disseminate his outlandish, homophobic, misogynist, nationalist, and racist politics.[6] Although initially many political commentators believed Bolsonaro's extreme, hate-filled positions left him with little chance of even competing, Bolsonaro eventually emerged as the frontrunner—especially after the leading candidate, former President Lula, was jailed on questionable corruption charges in the middle of the election cycle—and easily defeated Fernando Haddad, Lula's handpicked replacement.

Throughout the election, Bolsonaro and TV Globo maintained a contentious relationship, not unlike the one Trump cultivated with those media outlets not Fox News. However, whereas TV Globo's favor played an important role in Collor emerging to win the 1989 presidential election, and its disfavor, at least according to President Rousseff, intensified her political marginalization, the network's fairly explicit, adversarial stance against Bolsonaro's candidacy was not enough to, in Rousseff's words, "manipulate the opinion of the Brazilian people" to vote against Bolsonaro (Brasil 247, 2017). Indeed, leading up to the decisive vote, Arick Wierson, Bolsonaro's campaign manager, summed up their media strategy and their understanding of the contemporary Brazilian mediascape: "The Brazilian voter is tired of the traditional formats that produced old and outdated content . . . Allotted a mere seven seconds of television airtime, it is not possible to emphasize adequately any of Jair's many qualities. But *he did not need television* to become the leader in the polls . . . Jair is not trying to fool anyone, and some people are frightened by his frankness. With the growth of social networks, lies and false promises are soon unmasked" (Dantas, 2018, emphasis mine). Wierson's words suggest that Bolsonaro's campaign essentially dismissed television as a whole. However, considering the campaign's mutually beneficial relationship with the conservative broadcast network, Rede Record, it is safe to assume that what Wierson really means is that, unlike past elections where TV Globo served as *the* primary gatekeeper to the television audience and electorate, Bolsonaro focused primarily on disseminating his messages through upstart social media services and applications like Facebook, Twitter, YouTube, and WhatsApp.[7]

Despite what the preceding examples might suggest, this book is not about postmilitary dictatorship politics in Brazil. Rather, they help to illustrate the extent to which the Brazilian mediascape has undergone foundational shifts in recent years. When President Collor was elected to office in 1989, it would have been almost unthinkable that he—or any candidate, for that matter—could have been successful without access to TV Globo and its tens of millions of spectators. At that time, pay-television and the Internet had not yet arrived in Brazil. In this period of limited competition, according to every meaningful measure, TV Globo far outpaced all other Brazilian over-the-air broadcast networks. In short, TV Globo was *the* hegemonic media company in Brazil. Broadly speaking, the same was true for the elections that followed. Though the mediascape became more competitive between 1989 and 2011, when President Rousseff was elected for the first time, the overall status of the field had changed little. That is, pay-television and the Internet were still largely available only in affluent households, and TV Globo remained the dominant leader in terms of audience share, production, and advertising revenue. However, by 2016—the exact year in which President Rousseff was impeached and future President Jair Bolsonaro announced his intention to run for office—legal, technological, and economic developments, both local and global, were busy pushing the Brazilian mediascape into a new era.

This book focuses on these changes through the creation, production, distribution, and consumption of a selection of television and Internet fiction, exploring the new Brazilian mediascape that has taken root since 2011. The objective is not to predict what that mediascape will be in the coming decades but to shed light on the emergence and the consequences of the post-2011 mediascape as a particular conjuncture.[8] Ultimately, I argue that the ongoing transition from the nearly five-decade, TV Globo–dominated Network Era (1968–2011) to the increasingly competitive and fragmented post-2011 mediascape has given way to fundamental changes to the economic models, modes of production, producers, distribution windows, and consumption that have largely defined the Brazilian mediascape since the late 1960s. Such changes, I contend, also have major implications for the symbolic construction of the national social imaginary.

Television, TV Globo, and the Nation

Audiovisual production the world over is experiencing significant shifts. In the United States, for example, industry-wide pivots resulting from technological advancements have given way to new economic, production, and distribution models. Such developments have dramatically transformed the television landscape, ushering in the early stages of what Amanda D. Lotz (2014) has referred to as the Post-Network Era. The confluence of novel forms of technology, distribution, and reception has taken root to alter what the industry creates, what the audience receives as content, and the channels through which it is received (Lotz, 2014: 4). Consequently, excluding live sporting events such as the Super Bowl or the FIFA World Cup, the spatiotemporally fixed and collective viewings of content that defined the Network Era in the United States are now largely a thing of the past. Instead, the solidification of the digital era and the multiplication of screens have freed television viewing from domestic confinement and pre-established linear programming, providing viewers with greater control over when, what, and where they consume content (Lotz, 2014: 4). Shifts in distribution possibilities have also expanded "previously standard models for financing shows and profiting from them, thereby creating a vast expansion in economically viable content" (Lotz, 2014: 5).

Similar transformations are afoot in Brazil. Nonetheless, although audiovisual production, distribution, and consumption are increasingly tangled in flows of global capital and technology, changes to local media ecologies are embedded in specific socioeconomic, legal, and cultural contexts and therefore occur at varying degrees and at different paces. As such, it would be a mistake to take the transformations outlined by Lotz as universally applicable. In fact, following Graeme Turner and Jinna Tay, Lotz herself recognizes that what television is "very much depends on where you are." Focusing, then, on the changes developing in specific contexts provides important pieces to the global media ecology puzzle. At the same time, it also anchors the local-global dialectic that informs the broader construction of the ever-connected global mediascape (Straubhaar, 2003 and 2007).

In the case of Brazil, television arrived relatively early. Despite an almost total lack of infrastructure and a dearth of television sets, on September 18, 1950, radio and newspaper mogul Assis Chateaubriand inaugurated TV Tupi Difusora de São Paulo—the first television channel both in Brazil and in South America as a whole. The following day, from its precariously installed studios in São Paulo, TV Tupi transmitted the country's first program, *Imagens do dia (Images from the Day)*, to the approximately two hundred existing television sets, most of them located in São Paulo (Mattos, 1992: 49, 170). By comparison, drawing from Lynn Spigel's work, Esther Hamburger notes that by the mid-1950s nearly two-thirds of American households already had a television set, and in that same decade television broadcast signals reached the majority of the United States' territory (Hamburger, 2005: 21).

Although Brazilian television expanded much more slowly than that of its neighbor to the north, that did not stop existing channels from adopting the advertiser-based model that characterized television in the United States from the early 1950s to the mid-1980s, when the "Big Three" networks (ABC, CBS, and NBC) dominated that country's television landscape (Mattos, 2002: 70). In general terms, under this model broadcast networks aired content designed to attract the largest possible audiences, which they then sold to advertisers through thirty-second commercials.

Initially, the implementation of such a model in Brazil was out of place—or what Roberto Schwarz (2014) has referred to in another context as an *"ideia fora do lugar"* (an idea out of place). This is because early television in Brazil was very local and its audiences were small. In fact, in the period between 1950 and the military coup in 1964, the period scholars refer to as the *Fase Elitista* (Elitist Phase), access to television was mostly limited to the cities of São Paulo and Rio de Janeiro and to the relatively small portion of the population who had the means to purchase the expensive technology.

During this period *teleteatros*—television adaptations of canonical European plays—were integral to programming-grids aimed at a small, affluent, and cultured audience. Following fifteen years of slow growth, the earliest signs of a national Network Era in Brazil appeared in the mid-1960s when Roberto Marinho, another radio and newspaper mogul, founded TV Globo. Only a few years later, aided by the professional expertise and financial backing provided by an illegal partnership with Time-Life, by substantial political support from the recently installed military dictatorship, and by the subsequent decline of TV Excelsior and TV Tupi, TV Globo's primary competitors,[9] Marinho's network had become the country's preeminent source for locally produced television content.[10] Importantly, it was during this period—often referred to as the *Fase Populista* (Populist Phase, 1965–1975)—that TV Globo "North Americanized" Brazilian television by adopting the management, production, and programming standards of its neighbor to the north (Caparelli, 1982: 32; Mattos, 1990: 16).

While these and other factors contributed to TV Globo's subsequent five-decade domination of Brazil's television industry, nothing was more important to the network's rise, in terms of content, than the production of *telenovelas*. Throughout its history, TV Globo has produced and aired *teleteatros,* mini- and microseries, and the occasional series. None of these genres, however, comes even close to comparing to the ubiquitous presence and importance of the *telenovela*. Consider the following numbers: between 1965 and 2018, TV Globo produced a total of ninety-nine series. Of that total, forty were produced relatively recently, between 2010 and 2018. In other words, during TV Globo's first forty-five years of existence, the network created an average of slightly more than one series per year and an overall average of approximately 1.9 per year for the entire period. By comparison, from 1965 to 2018, TV Globo developed 93, 93, 89, and 36 *telenovelas* for the 6, 7, 8, and 10 PM slots, respectively—a yearly average of six *telenovelas*.[11]

Though significantly greater than that of the series, these yearly averages do not reveal the extent to which the TV Globo *telenovela* has historically overshadowed the series for the network, and, more broadly, for Brazilian television as a whole. Like the studio system that reigned in Hollywood during the 1940s, TV Globo has continuously produced all of its *telenovelas* in-house since the late 1960s, making the network far and away the largest producer of fictional content in Brazil. In an uninterrupted cycle of production that is evocative of Adorno's (2001) description of the culture industry,[12] TV Globo churns out four one-hour prime-time *telenovelas* Monday through Saturday for every week of the year. Discounting the genre's standard inclusion of five approximately three-minute commercial breaks, during which a thirty-second spot can fetch upward of $100,000, effectively covering the costs of that day's production, all together the network produces the rough equivalent of a two-hour film 312 days a year. Put differently, if a series generally airs once a week for thirty to sixty minutes, and a single season maxes out at twenty-four episodes (a rarity in present-day television production), TV Globo's yearly average of producing slightly less than two series per year would represent at most forty-eight hours of content. By comparison, the network's six daily *telenovelas* per-year average represents approximately 780 hours of content, the equivalent of more than thirty-two one-hour episodes in a twenty-four-episode season series.

Over the years, TV Globo's high-quality, *melorealist* (Rodríguez, 2016) depictions of Brazilian culture, combined with a general lack of competition from other domestic players, have established the *telenovela* as Brazilian television fiction par excellence.[13] In addition to employing and featuring the nation's most famous writers, directors, and actors, TV Globo's *telenovelas* put the network's celebrated *padrão Globo de qualidade* (The Globo Standard of Quality) on display. Initiated in the early 1970s to appease the military dictatorship's concerns about what it perceived as the network's increasing use of low-brow humor and violence—both of which contradicted the conservative family values of the regime's desired Brazil—the Globo Standard of Quality replaced informality and improvisation with stringent management and a qualitative standardization of content (Mattos, 2002: 98; Hamburger, 2005: 35; Fechine, 2007: 5). Videotape, color, and cutting-edge graphics, among other technological

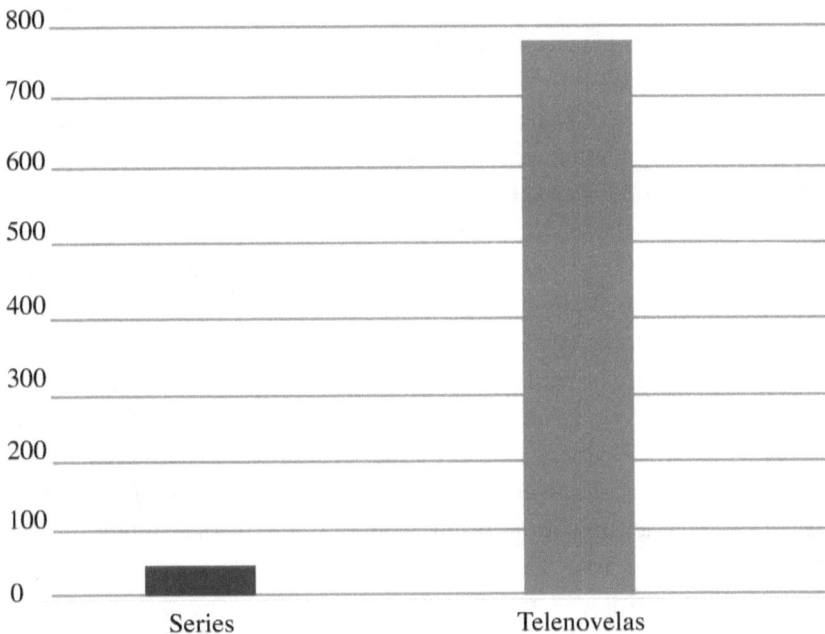

Figure 0.1. Average number of yearly hours produced of *telenovelas* and series, 1965–2008.

advancements, were central to the network's reevaluation of its style and production. The acquisition and use of such cutting-edge technology further established and distinguished the TV Globo brand from those of other networks and among television audiences. Indeed, as Hamburger (2005: 32) points out, by the late 1960s and early 1970s, although TV Globo was a privately run company, it had essentially secured the kind of audience monopoly generally reserved for publicly run networks in nations where vehicles of mass communication are controlled by the state.

In short, the combination of TV Globo's professionalization, political support, its star system (Johnson, 2017), and the consistently high production value on display in its television fiction has continued to differentiate the network, in qualitative terms, from its competitors, arming the media conglomerate with significant amounts of symbolic, economic, and political capital (Bourdieu, 1993). Consequently, millions of Brazilians in every corner of the country's vast territory and from all classes and races have faithfully tuned in to watch TV Globo programming, especially its *telenovelas*. In turn, the network has profited greatly by selling its massive audiences to advertisers interested in expanding their consumer bases and hawking their products (Straubhaar, 2012: 165).

From roughly 1968 to 2011, no other cultural product defined, influenced, or shaped the Brazilian social imaginary more than TV Globo's *telenovelas*. Indeed, scholars such as Kehl (1986), Ortiz (1988), La Pastina (1999), Borelli and Priolli (2000), and Bolaño and Brittos (2005), to name but a few, have argued that TV Globo's relatively unchallenged position among other domestic media companies and its audiences' preference for and dedication to the network have helped to situate the company's *telenovelas* as the primary source for the symbolic construction of what it means to be Brazilian. In fact, it is difficult to encounter a scholarly study of Brazilian television that does not at least mention TV Globo's primary role in helping to establish and perpetuate contemporary iterations of Brazil as an imagined community (Anderson, 2006). In his seminal study on imagined communities and the spread of nationalism during the nineteenth century, Benedict Anderson (2016: 133) notes that "the most important thing about language is its capacity for generating imagined communities, building in effect *particular solidarities*." But, it is not simply language that generates imagined communities; rather, according to Anderson (2016), it is a specific *type* of language. For example, in the period studied by Anderson, it was "print-language" that invented "nationalism, not a particular language per se" (2016: 134).

If print-language invented nationalism by creating the conditions for people to imagine communities that existed within broad territories across space and time, then audiovisual forms of media—that is, film, television, and more recently the Internet—ensure its continuation, even as they challenge its current iteration. In Brazil, nothing has done this more than the common language of the TV Globo–produced and distributed *telenovela*, which, as Butcher notes, has situated itself and its fictional content firmly against imported culture as the generator of an authentically Brazilian identity (2006: 39).

Along these lines, Ana M. López has also argued that the "telenovela served to create a televisual 'national' in which the imagined community rallies around specific images of itself" and that TV Globo *telenovelas* in particular "have been based upon specifically Brazilian themes, characters, and landscapes, and have featured the topography, culture, and characters of the entire nation" (1995: 262). For her part, Hamburger maintains that *telenovelas* enact a sense of membership to a community, constituting what she refers to as a "virtual everyday life domain" (2000: 173). According to Hamburger, the community that exists in and emerges from this virtual domain is national, "but instead of a flag or national colors," it defines itself by the "shared knowledge of plots and conventions of a television genre and by the debate of controversial subjects in the plot" (2000: 173).

Similarly, Mauro Porto astutely notes that in the Latin American context, though novels maintain an important function in shaping national imagined communities, film and radio have also been highly influential. Nonetheless, "in the specific case of Brazil," Porto rightfully contends that "television has established mass ceremonies much broader and more significant in scope than the public forums created by print media" (2011: 55).[14] Last, as is characteristic of all of his foundational work on Brazilian television, Joseph Straubhaar succinctly elucidates the communicative, hegemonic, and symbolic link between the nation and Brazil's largest broadcast network: "Television is *still* the dominant institution in Brazil for news, information, and culture. TV Globo's evening news and prime time *telenovelas still* hold sway in over half the homes in the country. They have served as a unifying force in a nation with extremely diverse regions since the early 1970s; they are *still* the dominant means by which Brazilians imagine themselves as a country" (Straubhaar, 2013: 63, emphasis mine).

But as Robert Burgoyne points out, there is no one single national identity: "Nation-states contain within themselves 'two or more nations,' though they 'have generally succeeded in concealing or eradicating the cultural particularity of these 'hidden nations'" (Burgoyne, 2010: 38). In the case of TV Globo, it is clear that its *telenovelas* deal with and portray a wide array of socially relevant topics, ranging from domestic violence and political corruption to the transgender community and social movements such as the Movimento Sem Terra (MST, Landless Worker's Movement). Problematically, however, to Burgoyne's point about Hollywood, the *telenovelas* broadcast by TV Globo have long emphasized whiteness, middle and upper-middle-class consumerism, and modern urban spaces such as Rio de Janeiro and São Paulo as the standard or, at the very least, the preferred version of the nation. At the same time, TV Globo's *telenovelas* frequently oversimplify matters pertaining to race and marginalized spaces such as the *favela* or *sertão*. Often, such spaces are either conspicuously absent, constructed as idealized or model communities, or portrayed as home to the violent or folkloric other, who is all too often a person of color.

This is not to suggest that TV Globo simply produces monolithic representations of Brazil that are passively or uncritically consumed by its viewers. As Marshall C. Eakin argues, while the vast majority of Brazilians are commonly aware of the symbols, rituals, and beliefs at the core of the symbolic construction of Brazilian identity, "they are not fully embraced by everyone in the same fashion" (Eakin, 2017: 138). Nonetheless, Eakin concedes that "what is important for the formation of a national imaginary is that everyone is aware of those symbols, rituals, and beliefs—that they resonate—not that everyone embraces them with the same intensity and understanding" (138). There can be no doubt that in Brazil TV Globo's fictional portrayals of the nation have made nearly all Brazilians aware of the network's conceptualization of the symbols, rituals, and beliefs *it* deems suitable for the reproduction of the productive consumer whom advertisers so desperately want to reach. And while such portrayals have evolved over the years, the network has, to borrow from Theodor Adorno, maintained and therefore been upheld by "a scaffolding of rigidly conservative basic categories" (2001: 100). Thus, continuing with Adorno, what TV Globo offers as progress in its *telenovelas* is often "the disguise for an eternal sameness; everywhere the changes mask a skeleton which has changed just as little as the profit motive itself since the time it first gained its predominance over culture" (100).

With the TV Globo, *telenovela*-centric Network Era as a backdrop, the chapters that follow focus on a selection of television and Internet fiction produced since 2011. Through the analysis of the individual works and the broader mediascape within which they unfold, I argue that factors having to do with legislation, production, technology, distribution, and access have combined to not only push the Brazilian mediascape into a new era but also to help create the conditions for an expansive, ongoing challenge to TV Globo's hegemonic representations of Brazil and, by extension, to what it means to be Brazilian. To put it simply, as a result of legislative and technological advances that have led to the appearance of new competitors, including pay-television channels, YouTube channels, and Internet-distributed television, an ever-growing portion of the population has moved far beyond the days when broadcast network television was the only game in town and when pay-television, the Internet, and over-the-top (OTT) content,[15] among other increasingly personalized forms of entertainment, were either nonexistent or accessible only by a select few. Though they have not disappeared entirely, the business practices that structured the field and resulted primarily in the uninterrupted creation of *telenovelas* have found themselves crowded by new practices aimed at reaching smaller, niche audiences. Thus, I contend that the rise of conditions for more symbolic forms like the series, for example, to exist alongside the *telenovela* and for these forms to be increasingly available in rising numbers of both linear and nonlinear distribution channels results in the expansion of the imagined realities of the average Brazilian citizen.

Along these lines, I will show that works in question, in varied ways and to varying degrees, offer more diverse portrayals of Brazil than have traditionally been on display in TV Globo's *telenovelas* during the Network Era. To this end, chapter 1—which serves as the base for the book's broader argument—establishes the 2011 Pay-TV Law (Law 12.485/11) as the marker of the onset of the new, still-developing Brazilian mediascape. The chapter outlines the major tenets of the Pay-TV Law while also situating its development and adoption within the larger political milieu beginning in 1990. By analyzing a wide array of data during the period between 1990 and 2018 and by emphasizing the increased presence of independent production companies, the number of hours produced, the number of distribution channels, funding sources, and the uptick in the creation of series, the analysis reveals the significant extent to which the Brazilian mediascape has expanded and become increasingly competitive since 2011.

Chapter 2 turns its attention to the pay-television sector. Though it first arrived to Brazil in 1990, for the better part of two decades Brazilian pay-television was largely characterized by slow growth, access limited to the country's most affluent classes, and a programming-grid chock-full of content imported from the United States. The Pay-TV Law's establishment of quotas for locally produced content, however, has helped to carve out a space for the production and distribution of Brazilian content. With this in mind, the chapter analyzes *1 contra todos* (*1 Against All*, Fox Brasil) and *Lama dos dias* (*Mud of the Days*, Canal Brasil). In addition to satisfying the content quotas outlined in the Pay-TV Law, both series benefited from government financing mechanisms, were directed by celebrated Brazilian filmmakers, and explicitly, albeit in distinct ways, contemplate the nation and *Brazilianness*.

Chapter 3 explores the expansion of Internet access in Brazil since 2011 and analyzes three critically acclaimed web series: *Septo (Septum,* YouTube), *Marcos: Uma websérie quase original (Marcos: An Almost Original Web Series,* Instagram and YouTube), and *3%* (YouTube and Netflix). The former two were made exclusively for Internet distribution and are the products of recently formed production companies in cities far from the Rio-São Paulo axis of production: Natal and Caxias do Sul. While they differ in genre, tone, length, and themes, both *Septo* and *Marcos* stand out for representing regions of Brazil not often portrayed on the small screen during the period leading up to 2011. For its part, *3%* eschews regional and national differences, focusing instead on a post-apocalyptic world. Unlike *Septo* and *Marcos,* both of which emerged within the context of the new Brazilian mediascape, the production of *3%* spans the pre-and post-2011 mediascapes.

Chapter 4 begins by delving deeper into the Brazilian mediascape during the period between 1990 and 2011, revealing the early appearance of developments that challenged TV Globo's audience shares over the two decades. This first part of the chapter sets the stage for the subsequent emergence of Porta dos Fundos, a recently formed independent production company and YouTube sensation. The remainder of the chapter explores the Pay-TV Law and the post-2011 mediascape through an analysis of Porta dos Fundos' formation, founders, partnerships, and multimedial production. A continuation of chapter 4, chapter 5 expands on the structural analyses of the previous chapters by emphasizing the interrelatedness of developments occurring within the post-2011 mediascape and a broader theme: blackness in two contemporary Brazilian serial comedies: *Mister Brau (Mr. Brown)* and *O Grande Gonzalez (The Great Gonzalez).*

Last, chapter 6 turns its attention to Globo's efforts to reposition itself within the increasingly complex and competitive new Brazilian mediascape, particularly as those efforts pertain to strengthening its streaming service, Globo Play. With the growth of Netflix Brasil in recent years and the streaming platform's emergence as one of Globo's biggest threats, chapter 6 considers some of the tactics employed by Globo to remain competitive. Namely, such tactics center on the media conglomerate's experimentation with its over-the-air and over-the-top businesses and an increased production in series. To illustrate Globo's efforts in this arena, the chapter focuses on the production and rollout of two Globo original series: *Supermax* and *Assédio*.

Together, the six chapters spotlight the still-developing transformations to the Brazilian mediascape that began in 2011. Although more changes will certainly arise as those transformations continue to take hold, it is clear that the confluence of legislative, technological, economic, and creative factors during the post-2011 context have given way to the most competitive mediascape in the history of Brazil. As I aim to show in what follows, this particular moment represents a snapshot of Brazil, where the increasingly diverse field of television and Internet fiction is altering the relationships between distributor and producer and producer and viewer, and where a hegemonic force like Globo struggles to maintain and reproduce its audiences in the face of a number of subnational, transnational, and global movements, organizations, and technologies (Appadurai, 1996: 188). In short, in the new Brazilian mediascape, while Globo competes with national and international pay-television channels, YouTube, and Netflix and while *telenovelas* compete with series, both local and foreign, more Brazilians in more parts of Brazil are faced with more symbolic portrayals of the nation than ever before. The result, I argue, is a Brazil *reframed* by the small screens.

The Pay-TV Law and the New Brazilian Mediascape

Analyzing the contemporary mediascape is a difficult task. Incipient policies, technological advancements, emergent forms of distribution, new revenue models, and a proliferation of producers and content combine to create a dynamic, complex field of production that is perhaps best characterized by its state of flux. In Brazil, a clear picture of the transitional moment of the contemporary mediascape is muddied by traditional television practices of the Network Era meeting head on with disruptive practices of new media. The clash of "old" and "new" media give way to a temporary, hybrid state that is neither fully one nor the other and is constantly experiencing tweaks and developments that push it toward the solidification of an as yet unknown new norm. Despite the challenges presented by Brazil's still-developing contemporary mediascape, our analysis is an important and necessary undertaking and must begin by outlining and examining the numerous factors that pushed Brazilian television out of a Network Era that lasted more than five decades (1968–2011).

Though this shift has slowly been taking root since the early 1990s and spans television and film, I contend that the passage of the Pay-TV Law (Law 12.485/11) in 2011, its broad impact on the field, and the increased access to the Internet in the years that followed have combined to establish a new, transitional era. Insofar as traditional Network-Era characteristics co-exist alongside Post-Network Era characteristics,[1] this new era occupies a liminal space. It is not simply a multichannel transition like the one that took form with the growth of pay-television in the United States between the mid-1980s and mid-2000s, propelling the country out of its own Network Era that lasted three decades (Lotz, 2014). Instead, in the Brazilian case, the relatively late growth of the pay-television sector develops *alongside* the rise of Internet access, both of which have current penetration rates that still lag behind those of the United States of a decade prior.

With this in mind, the "new Brazilian mediascape" or the "post-2011 mediascape or era," as I will interchangeably refer to it throughout this book, is marked by the continued presence of broadcast networks, especially TV Globo. However, within the post-2011 mediascape, for the first time since Brazil's largest broadcast network and producer took hold of its dominant position, TV Globo increasingly exists in a space characterized by new distributors and delivery mechanisms, an influx of independent production companies, an expansion of viewing options and screens, and new economic models. The increased competition of the new mediascape has accelerated the fragmentation of TV Globo's hegemony over the symbolic constructions of Brazil as an imagined community (Anderson, 2006). Considering the media's roles in the "*work of the imagination* as a constitutive feature of modern subjectivity" (Appadurai, 1995: 3), the result of this fragmentation should be understood as the expansion of the social imaginary and the emergence of new models of citizenship that move beyond those offered by Globo and its broadcast network.

Television *and* Film: The Audiovisual Law and the Centrality of Globo

As discussed in the introduction, TV Globo has sustained a dominant position as Brazil's hegemonic broadcast network and, as a result, has forced both its domestic and foreign competitors to fight for a distant second place within the local market. In contrast, Brazilian film has traditionally occupied a subordinate position within its own market. In fact, apart from the brief period between 1908 and 1911 commonly referred to as the Golden Age (Bernardet, 2008; Johnson, 1987; Ramos et al., 1990), a short box-office boom in the mid-to late 1970s, and the commercial and critical success of a few recent works, Brazilian films subsist in the shadow of TV Globo's *telenovelas*' massive audiences, while also lagging behind imported North American and European films in terms of box office and prestige.

Throughout the second half of the twentieth century different government administrations made multiple attempts to create and promote a domestic film industry. In March 1990, however, President Fernando Collor de Mello effectively eliminated government support for the film industry. In line with the tenets of the neoliberal Program for National Privatization (*Programa Nacional de Desestatização*), President Collor announced Provisional Measure 151/90 (MP 151/90), which marked for permanent closure eleven state-run companies. Among others, one of the companies to be shuttered was the Brazilian Film Company (Embrafilme), a state-run financier, co-producer, and distributor whose initial aim was to promote and distribute Brazilian films abroad (Ikeda, 2015; Johnson, 1987; Lima, 2015; Santos, 2009). By the time any substantial government support returned in 1993, the Brazilian film industry had collapsed, releasing only three commercial films, which on average attracted a measly 36,000 spectators (Butcher, 2006; Ikeda, 2015; Johnson, 2007; Nagib, 2002; Rêgo, 2005; Santos, 2009). As a point of comparison, *Renascer*, a 1993 TV Globo *telenovela* directed by Luiz Fernando Carvalho, attracted an average nightly audience of over five million in the city of São Paulo alone (Sabbatino, 2013).

By 1995, many in Brazil pointed to Carla Camurati's box-office hit *Carlota Joaquina* as evidence that the film industry had begun to recover. Moreover, the local commercial success of Camurati's film was quickly followed by international recognition of three Oscar-nominated films: Fábio Barreto's *O quatrilho* (*The Quatrilho*, 1995), Bruno Barreto's *O que é isso, companheiro?* (*Four Days in September*, 1997), and Walter Salles's *Central do Brasil* (*Central Station*, 1998). For a number of scholars, Brazilian cinema's reemergence (*retomada*), symbolized by these important films, was the direct result of a new audiovisual landscape—one characterized in broad terms by the return of state support (Bahia, 2008; Bentes, 2007; Butcher, 2006; Johnson, 2005, 2007; Nagib, 2002).

Marcelo Ikeda (2015), for example, separates public policy directed at the film industry during the period between 1990 and 2010 into three phases: President Collor's Minimal State (*Estado mínimo*, 1990–1992); President Fernando Henrique Cardoso's Regulatory State (*Estado regulador*, 1995–2003); and President Lula Inácio da Silva's Propositional State (*Estado propositivo*, 2003–2011). While Ikeda (2015) notes that many factors led to the revival of Brazilian cinema in the mid-1990s, he argues that none was more important than the implementation of indirect financing mechanisms articulated in Law 8.685/93, more commonly referred to as the Lei do Audiovisual (Audiovisual Law). Passed in 1993, the Audiovisual Law represented an urgent attempt to save the film industry from the collapse that followed President Collor's neoliberal initiatives. For Suzy dos Santos (2009), however, even more important than the Audiovisual Law to the survival of the film industry was Globo's expansion of its reach through the founding of Globo Filmes in 1997.

Among other measures, the Audiovisual Law contained two indirect financing mechanisms: Articles 1 and 3. The following discussion emphasizes the latter, since Globo Filmes frequently produced or co-produced films utilizing that Article. According to the Audiovisual Law, any company that maintains the rights to commercialize an audiovisual work in Brazilian territory must pay taxes on monies it receives from or remits abroad. However, under Article 3, such companies—predominantly major Hollywood studios—may invest up to 70 percent of taxes owed on credits or remittances in Brazilian audiovisual works, which they then co-produce with a local independent production company (Cesnik and Juca, 2014; Ikeda, 2015).

Initially, Hollywood studios with operations in Brazil did not find the financial benefits offered by Article 3 sufficiently attractive to convince them to invest due taxes in local productions, especially because the studios often received more substantial tax incentives on their remittances from the United States government (Ikeda, 2015). Nonetheless, a more effective incentive came in 2001 in the form of Provisional Measure 2.228-1, which created a hefty 11 percent tax known as the Contribuição para o Desenvolvimento da Indústria Cinematográfica Nacional (Contribution to the Development of National Cinema Remittance Fee, CONDECINE Remessa) (Ikeda, 2015; Silva, 2013). The Provisional Measure allowed Hollywood studios operating in Brazil to avoid paying the 11 percent remittance tax if they invested 70 percent of taxes due in local co-productions, as stipulated by Article 3 (Lei do Audiovisual, 1993). The measure proved successful in meeting its objective: investments related to Article 3 grew from slightly under $3.44 million (R$11 million) in 2001 to an average of $11.89 million (R$38 million) per year during the period between 2002 and 2008 (Ikeda, 2015: 83).[2] As figure 1.1 shows, Globo's newly established film production company quickly emerged as Hollywood studios' most sought-after partner for investments related to Article 3.

The widespread involvement of Globo Filmes in film production via Article 3 sheds light on why Santos (2009) correctly described the audiovisual landscape in the late 1990s and early 2000s as one that created barriers, making it difficult for new agents to participate while also reinforcing Globo's dominance. Specifically, in the case of Article 3, while

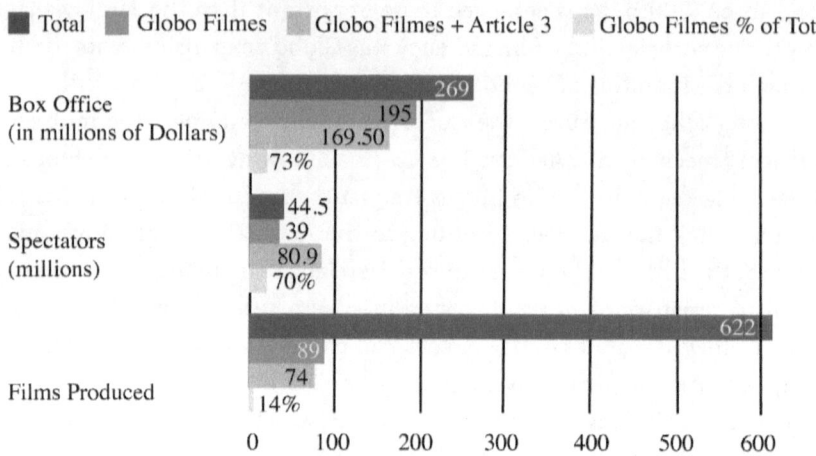

Figure 1.1. Brazilian cinema, 1995–2004 (US dollars calculated using an exchange rate of 3.2 reais to 1 dollar). Created from data from Ikeda (2015).

the participation of major Hollywood studios effectively guaranteed distribution for Brazilian films, it also marginalized Brazilian independent distributors, established box-office success as the preferred economic and production model, and increased Hollywood studios' shares in films to the detriment of the shares held by the local independent production companies (Bahia, 2008; Butcher, 2006; Ikeda, 2015; Santos, 2009). In other words, Article 3 marginalized nearly all players not Globo or those not associated with the media conglomerate. For Santos, the concentration of power—political, economic, and symbolic—in the hands of a few established producers and distributors was due to the absence of a more holistic public policy toward the audiovisual sector (2009: 707). Importantly, the lack of such a policy, she argues, allowed broadcast television to occupy a central role in the broader audiovisual chains (film and television) of production, distribution, and exhibition (707). In line with Santos's position, Silva notes that the creation of Globo Filmes resulted in a new relationship between Brazilian film and television—that is, not only did Brazilian cinema have to compete with Hollywood, as it had unsuccessfully attempted to do for nearly a century; it now had to also compete with TV Globo's standard of quality transferred from their famed *telenovelas* to the big screen (Silva, 2015: 70).

Indeed, in addition to TV Globo's dominant position as Brazil's premiere broadcast television network, the numbers cited in figure 1.1 demonstrate Globo Filmes' rapid rise to become a—if not *the*—major player in the Brazilian film industry. However, those numbers as well as Santos's argument are embedded in an audiovisual context that had not yet been impacted by the Pay-TV Law and technological advancements that have since become increasingly a part of everyday life in Brazil. If Article 3 of the Audiovisual Law played out during President Cardoso's Regulatory State, then President Lula's Propositional State characterized the period leading up to the implementation of the Pay-TV Law (Ikeda, 2015). As José Guibson Delgado Dantas and Gárdia Rodrigues point out, during President Lula's administration, culture began to be understood as a matter of national politics. More specifically, the administration conferred a heightened importance upon the audiovisual sector, at the core of which was a proposed relationship between television *and* film (Dantas and Rodrigues, 2016; Ikeda, 2015; Lima, 2015; Sousa, 2018).

To this end, beginning in 2004 when the legislation was first introduced to Congress, a concerted effort took place on the part of the Lula administration to create the Agência Nacional do Cinema e do Audiovisual (National Agency of Film and the Audiovisual, ANCINAV). Aware of the important role of the audiovisual sector in the formation of contemporary society, under the leadership of Minister Gilberto Gil, the Ministry of Culture proposed that the Agência Nacional do Cinema (National Film Agency, ANCINE) be transformed to include the oversight and regulation of the audiovisual field as a whole, ranging from broadcast television and film to pay-television and the Internet (Dantas and Rodrigues, 2016; Ikeda, 2015; Maurício, 2015; Sousa, 2018). According to Ikeda, "ANCINAV represented the first systematic attempt by the Brazilian government to regulate content and *promote cultural diversity* in the field of communications" (2015: 107, emphasis mine).[3] Ultimately, however, due to strong resistance from nearly all business sectors to the generalized surcharge proposed by the legislation and, more specifically, to resistance from TV Globo, other broadcast networks, and major Hollywood studios, who saw the proposal as a threat to their hegemonic positions, Congress withdrew the legislation in 2006 (Autran and Fernandes, 2017; Dantas and Rodrigues, 2016; Geraldes and Caribé, 2016; Ikeda, 2015; Tavares, 2015; Sousa, 2018).[4] Nonetheless, the idea of restructuring the audiovisual field played an important role in the eventual passage of the Fundo Setorial do Audiovisual (Audiovisual Sector Fund, FSA) and of the Pay-TV Law (Ikeda, 2015; Tavares, 2015). Together, these legislative developments have played integral roles in the expansion of the Brazilian mediascape since 2011.

Pay-Television: A Long Road to Growth

The preceding discussion considers broadcast network television and the film industry in Brazil with the objective of locating Globo's central position within the mediascape that characterized the years between 1990 and 2004. Though implied by the mention of the Law 12.485/11, the pay-television sector itself is conspicuously missing from the discussion. This is largely because the sector would come to occupy a meaningful position in the Brazilian mediascape only after the passage of the Pay-TV Law in 2011. Before we proceed to the Law itself, the following section contextualizes the trajectory of the pay-television sector beginning in 1990 and leading up to 2011, when Law 12.485/11 was passed.

In *TV por assinatura: 20 anos de evolução* (*Pay-Television: 20 Years of Evolution*), almost certainly the most complete study of the history of the Brazilian pay-television industry to date, Samuel Possebon notes that one could, at least in theory, trace back the origins of the sector to as early as the late 1950s (2009: 19). Indeed, according to Possebon, by 1958 Community Antenna Television (subscription communal antennas, CATV) were already in use in Petropolis, a mountainous municipality located approximately forty miles north of Rio de Janeiro. However, as was the case for much of the remainder of the twentieth century, these distribution signals served primarily to provide homes with higher-quality access to broadcast network television programming such as TV Globo. Despite the early seeds planted in the middle of the twentieth century, the pay-television sector as currently constituted truly began to take form only in the late 1980s.

Not unlike the case with broadcast television in the 1950s, when media mogul Assis Chateaubriand took on the herculean task of making the incipient technology a reality, beginning in the 1980s, a number of regional entrepreneurs worked tirelessly to implement varied forms (e.g., UHF, cable, satellite) of pay-television throughout the country. For the early development of pay-television in Brazil, perhaps the most important of these entrepreneurs was the Civita family, owner of the Abril Group, one of the largest media companies in South America. Headed by founder Victor Civita and his son Roberto, the Abril Group in the early 1980s sought to add to its publishing activities by entering the television industry. More specifically, Abril had its eye on securing the broadcast license of the recently shuttered TV Tupi. However, the military dictatorship—then still in power—split TV Tupi's license in two, eventually awarding the two parts to friends of the regime: Sílvio Santos's Sistema Brasileiro de Televisão (SBT) and Adolpho Bloch's TV Manchete. Disappointed but not deterred, Victor and Roberto decided to explore alternatives to broadcast network television (Possebon, 2009: 30). According to Roberto, rather than being the last to secure a broadcast license, he preferred to be the first to enter the pay-television industry (Possebon, 2009: 250).

As a result, the Civitas turned their attention to the virtually nonexistent pay-television sector. Following the model established in France by Canal+ and implemented in Brazil by Matias Machline, in 1985 the Abril Group secured a single UHF (Ultra High Frequency) channel in the city of São Paulo with the intent of commercializing it as a subscription option to Brazil's largest urban population. Those plans, however, were doubly frustrated. First the Ministry of Communication informed the group that prior to implementing their business plan, policies regulating the sector would need to be developed and approved by the appropriate government channels. Finally, in 1988, after the Civitas had spent two long years working alongside the Ministry of Communication to develop the necessary regulatory policy, Decree 95.744 created the Serviço Especial de Televisão por Assinatura (Special Service Subscription Television, TVA), effectively authorizing the Abril Group to proceed with its UHF subscription channel. Nonetheless, although Abril had worked directly with the Ministry of Communication to help create the conditions for the company to operate its channel, to the Civitas' dismay they were but one of four groups to receive such an authorization. Importantly, among the three other groups was Brazil's media behemoth, Globo (Possebon, 2009: 31–32).

The Abril Group's centrality to the early development of the pay-television sector in Brazil goes beyond the company's wide-ranging efforts to establish its business. This is because one of the primary effects of the Abril Group's interest in pay-television was that it spurred Globo to action. Unlike the numerous regional entrepreneurs struggling to piece together pay-television operations toward the end of the 1980s and early 1990s, the Abril Group was financially stable and large enough to attract the attention of Brazil's largest media group. In short, in an audiovisual landscape dominated by Globo, the Abril Group introduced a level of competition that was important for pushing the sector out of its infancy. The ongoing market dispute between the two groups and their employment of very different economic logics shaped the development of Brazilian pay-television in those early years. Possebon highlights the fact that each of the two groups adopted positions that were in large part determined by what it speculated the other was doing: "At Abril, decision makers imagined that Globo was mounting an operation that would include everything it could muster, from its capacity for production and the use of archival material to its technical know-how" (Possebon, 2009: 40). According to longtime Globo executive Joe Wallach, however, the truth was actually the exact opposite: "only upon seeing Abril set up its pay-television strategy did Globo decide to react" (40).

While the two groups speculated as to what the other was doing, there was an important difference in the way they structured their respective businesses: early on, Globo believed that, due to national coverage and the ability to reach subscribers more quickly, satellite or direct to home (DTH) was the best mode of distribution. Abril, on the other hand, decided it best to employ the TVA (TV por assinatura) model, transmitting its signal via UHF and SHF (Possebon, 2009: 39–40).[5] Over the following years, as the sector developed, the two groups revised their business models and pivoted as necessary. Globo, for example, had separated its interrelated pay-television business interests into content production and distribution. To this end, the Globo group created Globosat, which focused on production.[6] The group diversified its distribution services into satellite, through a partnership with Rupert Murdoch's Sky, and cable, through Net Brasil, which would later become Globo Cabo, before finally settling on Net Serviços in 2002 (Possebon, 2009: 147, 162, 187).[7]

By 1997, when the highly anticipated second wave of the government administered bidding for pay-television distribution licenses (*editais*) finally came to fruition, Globo had secured a position for itself as the most important actor in the sector. Despite Globo's strengthened position, the Abril Group pushed forward with its plan to challenge its primary competition for supremacy in the pay-television industry. Nonetheless, with the stakes increasingly higher, Possebon notes that the Abril Group became cautious about carving out a path distinct from that of Globo (2009: 148). Instead, as the decade drew to a close the Civitas modeled their company's plan-of-action after Globo's, seeking to establish a widespread network along the lines of Net Brasil.[8]

The competitive back and forth between the Abril Group and Globo played a central role in defining market strategies during the first decade of the pay-television industry in Brazil. The strategies available to these and other media groups, however, were regulated by Law 8.977/95, more commonly called the Lei do Cabo (Cable TV Law). Signed into existence in 1995 by President Fernando Henrique Cardoso, the first such act of his two-term tenure, the Cable TV Law established fifteen-year licenses, to be granted to cable operators by the government through formal bidding cycles. Such concessions, as they are referred to, would be given only to private legal entities that maintained the offering of television subscription as their main economic activity. What is more, such entities would need to be headquartered in Brazil, and at least 51 percent of the cable provider's share capital and voting rights needed to belong to Brazilians either born in Brazil or naturalized for more than ten years. As a result, the law limited foreign capital to a maximum of 49 percent. At the same time, telecommunication companies could provide cable services only in regions where private companies showed no interest in securing a concession to establish and offer the service.

When the Cable TV Law was passed in 1995, regulation of the sector depended on the type of technology offered. Thus, the rules applied to cable television were not necessarily applied to multichannel multipoint distribution (MMDS), direct-to-home (DTH), or TVA services. For example, though participation of foreign capital in TVA services was banned, non-Brazilian capital was allowed to reach up to 100 percent in MMDS and DTH services. Additionally, telecommunication companies were authorized to offer MMDS, DTH, and TVA services without the stipulations that surrounded or applied to cable television. What is more, while the law stated that cable television operators "must carry," at no additional charge, "basic utilization channels" (*canais básicos de utilização*), which included a municipal or state legislation channel, a channel dedicated to the proceedings of Congress and one dedicated to the Senate, a channel centered on local universities, and a channel focused on cultural education, it freed DTH services from having to carry such channels.

With the Cable TV Law in place, and two of the largest Brazilian media groups taking the lead, the Brazilian pay-television industry had begun to take root, increasingly attracting the attention of domestic and foreign investors alike (Lima, 2015: 38). Among these investors, which included such national and transnational players as Garantia, Opportunity, ABC/

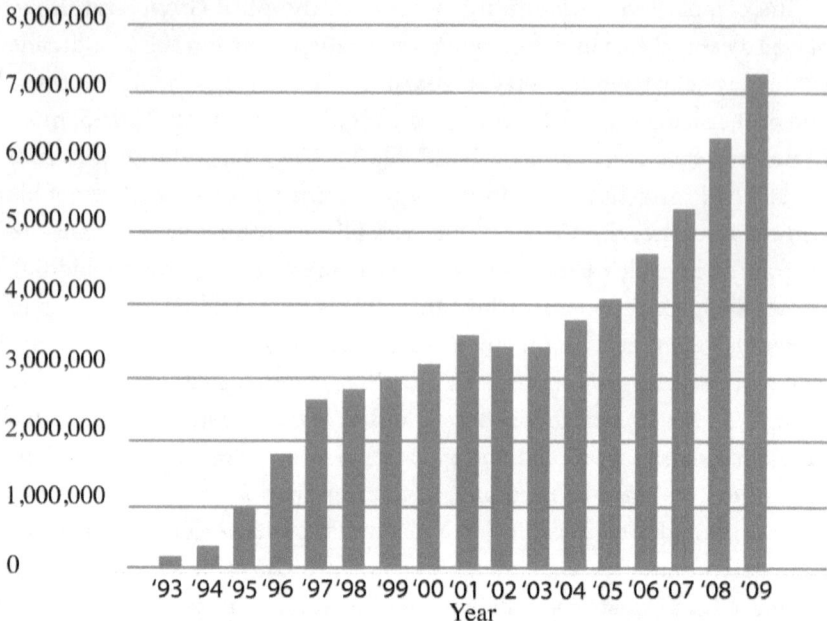

Figure 1.2. Number of households with pay-television, 1993–2009. Adapted from Dados do Setor (2018).

Disney, Horizon, and Sky, optimism was widespread that it was only a matter of time before the Brazilian pay-television industry realized the enormous potential presented by the country's large population.[9] In fact, industry-employed economic models projected that the sector would close out the 1990s with approximately ten million subscribers across all technologies (Possebon, 2009: 252). The reality was far different from the projections.

Although by 1999 in the United States pay-television had already surpassed broadcast network television, by the end of that same year slightly less than three million Brazilian households had some form of subscription television. The reasons the sector had not met industry projections are complex. Nonetheless, in broad terms, it is clear that costly subscription rates, geographically restricted access, and programming schedules largely comprised of foreign content were important factors in the unexpectedly slow growth during the industry's first decade.

However, as figure 1.2 shows, such slow growth was not restricted to the 1990s. Instead, it proved to be the norm for the Brazilian pay-television sector during the vast majority of its first two decades of existence. In 2000, for example, pay-television in Brazil had a household penetration rate of approximately 8 percent. By comparison, penetration rate was approximately 58 percent, 18 percent, 41 percent, and 15 percent in Argentina, Chile, Colombia, and Mexico, respectively (Silva, 2015: 57). By the end of 2010, Brazil's household penetration rate for pay-television had climbed to a still paltry 12 percent, paling in comparison to TV Globo's presence in over 98 percent of all Brazilian homes.

Nonetheless, writing in 2009, Possebon closed his detailed history of the Brazilian pay-television industry on an optimistic note, going so far as to deny that the number of subscribers was an important indicator of the sector's stability and future outlook (2009: 249). Within the broader context of an audiovisual landscape long dominated by the Globo group and within the specific context of the development of the pay-television sector, itself characterized in part by an uphill battle taken on by geographically dispersed entrepreneurs of varied sizes and economic capital, Possebon's conclusive analysis is not incorrect. Nonetheless, it is important to point out that Possebon was hand-picked by the Associação Brasileira de TV por Assinatura (Brazilian Pay-Television Association, ABTA), which, along with the Sindicato de Empresas de TV por Assinatura (Union of Pay-Television Companies, SETA), published *TV por Assinatura* to celebrate the industry's twenty years of existence. Thus, his general dismissal of the sector's middling number of subscribers in favor of highlighting economic factors such as commercial revenue and the development of new technologies can be seen as purposeful misdirection, thereby overemphasizing pay-television's limited impact on Brazil's mediascape in 2009. What Possebon could not have known, however, was that, despite an economic crisis that began in 2013 and worsened in subsequent years, the passage of Law 12.485/11 in 2011 and its gradual implementation between 2012 and 2014 would play a central role in nearly tripling the household penetration rate of pay-television to 30 percent by the end of 2016 (TIC Domicílios, 2017b).[10]

The Pay-TV Law: The End of the Network Era

Leading up to 2011, the Brazilian audiovisual landscape was fairly simple: TV Globo was the preferred viewing destination for the majority of the country's television audiences; Globo Filmes was the market leader for domestic films; and the pay-television sector and the Internet were not widely accessible. In terms of fictional content, though qualitatively more advanced, TV Globo's *telenovelas* were not vastly different from those that had come to solidify the network as the market leader in the late 1960s. For example, writing in 2010, Newton Cannito (2010: 110) argues that, despite the advent of the digital era, Brazilian networks insisted on a mode of production and creation aimed at capturing the largest possible audiences for their high-paying advertising partners. Though Cannito's characterization was accurate, the networks' refusal to pivot from a business model that had ensured them high profits for nearly five decades should be understood as the result of the Brazilian mediascape having not yet transitioned sufficiently enough to incentivize alterations, let alone transformations to their proven modes of operation.

Similarly, in the context of the United States, such change came about only in the mid-2000s, during television's multichannel transition to the Post-Network Era. Lotz argues that up until then, even though "network-era advertising practices" had long provided advertisers with decreasing returns, "the continued supply of capital from this sector discouraged change" (Lotz, 2014: 205). Such transitional periods, however, can create "'cracks' in successful organizational operations," disrupting hegemonic relationships and allowing for the establishment of new norms (200). Characterized by limited content choice, a dearth of technological advancements, and spectatorship restricted by time and place, Network-Era television produced a relatively uniform viewing experience. "This uniformity of use aided the industry's production processes," Lotz says, "because it enabled the industry to assume certain viewing conditions and rely on viewers to watch network-determined schedules" (56). During the multichannel transition, however, incipient technologies like the remote control, the VCR, and cable network distribution, combined with a proliferation of content aimed to fill the numerous channels made available by forms of subscription television, increased the audience's choice and control, profoundly altering their previously limited viewing experience (57–58). Nonetheless, these changes took decades to reach a point of economic crisis. Thus, it was not until the arrival of digital technologies and the onset of the Post-Network Era that Network-Era norms and business models were forced to adapt to the new reality, a process that continues into 2020.

Among other things, the digital technologies and distribution opportunities that ushered in the Post-Network Era in the United States enhanced the convenience, mobility, and theatricality of the television experience, enabling "storytelling forms that matched the emerging ways to engage with content" (Lotz, 2014: 59, 74). For example, Lotz notes that "convenience technologies encourage active selection, rather than passive viewing of the linear flow of whatever 'comes on next or is on,' and consequently led viewers to focus much more on programs than on networks—all of which contributes to eroding conventional production practices in significant ways and to producing the distinctions among prized content, live sports and contests, and linear viewing . . . Convenience technologies also increased the deliberateness in viewers' use of television, which allowed for adjustments in how programs were created, funded, paid for, and distributed" (68).

With regard to content creation and advertising, the arrival of the Post-Network Era and its characteristic offering of choice and control to viewers in the United States challenged broadcast networks and their long-established norms to reconceptualize how to best attract, keep, and reproduce the ever-fragmented audiences. Forced to adapt, Lotz maintains that "advertisers' willingness to finance experiments with different advertising strategies was the first domino to fall in the chain of events advancing transformation, and *it influenced many subsequent aspects of production and financing*" (Lotz, 2014: 205, emphasis mine). Lotz uses "production" to signify a larger process that includes the interrelated components of technology, creation, distribution, and audience research, exploring the ways in which these components interact within specific sociohistorical contexts to create distinct *types* of "production" (50). Along these lines, then, the different advertising strategies mentioned by Lotz "led to different business models; different business models led to different funding possibilities; different funding possibilities led to different programing; different programming redefined the medium's relationship with viewers and the culture at large" (205).

Thus, as is made clear by Lotz's example of the United States, the mediascape about which Cannito was writing in 2010, even despite the digital and technological advancements that serve as the basis of his discussion, was still entrenched in a Network-Era logic informed and shaped by a field characterized by limited choice and control and by audience reproducibility. Nonetheless, over the subsequent decade, the onset of an increasingly competitive marketplace allowed more Brazilians more choice and control of what and where they watch television, which, in 2020, has resulted in an uncertainty among networks like TV Globo regarding whether their enormous audiences are going to tune in as they previously did. Not unlike what occurred in the United States, Brazil's own multichannel transition as well as TV Globo's recognition of it and of its effects on the domestic market have resulted in a general restructuring of field norms (Brittos and Simões, 2010: 220).

The Pay-TV Law (12.485/11) spurred and has been at the center of this ongoing restructuring. The expansion of pay-television (and the broader Brazilian mediascape) from 2011 to the present (2020) stems from Law 12.485/11's promotion of the sector as a whole. The comprehensive approach to growth is articulated in the three primary interrelated objectives of the Law: to increase the number of competing companies and agents by eliminating bureaucratic barriers; to promote *Brazilian culture* and *bolster the local independent production sector*; and to expand access to pay-television to all classes (emphasis mine). To achieve these objectives, the Law outlines a number of initiatives from production and distribution to technology and consumption. The most widely discussed of these is the Law's establishment of quotas for both the presence of Brazilian channels in pay-television packages sold to the consumer and the requirement that content produced by local Brazilian production and independent production companies be aired on *all* qualifying pay-television channels, whether foreign or Brazilian.

Under previous legislation, namely the aforementioned Cable TV Law, distributors had to carry at least one channel with programming exclusively comprised of independently produced Brazilian films and audiovisual works. However, through the introduction of the concepts of *canais de espaço qualificado* (qualified space channels) and *canais brasileiros de espaço qualificado* (Brazilian qualified space channels), Law 12.485/11 established a much broader and more permanent space for locally produced content. To put it simply, qualified space channels refer to those that air films, miniseries, series, and narrative specials. According to the established quotas, during the daily prime-time window between 11 AM and 2 PM and 5 PM and 9 PM (if directed at children or adolescents), and between 6 PM and 12 PM for all other programming, each of the qualified space channels must air a weekly total of 210 minutes (3.5 hours) of

Qualified Space Channel (CEQ)
3 CEQs
Brazilian Qualified Space Channel (CBEQ)*
1 CBEQ
* The Pay-Tv Law requires that for every 3 CEQs, pay-television packages must include 1 CBEQ
* One-third of all CBEQs must be independent (CBEQIs)
* Of all the CBEQs, pay-television packages must include at least 2 super Brazilian channels (CSBEQs), one of which must be independent

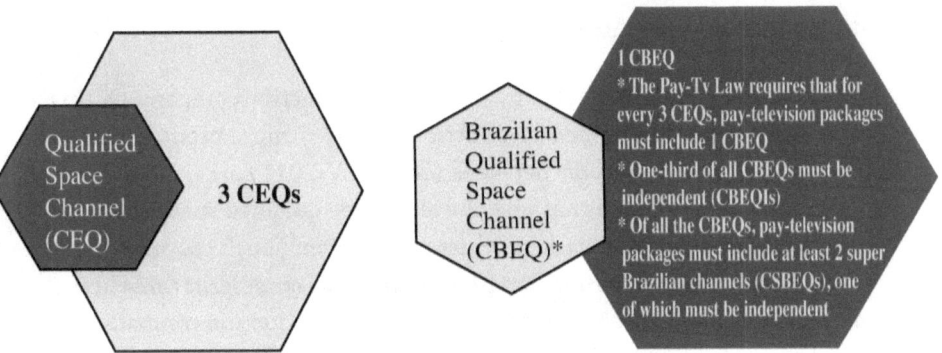

Figure 1.3. Qualified space channels (CEQs).

Qualified Space Channels (CEQs)
AMC
AXN
Comedy Central
Fox
HBO
Studo Universal
TBS
TNT
Warner Channel
Super Brazilian Channels (CSBEQs)
Canal Brasil
Brazilian Qualified Space Channels (CBEQs)
Arte 1
BIS
Globosat
GNT
Off
Play TV
Independent Brazilian Qualified Space Channels (CBEQIs)
CineBrasil TV
Fashion TV Brazil
Prime Box Brazil
TV Rã Tim Rum!

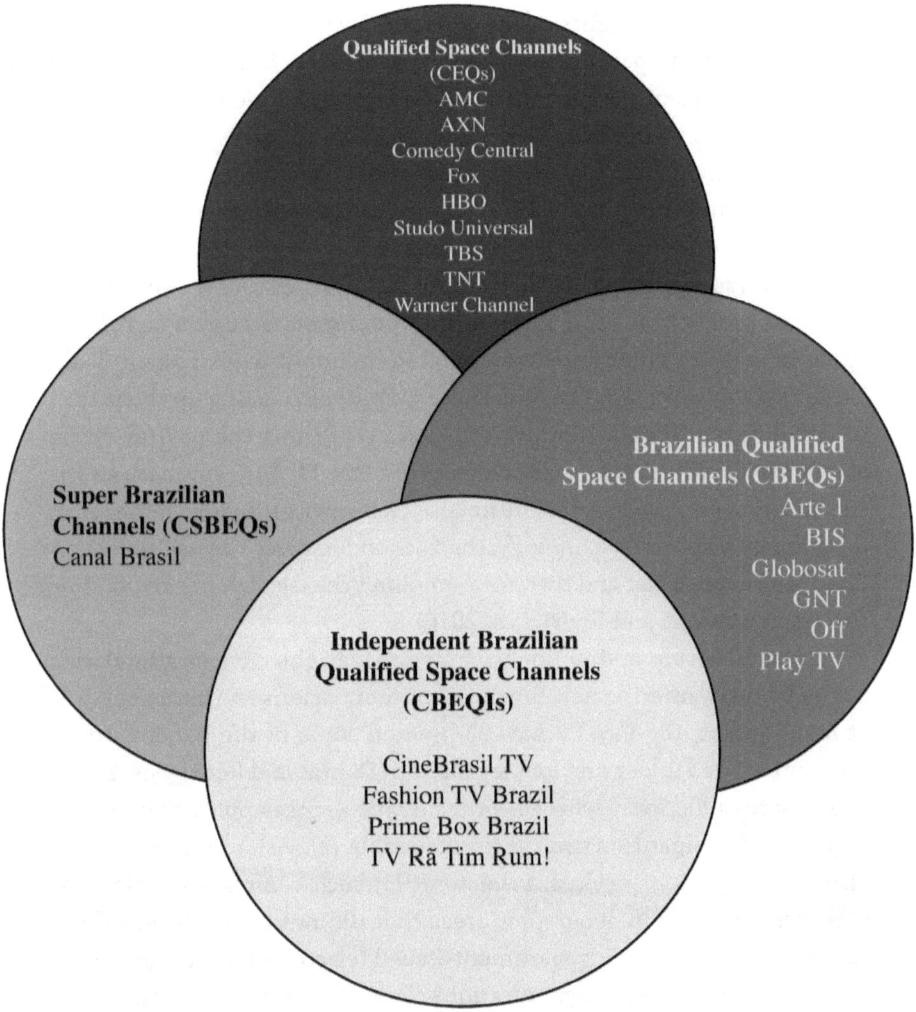

Figure 1.4. List of qualified space channels.

qualified space content created by a Brazilian production company. Of this total, a Brazilian *independent* production company must produce half of the content, or 105 minutes per week (Lei da TV, 2011; Lima, 2015).[11]

The Law also requires that one of every three qualified space channels in a given pay-television package must be *Brazilian*.[12] Such channels must (1) be programmed by a Brazilian programmer; (2) air at least three hours of qualified space content, created by a Brazilian production company, per day during the six-hour prime-time window, half of which must be the product of a Brazilian *independent* production company; and (3) not be involved in a contract of exclusivity that prohibits the programmer from commercializing the rights of the channel's exhibition and transmission to any interested operator (packager or distributor). As outlined by the Law, at least two of the Brazilian qualified space channels must be *canais super brasileiros* (super Brazilian channels). Such channels are required to air a minimum of twelve hours of Brazilian *independently* produced qualified space content per day, with a minimum of three of these hours coming during the six-hour prime-time window.

The quotas regulating production and the airing of content ensure that Brazilian production companies and programmers occupy a significant space in a sector traditionally dominated by non-Brazilian agents. Law 12.485/11, however, goes beyond these quotas, also taking up the matter of technology. Whereas the previous laws governing the pay-television sector regulated existing technologies, the Pay-TV Law emphasizes *serviço de acesso condicionado* (conditional access service). That is, rather than focusing on a specific technology, the Law underscores the usefulness offered to the consumer and therefore simplifies the legislation surrounding the sector (Dantas and Rodrigues, 2016).

In a similar vein and in line with its broader objective of stimulating competition by offering new Brazilian content options and better services at lower prices, the Pay-TV Law eliminated some of the barriers to access that existed under previous legislation (Dantas and Rodrigues, 2016). The Law thus did away with the bureaucratic license application process required of companies wanting to offer cable television and other television subscription services. Prior to 2011, such companies could offer their services only in geographic areas that did not coincide with those regions outlined in their government-issued telecommunications concessions. Because the telecommunications companies were legally restricted, they could not use their transmission networks to explore technological convergences like triple-play packages (television, broadband Internet, and telephone) (Lima, 2015). No longer limiting where those companies with telecommunications concessions could operate, Law 12.485/11 created the conditions for the broad commercialization of triple-play packages (Roppa et al., 2016). Indeed, this freedom has played an important role in expanding the total number of homes with broadband Internet access. Though this subject is discussed in greater detail in chapter 3, for now it suffices to point out that data show that since 2010, when only 27 percent of all households had some type of Internet access, that rate had doubled by the end of 2016 to 54 percent, 64 percent of which is in the form of broadband access (TIC Domicílios, 2017a).

The legislation preceding Law 12.485/11 also limited foreign capital in cable television companies to 49 percent and barred foreign capital altogether in other television subscription companies. The Pay-TV Law, however, opened up all sectors, independent of technology, to the participation of foreign capital. This change effectively allows telecommunications companies to offer pay-television packages. At the same time, however, these companies are limited to distribution—they cannot produce, program, or package content. Moreover, foreign telecommunications companies are prohibited from owning more than 30 percent of the total capital and voting power of broadcast networks, producers, and programmers with headquarters in Brazil (Roppa et al., 2016). Conversely, none of these is allowed to own more than 50 percent of the total capital and voting power of telecommunications companies (Roppa et al., 2016). Thus, while Law 12.485/11 takes measures to open the domestic market to global flows of capital and technologies, it ensures that programming and production remain under the control of national companies or media groups, which are in turn disconnected from distribution. In this way, the Law bets on owning the rights to intellectual property—that is, to locally produced symbolic goods—as being more desirable than the means to distribute such property (Roppa et al., 2016). Indeed, the possession of intellectual property rights as economic leverage and cultural capital has proved to be one of the central objectives of subscriber-funded Internet "portals" such as Netflix, a subject discussed further in chapter six (Lotz, 2017, 40, 62).

Another result of Law 12.485/11 has been to strengthen the Fundo Setorial do Audiovisual (FSA). Created by Law 11.437/06 in 2006, the FSA is a state-run investment fund directed at the development of all phases of the audiovisual production chain. As Sousa points out, while the Audiovisual Law ultimately leaves the power with the sponsoring company (e.g., Petrobras) to decide what works do and do not get made, the FSA situates the State as a decisive figure, insofar as it *directly* funds projects (Sousa, 2018: 166).[13] What is more, the FSA goes beyond merely supporting artistic production to also include the business side of creation. Along these lines, Sousa notes that historically, public resources were directed to filmmakers (167). However, the FSA expands the realm of beneficiaries by including distributors, television series producers, and infrastructure projects (167). The fund's money comes from the economic activity of the audiovisual sector itself: namely, from the aforementioned Contribution to the Development of National Cinema (CONDECINE). Three types of contributions are made to the FSA. For our purposes, the most important of these is the "Teles Contribution." According to Morais, this particular contribution currently makes up approximately 90 percent of all of the resources invested in FSA-approved projects (2019: 276). Established by Law 12.485/11, this contribution must be made by telecommunications companies that distribute audiovisual content. Assisted by the Banco Nacional de Desenvolvimento (National Bank of Development), ANCINE administers the allocation of monies from the fund, directly investing in projects that fall under one of four Lines of Action (*Linhas de ação* A-D). Of particular importance are those funds distributed from Line B-PRODAV, which covers the independent production and development of audiovisual works for broadcast and pay-television (Brazil *Mecanismos*, nd). By allowing foreign telecommunication companies to operate as distributors and making them contribute to the FSA, the Pay-TV Law expanded consumer access to subscription packages and the Internet, while also providing the production sector with unprecedented funding for the creation of content.

Beyond Globo: The Impact of the Pay-TV Law

The preceding discussion highlights the primary objectives of the Pay-TV Law and its attempt to diversify an audiovisual landscape dominated by TV Globo and its film production company, Globo Filmes. Indeed, prior to 2011, with limited competition from the pay-television sector and from other broadcast networks, Globo continued as television's undisputed leader, as it had since the late 1960s, producing *telenovelas* that attracted tens of millions of spectators nightly. Moreover, through Globo Filmes, the media group expanded its dominance to film, playing a central role in transferring its televisual aesthetic to the big screen (Johnson, 2005; Santos, 2009). In short, prior to the passage of the Pay-TV Law, the vast majority of Brazilian producers and consumers of audiovisual content had few alternatives: for both those who wanted to work in the industry and those who consumed audiovisual content, their best and most accessible options were directly linked to Globo.

Writing in 2010, Sabrina Nudeliman and Daniela Pfeiffer highlight the restricted nature of the audiovisual landscape and the hold gatekeepers such as TV Globo maintained over access, production, and distribution. As with other Latin American countries, they argue, Brazilian television grew out of a model that prioritized in-house production over partnering with and acquiring content from independent production companies. Despite policy attempts to foment such partnerships—with the rare exception of O2 Filmes or Conspiração Filmes, two of Brazil's largest production companies—content created by independent production companies for either network or pay-television was sparse.[14] Regarding pay-television in particular, Nudeliman and Pfeiffer (2010: 112–113) note the low penetration rates, which they attribute to high subscription costs. In fact, as others have before them, the authors go so far as to point out that a significant portion of existing pay-television customers subscribed to the service in order to ensure a higher-quality transmission of the broadcast channels (e.g., TV Globo). Though correct at the time, Nudeliman and Pfeiffer's depiction of the audiovisual landscape must be understood as one existing prior to the onset of the new Brazilian mediascape. In direct contrast with the period that preceded it, during the post-2011 era production of local content, production companies, distribution channels, available funding, and consumer access have never been so numerous and diverse. The data that follow reveal the way in which the implementation of the Pay-TV Law has played a central role in diversifying the Brazilian mediascape beyond Globo.

Attracted by cultural proximity, Brazilian television audiences have historically been accustomed to consuming locally produced content (Straubhaar, 1991, 2003). Consequently, for the pay-television sector to compete with TV Globo, audiences would have to be enticed with nationally produced works. It follows, at least in theory, that the Pay-TV Law's quotas for the inclusion of Brazilian qualified space channels, Brazilian producers, and certified Brazilian content would provide subscribers not only greater access to more content but to more local content produced by Brazilians. Broadly speaking, what was true in theory has proven true in practice.

The data suggest significant growth not just in the production of local content but, more specifically, in the production of Brazilian series. The growth in this genre, traditionally underrepresented in the Brazilian context, represents an important shift in a field long dominated by the highly formulaic *telenovela*, produced on an industrial scale. Additionally, the data clearly show an increase in the number of production companies, suggesting the rise of an industry existing beyond and in competition with Globo.[15] For example, the total number of certified hours of content produced for the pay-television sector—that is, programming vetted by ANCINE to meet the stipulations of Law 12.485/11—rose from 1,690 in 2008 to 4,288 in 2014 (Zeidan et al., 2016: 29, 52–56). Moreover, the most significant growth during the period came from the production of serial works, which increased from 703 hours in 2008 to 2,943 in 2014. The data also reveal that the jump in growth occurred precisely in 2012, the first year of the implementation of the Pay-TV Law. For example, from 2006 to 2011 there were 15, 21, 17, 27, 25, and 15 fictional series produced. Thus, the total number of fictional series produced for the six-year period was 120, for an average of twenty per year (Lista de CPBs, 2018). However, in 2012 alone, that number jumped to eighty-seven, an increase of 435 percent. In the five years that followed there were 108, 101, 89, 95, and 76 fictional series produced. Thus, the overall total for the six-year period between 2012 and 2017 was 556, an annual average of 92.67 fictional series produced (Lista de CPBs, 2018).

Similar growth occurred for the total number of hours produced. In the four years between 2008 and 2011, an average of 910 hours of serial content was produced (Zeidan et al., 2016: 55). Again, an exponential spike in production began in 2012. From 2012 to 2014, the total number of hours of serial content produced annually jumped to a yearly average of 2,512 hours, far outpacing the production of nonserial content, which averaged 1,144 hours per year (55). The overall growth in the total number of hours produced was the result of increased production from both Brazilian production and *independent* production companies (Zeidan et al., 2016).

In the case of the former, production jumped from 543 hours in 2008 to 1,608 hours in 2014, an increase of 196 percent (Zeidan et al., 2016: 57). The growth coming from Brazilian independent production companies

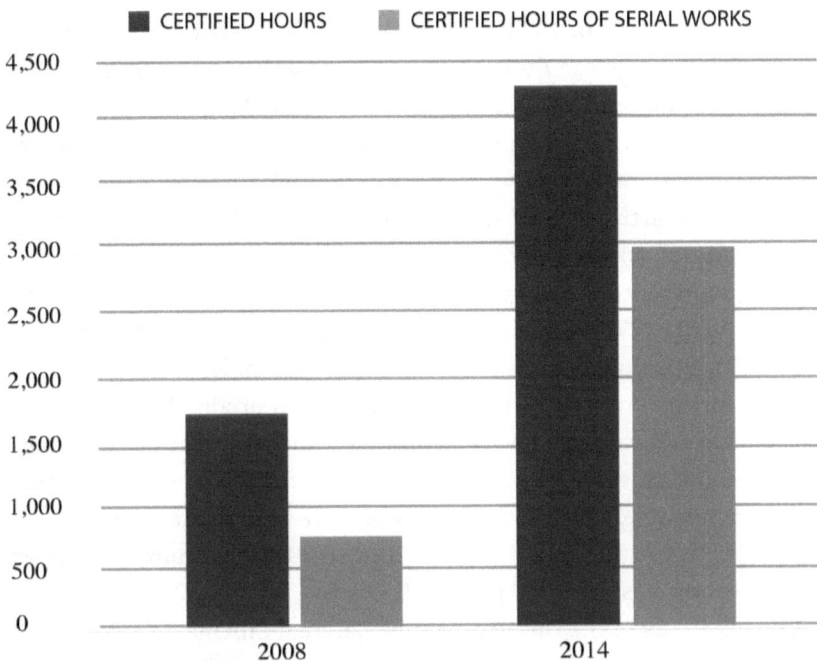

Figure 1.5. Total number of certified hours of pay-TV content, 2008 and 2014. Created from Zeidan et al. (2016).

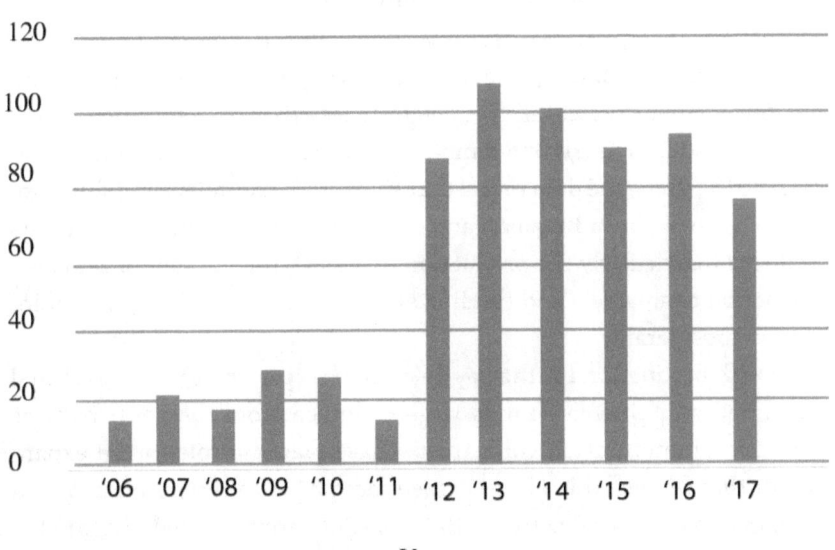

Figure 1.6. Total number of series produced for pay-TV, 2006–2017.

was even greater: from 303 hours in 2008 to 1,930 hours in 2014, an increase of 536 percent (57). The same data show that the number of registered Brazilian production companies has risen along with the growth in the production of local content. As of 2016, a total of 7,312 production companies were registered with the National Film Agency (268). From the first year of the Pay-TV Law in 2012 through 2015, the regulatory body registered an average of approximately 972 production companies per year, representing an increase of 280 percent over the period between 2002 and 2011 (270). Finally, there was a dramatic shift regarding production for Brazilian qualified space and Brazilian independent qualified space channels. From 2006 to 2011, thirty-seven production companies produced content for the former. From 2012 to 2017, that number grew to forty-eight, a nearly 30 percent increase. As for production for Brazilian independent qualified space channels, there were thirteen production companies from 2006 to 2011. From 2012 to 2017, that number jumped to 146—an increase of 1,023 percent (Lista de CPBs, 2018).

Contributions to the Development of National Cinema (CONDECINE) also experienced significant increases beginning in 2012 (Brazil, CONDECINE, 2016). While some of the other areas of contribution also increased after 2012, the overwhelming portion of the exponential growth during the period stemmed from those made by the telecommunications companies. Not surprisingly, flush with unprecedented funds, the FSA significantly increased its direct investment in the different Lines of Action. As figure 1.7 shows, television investments related to production and development increased from slightly less than $6.24 million (R$20 million) in 2011 to nearly $58.8 million (R$190 million) in 2015 (Brazil Valores, 2016). Thus, the data reveal that since 2011, pay-television subscriptions, channels (both Brazilian and non-Brazilian), the number of hours produced (particularly the production of series), the number of Brazilian production companies, and funding stemming from the FSA have all increased considerably.

As with production for the pay-television sector, the FSA's augmented investments in cinema—funds largely derived from the contributions from telecommunication companies—have played a role in the expansion of that sector, which has released more films in recent years. When compared to the period between 1995 and 2004, represented in figure 1.1, the numbers from figure 1.8 suggest a slightly more competitive milieu beginning in 2012.

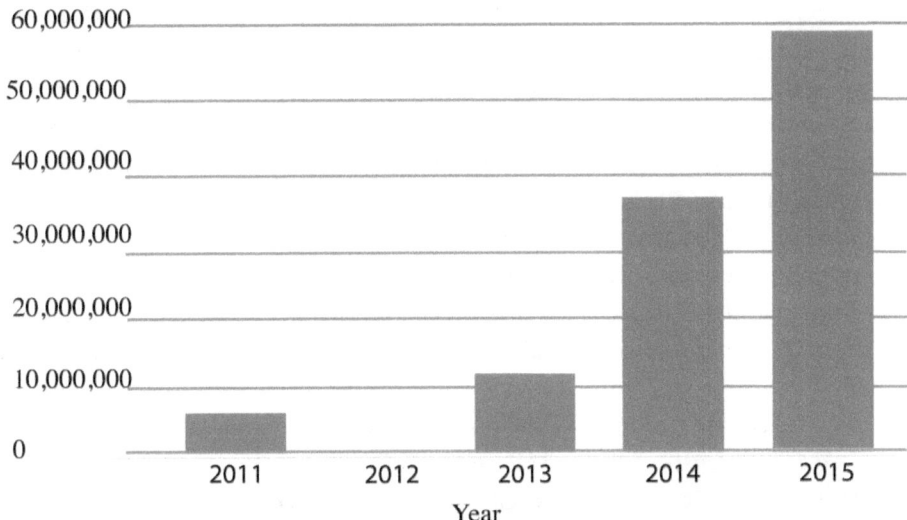

Figure 1.7. Audiovisual Sector Fund (Fundo Setorial do Audiovisual) (US dollars calculated using an exchange rate of 3.2 reais to 1 dollar). Created from Brazil, Agência Nacional do Cinema (2016).

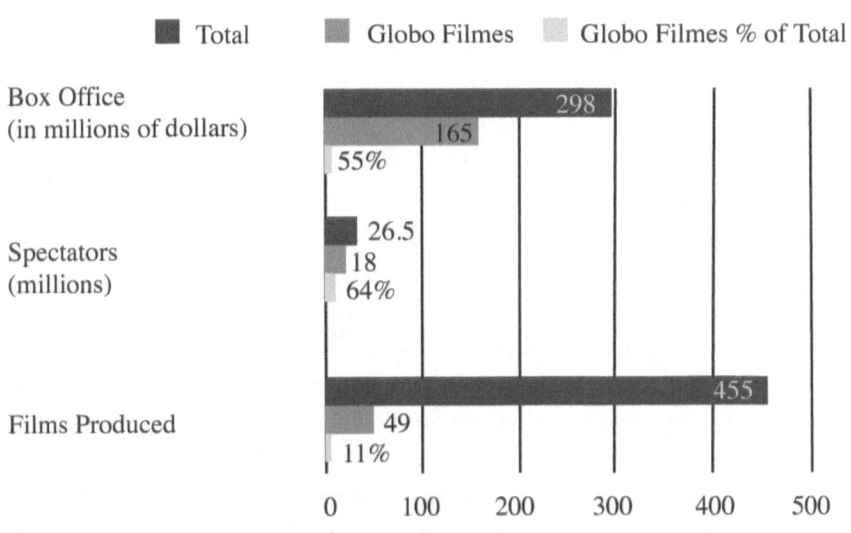

Figure 1.8. Brazilian cinema, 2012–2015 (US dollars calculated using an exchange rate of 3.2 reais to 1 dollar). Created from data from Brazil, Observatório Brasileiro do Cinema e do Audiovisual (2016).

Though opportunities across the industry have experienced a clear increase, it is important not to take these to indicate that the industry has suddenly become accessible to all. Rather, the economic and cultural concentration that long characterized Brazilian audiovisual production (and in broader terms, Brazil itself) leading up to the Pay-TV Law continues, albeit to a lesser degree, in symbolic and practical terms. Most of the important increases mentioned above have largely occurred in Brazil's audiovisual capitals, Rio de Janeiro and São Paulo. Despite the Law's attempts to foster regional diversification, the field continues to cling to the economic and cultural centers in the Southeast. For example, between 2014 and 2016, approximately 53 percent of all distributors, 53 percent of all registered production and post-production companies, 76 percent of all certified programs, and 52 percent of all pay-television subscribers were concentrated in Rio de Janeiro and São Paulo (Zeidan et al., 2016: 54, 72–73, 126–127, 130, 133–134, 137–138). What is more, Sousa correctly highlights the continued economic concentration of channels and distribution (2018: 202). As an example, Sousa points out that the American and Brazilian media behemoths, Time Warner and Globo, own a combined 60 percent of the over two hundred pay-television channels and that Mexican telecommunication giant, Telecom Americas (Claro, Embratel, Net), and California-based satellite provider, DirecTV, together possess 81 percent of the market share (200). Thus, notwithstanding the Law's efforts to diversify the industry, the historical, economic, and cultural formation of Brazil, which since the second half of the eighteenth century has centered largely on the southeastern portion of the country, has not disappeared.

Nonetheless, it is clear that the Pay-TV Law's establishment of quotas for Brazilian content and channels, the deregulation of telecommunication companies, and the mandate that these contribute to the FSA have resulted—for both new agents and spectators alike—in the creation of an audiovisual space outside of TV Globo's exclusive vertical production model.[16] In fact, even Sousa admits that, while there continues to exist an underlying concentration of power in the hands of a few players, the Law has undeniably resulted in the opening up of the field to more participants than ever before: "Even if it is restricted to pay-television, the obligation to display national content has become a landmark in the relationship between cinema and television and between independent production and commercial channels in Brazil. The measure, created by Law 12.485/11, has had a considerable impact on the Brazilian audiovisual market. The demand for over a thousand hours of annual programming has allowed the emergence of new agents and has exponentially expanded the labor market" (2018: 198, 200).

Indeed, in the years since its implementation, the Pay-TV Law has significantly impacted the audiovisual industry in Brazil while also aiding in the expansion of the power of the country's imagination (Appadurai, 1996: 54). As I have argued elsewhere (Carter, 2018), though the Brazilian audiovisual industry is still a ways off from entering a Post-Network Era, the Pay-TV Law has not only pushed Brazil out of its Network Era but increasingly closer to the onset of the Post-Network Era. The importance of this shift cannot be understated. As discussed in the introduction and throughout this chapter, Brazil's mediascape has historically been dominated by a single family-owned company that positions its narrative production (*telenovelas*) as the primary symbolic source for the construction and representation of what it means to be Brazilian. Put differently, over the years these long-form serial narratives have become the most important source for the "mediation" of Brazil as an imagined community (Martín-Barbero, 1993). Problematically, however, TV Globo's dominance, characterized by narratives and an aesthetic that have historically emphasized well-to-do whiteness based in Rio de Janeiro and São Paulo, has made it difficult for a substantial section of the population to recognize itself in the network's representation of what it means to be Brazilian (Araújo, 2000). As La Pastina, Straubhaar, and Sifuentes put it, that representation has led many Brazilians to ask: "Why do I feel I don't belong to the Brazil on TV?" (2014). In the chapters that follow, I examine a selection of television and Internet fiction. All of the works share in common that they emerged out of the newly established Brazilian mediascape and that, to a large degree, they owe their existence to the mediascape the Pay-TV Law helped to bring about. In analyzing the individual productions, I intend to demonstrate how, in their own unique ways, they derive from a proliferation of voices and offer more diverse portrayals of Brazil and the Brazilian population than was otherwise the case prior to the onset of the post-2011 mediascape.

2

Pay-Television Welcomes Brazil

As touched on in chapter 1, for most of its three decades of existence pay-television in Brazil has largely been home to non-Brazilian content. That is, historically, it was where the economic and cultural elite could watch a non-Brazilian newscast, cooking shows, sporting events, or perhaps a recent film or series from the United States or Europe. To put it simply, leading up to 2011, *Brazil* was largely absent from pay-television's programming grid. However, the Pay-TV Law's channel and content quotas have shifted that reality, bringing more Brazilians in contact with more domestically produced content. Speaking in 2017 about the impact of the Pay-TV Law on the Brazilian mediascape, Manoel Rangel (Nitahara, 2017), then president of ANCINE, highlights the expanded funding from the FSA, the increase of Brazilian independent production, and the airing of this production on pay-television channels. For Rangel, the combination of financing, production, and distribution is not simply about bolstering a sector and generating revenue streams. More than this, it is, in Rangel's (Nitahara, 2017) words, about how the Law allows for "Brazilians to have contact with Brazilian audiovisual production," thereby intensifying "Brazil's ability to see itself on screen." Nowhere has this intensification been more apparent than in the production and distribution of series.[1]

The Accelerated Growth of Series

While *telenovelas* have long been Brazilian television's (if not Brazilian culture's) primary symbolic good, over the years TV Globo has also produced series, albeit to a much lesser extent. In 1965, for example, the network's first-ever fictional production was the six-episode *Rua da Matriz* (*Matriz Street*), the Brazilian version of *Coronation Street*. Seven years later, the network aired the first iteration of *Grande família* (*The Big Family*), a family sitcom in the mode of *All in the Family,* which totaled 105 episodes over four seasons between 1972 and 1975.[2] In the late 1970s, TV Globo produced *Carga pesada* (*Heavy Load,* 1979–1981)[3] and *Malu mulher* (*Malu Woman,* 1979–1980), registering forty-nine and seventy-six episodes, respectively. The time slots in which these respective episodic series aired tell us something about the early development of Brazilian television fiction as well as about the genre's position within Globo's programming hierarchy. In a period in which the Brazilian *telenovela* was still a few years away from becoming Brazil's most produced and coveted genre, *Rua da Matriz* was on at 6:30 PM. In contrast, *Grande família*'s weekly airing was already much later, at 9:30 PM. By the time *Carga pesada* and *Malu mulher* came along, both their weekly airings were in the 10 PM time slot. As Straubhaar (1984) demonstrates, over this nearly fifteen-year period the *telenovela* experienced significant growth, both in terms of production and audience share. Ultimately, the success of the genre led to it taking over Globo's prime-time programming with three original *telenovelas* airing each night between 6 and 10 PM. In turn, often marketed as prestige content, *teleteatros*, miniseries, and series were relegated to post-prime-time programming slots, which over time became a space for experimenting with talent (actors, directors, writers, etc.) and aesthetics and styles to determine what should and should not find its way to TV Globo's prime-time *telenovelas*.

Leading up to 2011, then, the vast majority of television viewers in Brazil found their options limited in terms of both genre and availability. For example, the numerous singular *teleteatros*, mini and microseries directed by Luiz Fernando Carvalho (Carter, 2018), or miniseries by experimental film and television director Guel Arraes always aired sometime after 10 PM and with far lesser promotion than is custom for *telenovelas*. Thus, in order to watch these, any of TV Globo's miniseries, which the network has consistently produced since the early 1980s, or Fernando Meirelles's uneven yet often excellent *Cidade dos homens* (*City of Men,* 2002–2005) or his superb *Som e fúria* (2009), an adaptation of the Canadian *Slings and Arrows* (2003–2006), one would have to either stay up until at least 11 PM on a weeknight, wait for the work to become available on DVD, or download a pirated version. In each instance, it is clear that one's socioeconomic status figures prominently. As TV Globo knows, and as is evidenced by the type of higher-end products (e.g., luxury cars, high-end chocolate and soaps, etc.) advertised during the commercial breaks that structure such prestige programming, viewers able to stay up later often have more professional flexibility, which is frequently related to, although not necessarily so, economic flexibility. The same can be said of DVDs, especially considering their high price tags in Brazil and the costliness of DVD players. In the last instance, in order to download a pirated version of a show, one would need to have broadband Internet access, which was both expensive and relatively uncommon prior to 2011.

Economic barriers certainly still exist in the post-2011 mediascape, even if they are not as exclusionary as they once were. The point here is that whereas the Brazilian series long occupied a subordinate position vis-à-vis the *telenovela*, the expansion of the pay-television, telecommunications, Internet, and streaming sectors has made the genre both more prevalent and more accessible than ever before. For example, Paulo Roberto Schmidt (Laporta, 2016), owner of the independent production company Academia de Filme, notes that prior to the implementation of Law 12.485/11, his company devoted the vast majority of its efforts to advertising campaigns. Since 2011, however, Academia de Filme's overall production for film and television has grown from 5 to 30 percent. Similarly, Eduardo Tibiriçá (Laporta, 2016), part owner of the production company Bossa Nova Group, points out that prior to the Pay-TV Law, 85 percent of the company's overall production was directed at advertising, with the remaining 15 percent for television. According to Tibiriçá, in the post-2011 mediascape, Bossa Nova Group's production for television has more than doubled to over 30 percent. Responding to the quickly changing mediascape, Globo executive Mônica Albuquerque also shines a light on the media group's own shift, which reorganized its corporate structure so as to be able to produce even more original content for the media conglomerate's pay-television channels and streaming service. To this end, Globo employs more than 250 writers who work to develop *series* that will meet the needs of the company's different platforms (emphasis mine, Globo inova, 2019).

Such a large number will likely stand out to those familiar with the Brazilian field of television production. This is because television writers in Brazil have historically been associated with the *telenovela* genre. Moreover, the *telenovela* writer, who over the years has come to occupy a god-like status within the field, has traditionally worked alone, writing up to forty pages a day, six days a week (Hamburger, 2005). Importantly, however, such a mode of production was the result of a particular type of ad-supported commercial model. As Lotz has argued, and as is implied by Albuquerque's comments, the emergence of new economic models, such as subscriber-supported platforms, creates the conditions for new modes of production (2014, 2017, 2018). The proliferation of writers, then, is significant in that it represents further evidence of ongoing economic and creative shifts regarding the types of fictional content produced in Brazil. In the words of Massarolo and Mesquita, "Historically, when content platforms were in the hands of a select few players, the distribution of content was strategically controlled and forms of visualization were circumscribed to the economic interests of large media conglomerates. With video streaming, distribution platforms move from the mass-market to the niche market, thinning boundaries between producer and consumer" (2016: 4).

Along these lines, in the post-2011 mediascape, the ever-diverse production sector finds itself increasingly closer to an ever-diverse pay-television audience. According to a 2002 ABTA-funded (the Brazilian Pay-Television/Telecom Association) study conducted by the Fundação Getúlio Vargas (FGV) and Accenture, pay-television penetration was low even among these, the country's most economically stable classes. The study found that penetration rates for the combined A and B Classes and for the C Class were a dismal 35 percent and 5 percent. The authors of the study concluded that for pay-television to achieve stability, the penetration rates needed to reach a minimum of 56 percent and 11 percent, respectively (Possebon, 2009: 192). In order for similar numbers to materialize, the study recommended that pay-television operators offer basic packages at the monthly rate of R$30 (~$12 US at the time). Such packages, however, would resolve only one of the challenges facing the pay-television industry. The issues pertaining to limitations on the participation of foreign capital and the overwhelming lack of domestic production would still need to be addressed.

As discussed in chapter 1, in an effort to bring about the long-awaited growth of this dormant sector, the Pay-TV Law dealt with precisely these and other issues. Though at the end of 2010 the pay-television industry had still not reached the symbolic 10 million mark—reporting the total number of household subscribers at 9.8 million—important socioeconomic transformations resulting from President Lula's aforementioned Propositional State were under way. Largely stemming from innovative social welfare programs like *Bolsa Família* (Family Grant),[4] Escosteguy and Coutinho show that the economic uptick occurring over President Lula's two terms equated to a per capita income growth rate of 23 percent (2017). Moreover, they note that during the Lula years minimum wage increased by 65 percent and approximately nineteen million people rose from poverty to the working middle-class, also known as the C Class.[5] Despite a recession beginning in 2014, the economic advancements made during Lula's Propositional State played an important role in nearly doubling total pay-television household subscriptions to approximately 17.8 million by the end of 2018 (Dados do, 2018). Perhaps not surprisingly, especially considering the growth of the C Class during Lula's tenure, of that total there has been a significant increase in the number of C Class subscribers: from only 5 percent in 2002 to nearly 49 percent by early 2018. Additionally, the D and E Classes—not even mentioned in the report from 2002—had climbed to 9 percent by the end of 2017. Growth also occurred among the A and B Classes, which rose from 35 percent in 2002 to 44 percent in 2018 (Mídia fatos, 2018). Such data reveal an ongoing socioeconomic diversification of a sector that has historically served and been linked to those members of Brazil's most financially secure classes. Simply put, not only are more Brazilians subscribing to pay-television in the post-2011 mediascape than they did previously, but those subscribers are more diverse than they have ever been.

Just as subscriber diversity has increased since 2012, so too has viewing. Data from Kantar Ibope Media show that average daily pay-television viewing has increased to three hours and eighteen minutes in 2017, up from two hours and twenty-nine minutes in 2011. The prime-time window-share of that total average increased from one hour and twenty-eight minutes in 2010 to one hour and fifty-eight minutes in 2017 (Mídia Fatos, 2018). Though growth has occurred among all genders, age groups, and socioeconomic classes, it is particularly strong among men and women between the ages of twelve and forty-nine, increasing by 46 percent since 2010. Over that same period, the C Class has outpaced the viewing time of the A and B Classes, registering an average of three hours and twenty-nine minutes compared to three hours and two minutes per day for the latter (Mídia Fatos, 2018). As with the increase in subscriptions among all classes, the numbers regarding viewership—particularly when placed alongside the declining audience shares of broadcast networks—imply that these subscribers are devoting an increased portion of their television viewing consumption to pay-television.

Contemplating Brazils

The increasingly diverse Pay-TV audiences are met with increasingly diverse programming, particularly when compared to the pre-2011 mediascape. The expansion of the mediascape since 2011 to include producers, works, and distributors in addition to and outside of Globo's vertically integrated structure provides the scaffolding for the creation of works whose narratives—to borrow from Tatiana Signorelli Heise (2012)—display the potential to reform, oppose, or propose alternative versions of what it means to be Brazilian. Analyzing a number of feature-length documentaries and fictional films, all of which "explicitly thematize nationhood" and were released during the *retomada* (reemergence of domestic film production in the mid-1990s), Heise explores the significance of Brazilian national identity in a context increasingly characterized by the rise of "'subnational' or 'transnational' identities based on race, ethnicity, gender, and sexuality" (2012: 3). Rather than arguing, as some scholars have, that such identities disrupt "the capacity of the nation to confer a sense of belonging and collective affiliation," Heise employs the aforementioned interpretive categories (along with what she refers to as the celebratory category), effectively demonstrating how, from varied positions, in varied ways, and to varying degrees, the films in question constantly reference "the hegemonic discourse of *brasilidade*" (167). For Heise, the centrality of the nation in these films, even among those that stake out highly critical positions, suggests that "there is no indication that a concern with national identity is receding in the face of social problems or the rise of other types of social identities" (167). Rather, Heise shows that ideas of the nation and the audiovisual representations of those ideas are dynamic, diverse, and adaptable to the defining sociohistorical context.

While Heise aims her attention at films produced during the *retomada*, the centrality of the nation in contemporary Brazilian cinema is not unique to recent production. As Lisa Shaw and Stephanie Denninson (2007) point out, from Humberto Mauro to Glauber Rocha to Ana Muylaert, portraying the nation has been one of the defining characteristics of Brazilian cinema's past and present. The same can be said of broadcast network television, albeit to an even greater degree. Whereas Brazilian films have lingered in Hollywood's long, suffocating shadow, both in terms of market share and perceived social and aesthetic value, Brazilian television, especially that produced by TV Globo, has consistently been the go-to option for local viewers. Thus, without discounting Brazilian cinema's aesthetic and cultural importance, it must, nevertheless, be noted that even the most-watched Brazilian films of all time pale in comparison to the size of an average audience captured by TV Globo's *telenovelas*. Indeed, since TV Globo first became the country's dominant broadcast network in 1968, no local cultural production has consistently been more frequently produced, attracted more spectators, and had a greater impact on the way Brazil imagines itself than the *telenovela*.

Nonetheless, TV Globo's near monopolistic presence over the five decades that followed 1968 played a fundamental role in reducing creative participation and limiting fictional portrayals of the nation. As such, in what might be understood as a hegemonic concession, even those few fictional works that "reform," "oppose," or "propose alternative" conceptualizations of the nation have more often than not come from TV Globo itself. More recently, the expansion of the Brazilian mediascape has paved the way for, among other things, new fictional works.

According to ANCINE's 2017 report on the pay-television market, depending on one's subscription package, the varied forms of pay-television offered their approximately eighteen million subscribers up to 166 total channels. Of these, 101 (60.8%) are registered with the regulatory body as either qualified space (CEQ), Brazilian qualified space (CABEQ), or super Brazilian qualified space (CABEQ SB) channels (Alves da Silva et al., 2018).[6] The reader will recall from chapter 1 that Law 12.485/11 stipulates that a CEQ air a minimum of 3.5 hours of Brazilian content (half of which must come from a Brazilian independent production company) during prime-time hours. CABEQs, on the other hand, which are by definition Brazilian controlled and operated channels, must air at least twenty-one weekly hours (half of the weekly prime-time total) of Brazilian content, with 10.5 of those hours stemming from the work of Brazilian independent production companies. Last, CABEQ SBs, also defined as Brazilian controlled and operated channels, must air a minimum of twelve daily hours of content produced by Brazilian independent production companies. Three of those twelve hours need to be made available during the prime-time window. Consequently, the least possible amount of Brazilian content these 101 channels could air each week without breaking the law would be 353.5 hours.

The obligation to meet Law 12.485/11's quotas changed the rules of the game. Consequently, in addition to ensuring their programming is in line with the current policy, pay-television executives who oversee one or more of the various types of CEQs must pose at least one very basic question: what type of *Brazilian* content do they believe their target audiences want to watch? In a landscape littered with imported content, prior to the passing of the Pay-TV Law, such a question was likely rare at best. However, within the new Brazilian mediascape, far and away the most common response has been series. The three leading serial genres in terms of percentage of programming hours in 2017 were varieties (38.6%), documentaries (29.4%), and fiction (11.8%) (Alves da Silva et al., 2018). Thus, at minimum, the different qualified space channels would have aired nearly 42 hours per week of Brazilian fictional series. By comparison, in 2011, when the Pay-TV Law was passed but not yet implemented, *all* fictional series—that is, Brazilian and non-Brazilian—made up only 17.33 percent of all the programming of channels that would later be classified under the category of qualified space (Flaksman et al., 2011).

This is not to suggest that domestically produced series had no place on Brazilian pay-television prior to 2011. For example, while relatively rare, one could point to HBO Latin America's original series. Between 2005 and 2011, the channel co-produced and aired four such series: *Mandrake* (2005–2007), *Filhos do carnaval* (*Sons of Carnival*, 2006 and 2009), *Alice* (2008 and 2010), and *Mulher de fases* (*Woman of Phases*, 2011). Between 2012 and 2017, HBO Latin America doubled its co-production of original series to eight. Based on the data outlined above and in chapter 1, it is clear that during the post-2011 era subscribers, channels, independent producers, series, and viewership have all substantially increased. Importantly, these increases have combined to expand the national mediascape in ways never before seen in Brazil. In simple terms, the new Brazilian mediascape has provided a space for more creators, more formats, more distributors, and more spectators than ever. In terms of fictional content, the rise of television and web series has been at the core of the post-2011 expansion. With this in mind, the remainder of this chapter focuses on two recent pay-television series: *1 contra todos* (*1 Against All*, dir. Breno Silveira, Fox Brasil, 2016–) and *Lama dos dias* (*Mud of the Days*, dir. Hilton Lacerda, Canal Brasil, 2018–).

Among the numerous possibilities from the period, I have selected these series for three main reasons. First, in addition to being fictional dramas, each was produced after 2012 under the auspices of the Pay-TV Law. Second, both were created by directors who have gained notoriety for their work in film. Third, whereas the narrative of *1 contra todos* centers on São Paulo and Brasília and aired on the international pay-television channel Fox, *Lama dos dias* was filmed and set in Recife, Pernambuco, and aired on the super Brazilian channel, Canal Brasil. It is important to note that TV Globo's vast production of television fiction deals with such wide-ranging issues as race, gender and sexuality, violence, politics, and the arts. However, each of the series analyzed in this chapter, as well as those discussed in chapters 3, 4, and 5, differ from Globo's broadcast network productions insofar as they are made for and distributed by the less content-regulated spaces of pay-television and the Internet. Related to this, unlike TV Globo's *telenovelas*, miniseries, and occasional series, all of which cater to the widest possible audience, the series discussed throughout this book are created and distributed with the understanding that they will be consumed by smaller, niche audiences.

1 contra todos—Brazil versus Brazil

Satisfying a portion of the international pay-television channel's quota requirement, the first of four seasons of *1 contra todos* premiered on Fox Brasil at 10:30 PM on June 20, 2016.[7] Co-produced by Fox Brasil and Conspiração Filmes, an established independent production company based in Rio de Janeiro, the series received approximately $6.7 ($2.1 US), $7.9 ($2.5 US), and $9 ($2.8 US) million for seasons two, three, and four from the aforementioned CONDECINE funding source.[8] Created and written by Gustavo Lipsztein, Thomas Starvos, and Breno Silveira, who, along with Daniel Lieff, also directed the series, *1 contra todos* has consistently placed among the most watched pay-television series in Brazil (*Um contra todos*, 2016). In addition to the commercial success, which extends to other markets in Latin America, especially in Mexico, *1 contra todos* has also received multiple International Emmy Award nominations for Best Actor (Júlio Andrade) and Best Dramatic Series.

Before discussing the series in greater depth, Silveira's professional trajectory and his involvement in *1 contra todos* deserves mentioning, as it highlights, at least in terms of expanded options, the opening up of the

Brazilian mediascape since 2011. Leading up to the first season of *1 contra todos*, Silveira's work in television occurred primarily early in his career, when he worked on commercials and directed music videos. After having served as a director of photography on a number of films in the 1990s and early 2000s, Silveira made his directorial debut in film in 2005 with *2 filhos de Francisco* (*2 Sons of Francisco*), which remains one of the highest-grossing Brazilian films since 1990.[9] The commercial success of *2 filhos de Francisco* brought more opportunities to Silveira, who went on to direct four additional films between 2008 and 2017.[10]

By late 2018, comments made by Silveira during a talk given at the Acadêmia Internacional de Cinema in São Paulo (International Academy of Cinema) suggested the director had become increasingly interested in television as a medium to explore his professional and creative interests. Confirming a point this book has sought to unearth, Silveira (2018b) said: "The [television] market has never been so in-demand. There is a need for professionals from all different areas. Today, one can make a living doing series in Brazil, a reality that simply did not exist until only recently. For example, we have already signed four contracts to produce series next year." However, as the following comments from Silveira show, his interest in creating and directing television series is not reduced simply to the fact there is a demand. As he had pointed out in another piece, while Brazilian cinema has become overly preoccupied with the perceived tastes of the movie-going public, all over the world smart and intelligent work is being done not in film but in series. Silveira (Breno, 2016) goes on to rave about the relative ease, quickness, and freedom he experienced making *1 contra todos*.

Since its debut in 2016, *1 contra todos* has been the most popular Brazilian series on pay-television and of the one most watched in Latin America (Furtado, 2018). What is it about the series that makes it so attractive to audiences in Brazil? To a large degree, it lies in the work's successful negotiation of global and local elements. Essentially, *1 contra todos* is a Brazilian version of AMC's *Breaking Bad* (2008–2013). However, whereas *Breaking Bad* broadly centers on Walter White's moral decline from model high school chemistry teacher to murderous drug lord, *1 contra todos* comments specifically on an imagined *Brazilian* morality through the figure of Cadu (Júlio Andrade), a hardworking, upstanding attorney who finds himself increasingly *bending bad*. The clear moral positioning in *Breaking Bad*—from good to bad—stands in direct contrast to the moral ambiguity in *1 contra todos*. Perhaps this is not surprising, especially considering that Brazilian anthropologist Roberto DaMatta (1979) has argued that whereas North Americans strive for clear definitions, Brazilians are comfortable with, and even celebrate, ambiguity. Thus, just as Cadu criticizes Brazil and Brazilians for being corrupt, he finds himself also engaging in such behavior, even if he remains disgusted by it.

In each of the three seasons released at the time of this writing, Cadu employs voiceover narration at key moments to inform the viewer of his moral struggle and the larger issue at hand: what does it mean to be good in a bad world? It was with a similar statement that Cadu opens season one: "I consider myself to be a good guy. I have always tried to do what's right. I must be the last honest idiot in this country. But in Brazil, being honest seems to be a defect." Throughout, the series puts forth the idea that insofar as law-abiding citizens like Cadu operate within a system characterized by corruption and illicit behavior, no one can escape without getting their hands at least a little dirty. In Cadu's case, every time he takes steps toward achieving his objective to change Brazil from outside or from within the political machine, either the machine itself or his unsolicited connection to the international drug trade pulls him ever closer to becoming a central reproducer of the very world he desires to change.

In a working-class neighborhood of Taubaté, São Paulo, a medium-sized city located between São Paulo and Rio de Janeiro, Cadu lives with his wife Malu (Júlia Ianina) and their son, Téo (João Fernandes). When we first encounter the couple, they are excitedly awaiting the arrival of their second child. Things take a turn for the worse, however, when Cadu unexpectedly loses his job. The situation becomes even more dire when, unannounced, the police appear with a warrant to search the couple's apartment, where they believe Cadu is hiding significant amounts of marijuana. Sure enough, the swarm of police officers finds one ton of marijuana hidden in the ceiling of the couple's recently remodeled nursery. Though unaware of how the drugs got there and innocent of any wrongdoing, Cadu is arrested and sent to prison. There, in a trajectory that evokes that of Walter White, Cadu begins his descent into a world of crime and violence.

While foregrounding Cadu and his family's gradual moral downfall, season one focuses on Brazil's corrupt legal system. For example, in "Caminho do crime" (Path to Crime), the third episode of the first season, Cadu experiences a turning-point in his life when he accidentally kills Macarrão, a dangerous inmate who threatened him. As a result of this accident and the constant television reports presenting Cadu as the "Doutor do tráfico" (Dr. Drug Trafficker), the warden, Demóstenes Alencar (Adriano Garib), and the other inmates come to see him as the boss, a role Cadu reluctantly accepts in the belief it will keep him safe. This, however, becomes a serious problem for Cadu when, during the sixth episode, "Verdade não se cria" (Truth Is Not Created), Pepe (Roberto Brindelli), the Bolivian drug lord for whom Cadu has been mistaken all this time, is now Tabuatê's newest prisoner. Terrified the truth will come to light and that Pepe, or perhaps the other inmates, will take revenge, Cadu arranges an illicit transfer by bribing the warden. However, before he is transferred, to his surprise, Pepe informs Cadu that he must continue to behave as if they are partners. In response, worried his family will go bankrupt and he will lose them, Cadu implies to Pepe that he needs money. Following the two inmates' conversation, Pepe's men deliver a briefcase full of money to Malu, who is initially reluctant to accept it.

Cadu's series of moral compromises finally arrives at his family's doorstep. With regard to the briefcase, Malu initially tells her father, JP (Xando Garcia), that he always taught her to be honest and do what is right and that taking the drug money would go against those teachings. As he himself takes money from the briefcase, JP asks, "And where has that ever gotten us?" Persuaded by her father's message, Malu uses the money to pamper herself like a princess. As she does so, Cadu similarly tracks to the opposite end of the moral spectrum, consuming copious amounts of cocaine, getting tattoos, and having sex with prostitutes.

By the end of season one, nearly three hundred days into his sentence, Cadu has his day in court. However, even though Pepe testifies that he had never even seen Cadu prior to their encounter in prison, the corrupt, yet not incorrect, warden outlines all the illicit acts committed by Cadu since his arrival to the facility. As a result, Cadu spends another eleven months in jail before he is able to go home. But even then Cadu is not yet in the clear. Two years following his release, Cadu is at home with his wife and children, seemingly reacclimated to his average, middle-class life, when two of Pepe's men suddenly appear at Cadu's home. Though, as his wife had done before him, he politely declines the briefcase the rough-looking men hand to him, they inform Cadu that he has no choice: Pepe needs him.

The second season, which turns its attention to Brazil's corrupt political system, begins nine years after Cadu was first imprisoned and three years after Pepe's men gave him the briefcase. Since he was released from prison, Cadu has struggled to find work as an attorney. Instead, he toils as a shoe salesman at his father-in-law's modest sidewalk store. To make matters worse, Cadu is unable to keep up with household bills and expenses. As a result, he experiences a constant interior struggle between doing what is right and following the law or doing whatever it takes to take care of his family. This moral dialectic is most clearly on display in "A prisão é para sempre" (Prison is for Life), the first episode of season two. In consecutive scenes, the viewer watches first as Cadu's desire to provide for his family leads him to reconsider dipping into the money in Pepe's briefcase. Malu dissuades her husband with a message of family togetherness—that is, money, especially if acquired illicitly, is secondary to their health and unity. They have already played this game, and it left scars. Nevertheless, a sequence of defeats increasingly pushes Cadu to a tipping point.

In the subsequent scene, highlighting the seemingly boundless reach of Brazil's systemic corruption, a municipal employee threatens to fine JP R$10,000 (~$3,000 US) for an electrical irregularity at his shoe store. When, in dismay, JP makes it clear that such a sum would be impossible to secure, the municipal employee says he will forgo the fine if given R$5,000 right then and there. From the stockroom, Cadu overhears the conversation, leading him to confront the municipal employee by citing the legal code. Taken aback by Cadu's knowledge of the law, the corrupt employee decides to shut down JP's store. The unjust decision infuriates Cadu, who grabs the man by the collar and before a mass of passersby on the sidewalk in front of the store declares: "Listen here you shit, when you ask for a bribe, you're not just fucking over my father-in-law's store, you're fucking over me, the people, all of society." Cadu goes on to inform the employee, and by extension those who have gathered to witness the spectacle, that Brazil has the highest tax rates in the world. When, in turn, the municipal employee responds, "I don't give a shit about the country," Cadu turns to the crowd and says, "It is because of filth like this guy that Brazil is in the shits!" Punctuating his position, which is reminiscent of the one he takes at the beginning of season one prior to imprisonment and then again at the end following his release, Cadu repeatedly shouts: "Corrupt!" In the next scene, the social critique of Brazil is picked up by Simões Lopes (Stepan Nercessian), a host of an afternoon television program. As Malu dines with her two boys at a local restaurant, they watch as Lopes informs his television audience that, in Brazil, the good guys are the ones who go to jail. As he says this, police officers appear ushering Cadu into the back of a police car.

Cadu's second run-in with the law ultimately propels him to political aspirations. However, as we (and Cadu) learn toward the end of the season, Cadu is nothing more than Pepe's puppet. Gael Marques (Erom Cordeiro), the director of *Outra chance* (Another Chance), a nonprofit organization that works on the behalf of individuals who have been treated unjustly by the law, is able to get Cadu out of jail. He also offers him an opportunity to use his experience and legal expertise to speak out against the system. The very next day, Cadu sits alongside Gael at the nonprofit's offices, where they listen to a Brazilian woman share a story of how she was arrested for no apparent reason other than for being black: "Then, the police officer looked at this black face of mine," she says, "inside my car, my own car! And asked, 'Where did this little black lady steal this car?' I responded, 'I stole it from your mother the whore.' He didn't like that, so he arrested me for contempt and for possession of marijuana, even though I have never even smoked once in my life!" Reluctantly attending to Gael's request, Cadu represents the woman before the judge. Keeping with the series' overarching critique of Brazil's legal system, Cadu asks the judge to spare this woman the kind of injustice he and so many other Brazilians have endured. Victory in this case sets off a number of successful defenses, which lead to media exposure portraying Cadu as the voice of the wronged. However, prodded by Gael, who—we later learn—is working on behalf of Pepe, Cadu begins to realize that more widespread change will come only if he runs for office.

Working to promote his candidacy for Congress, Cadu quickly realizes that the political machine runs on money. Lagging well behind the heavily financed campaign of the corrupt warden turned politician, Demóstenes Alencar, Cadu turns once again to Pepe's briefcase. Unlike in the first instance, Cadu takes the money and uses it to bolster his own campaign, which results in his ascension in the polls. In the end, it is not enough, as Cadu falls just short of one of the six seats. However, as Simões Lopes informs his viewers, Cadu is the candidate with the seventh-most votes. Consequently, if one of the top six were to fall out for whatever reason, Cadu would be their substitute. Aware of the situation, Pepe sees an opportunity to gain influence and power by orchestrating the death of warden Demóstenes Alencar, whose airplane "accidentally" crashes.

Thus, "A caça-deputado" (The Congressman Hunter), the second episode of the second season, begins in 2009 with Cadu arriving to Brasília to begin his work as one of the congressional representatives of São Paulo. There, already compromised by his relationship with Pepe and his own questionable behavior, Cadu encounters a political system whose inherent logic is not only corrupt, but corruption itself. As such, Cadu finds himself serving two diametrically opposed interests that in actuality operate according to the same rule—every person for him or herself. Initially, Cadu remains firm in his stance against injustice and corruption. Cadu has been tasked with investigating the Speaker of the House and at the same time blackmailed to find him innocent. However, in the closing scenes of "A caça-deputado," rather than bending to the will of his corrupt colleagues, Cadu follows his convictions, declaring the speaker to be guilty of numerous crimes. In a monologue that echoes the altercation with the municipal employee from season two and that fits perfectly within Brazilian citizens' present-day wide-ranging, partisan discontent with their politicians, Cadu says, "This commission is not theirs. This Congress is not theirs. This house is not theirs. This house is ours! It belongs to the people!" As Cadu proclaims these words, those present, excluding the accused and their allies, along with the millions of Brazilians watching at home on television, enthusiastically and cathartically cheer their newfound political hero's honesty and bravery.

As in the first season, however, the system moves swiftly to eradicate Cadu's moral stand against those who have made Brazil's public coffers their personal bank accounts. By the end of season two, Cadu is yet again deeply involved in multiple illegal schemes. The downtrodden shoe salesman who called out the corrupt municipal employee and the recently elected congressman who denounced the Speaker of the House in front of all of Brazil has been reduced to mere flashes of his previously upstanding self. Yet, despite all the illegal and immoral acts he has committed, at the end of "Fim de estrada" (End of the Road), the eighth and last episode of season two, Cadu maintains that he is not a criminal. However, as Pepe points out, Cadu has always had a choice, and he has consistently chosen the wrong path. In voiceover narration that concludes season two, Cadu realizes the folly of his ways: "I wanted to change Brazil. Power intoxicates; money compromises; and politics are blinding. I thought I was an honest man, now I am not so sure."

Cadu's vacillation and characteristic uncertainty are both remedied at the beginning of season three, which focuses on family as a microcosm of Brazil. At the beginning of the first episode, we encounter the on-again, off-again hero sulking in his backyard, among empty bottles of booze, dirty dishes, and trash. Though it seems Cadu has committed too many wrongs and that the system has finally broken him, he pushes back yet again. In voiceover, Cadu locates the root of his destruction in Brazil itself: "The first time I did it the wrong way but it turned out right. This country doesn't root for what is right or for the truth. Brasília survives on lies. It is that way in politics, it is that way with the people, it is that way in life. I tried to do everything right and it went wrong. I lost my wife, my family. My son is going to jail. I've lost hope. I became all that I hated. Now I am going to make it right." But what does it mean to make it right? As the season plays out, through not only the actions of Cadu but also through those of Malu, Téo, Pepe, and others, the narrative suggests that at least in Brazil and in Latin America, moral ambiguity reigns—that is, we are all both good and bad to varying degrees, depending on what the situation calls for.

Indeed, Cadu realizes this in the season's last scene, when yet again in voiceover he says: "I lived so much in a lie that I no longer know who I am. Lawyer. Congressman. Drug trafficker. An honest man, lost. A man on the run from the law. Perhaps it's time to forget all this—to embrace my destiny and whatever it might bring." Thus, returning to Heise's categories, *1 contra todos* presents an (anti-)hero who engages in a dialectic of "reform" (of the system, of himself) and "opposition" (to Brazilian corruption, of himself) to ultimately "propose" an alternative: that he is—that Brazil is—the locus of both Edenic and Satanic motifs (Carvalho, 2000). The confluence of the two results in a never-ending moral struggle for one or the other to win out. However, because neither one is ever able to establish a stronghold, they always coexist in a spectacle of ambiguity that pits Brazil (good) versus Brazil (bad).

Lama dos dias—Transforming "Mud" into Art

The first of *Lama dos dias'* seven episodes aired on Canal Brasil at 9:30 PM on September 23, 2018. Like *1 contra todos,* the series satisfied a portion of the super Brazilian channel's quota requirements. *Lama dos dias* was co-produced by Pacto Filmes and Carnaval Filmes. The former, which is partly owned by Hilton Lacerda, was founded in 2003 and is based in São Paulo, though much of the company's work takes place in Pernambuco. The latter was founded in 2017 by João Vieira Jr. and Nara Aragão and is based in Recife. In 2016, *Lama dos dias* received R$1.7 million (~$530,000 US) from the FSA PRODAV. More specifically, Lacerda and his production partners submitted their proposal to the Programa Brasil de Todas as Telas (Program for Brazil on All Screens). Launched only two years prior in 2014 as the result of a partnership between ANCINE and the Ministry of Culture in collaboration with FSA, the program aimed at transforming all of Brazil into a relevant center for the production and programming of audiovisual content, paying special attention to regions outside of the Rio-São Paulo axis of production (Programa Brasil, 2016).

Though *1 contra todos* and *Lama dos dias* take decidedly different approaches to thinking about and representing Brazil on the small screen, in addition to receiving funds through government financing mechanisms and meeting the Pay-TV Law's quotas, they both were created and directed by well-known filmmakers: Breno Silveira and Hilton Lacerda.[11] Prior to *Lama dos dias*, Lacerda, who is from Recife, was an active participant in the reemergence of *cinema pernambucano* (cinema from the state of Pernambuco). Among others, Lacerda wrote or co-wrote the screenplays for such influential Pernambucano films as *Baile perfumado* (*Perfumed Ball*, 1997),[12] *Amarelo manga* (*Mango Yellow*, 2002), *Baixio das bestas* (*Scourge of Beasts*, 2006), *A Festa da menina morta* (*The Party of the Dead Girl*, 2008), and *Febre dos ratos* (*Fever of Rats*, 2011). Additionally, Lacerda co-directed (along with Lírio Ferreira, who directed *Baile perfumado*) the documentary *Cartola—Música para os olhos* (*Cartola—Music for the Eyes*, 2006) and directed and wrote the critically acclaimed feature-length film, *Tatuagem* (*Tattoo*, 2013). In 2016, Lacerda made his television directorial debut with *Fim do mundo* (*The End of the World*), a five-part miniseries starring Jesuita Barbosa (who also starred in *Tatuagem*), which, as with *Lama dos dias*, aired on super Brazilian channel Canal Brasil.

Whereas *1 contra todos* levies a harsh critique at Brazil and its institutions, *Lama dos Dias* "celebrates" the country's singular creativity. Set in Recife shortly after the fall of the Berlin Wall and during the height of the neoliberal policies of then President Fernando Collor de Mello, *Lama dos dias* is inspired by Recife itself and the tragically short musical ascension of Chico Science & Nação Zumbi. The release of Chico Science & Nação Zumbi's first album, *Da lama ao caos* (*Fom Mud to Chaos*, 1994), signaled the beginning of a counterculture movement known as *manguebeats* (lit. mangrove beats). Characterized by socially conscious lyrics that spoke to the inequality of "Hellcife," as the northeastern urban center was often referred to at the time, *manguebeats* freely combined rock, funk, hip-hop, and electronic music with northeastern Brazilian genres to create a new musical form that was both specific to and spoke to that time and place. Lacerda's series celebrates the fictional origins of the *manguebeats* movement and its participants by focusing on the friendship, desires, and politics of Adriana (Isadora Gibson), Bill (Vitor Araújo), Farmácia (Geyson Luiz), Francisco (Thiago das Mercês), and Luli (Louise França[13]), all of whom are students at a local university. The friends eventually link up with EZK (Matheus Tchôca), a young aspiring music producer from Recife's periphery. Through EZK, the group of college students also befriend Psicopasso, a band whose members include Boyzinha (Débora Leão, aka Negrita MC), Cruzado (Enio Damasceno), and Nego Queen (Edson Vogue), each of whom is also from the periphery of Recife.

Lama dos dias opens with a rapid, quick-hit montage comprised of black-and-white archival footage, artistic drawings, legal documents, newspaper clippings, posters, and propaganda. Though they disappear as quickly as they flash on screen, together the collection of images situates Brazil—at the varied levels of the local, regional, national, and transnational—as the overarching focus of what is to come. For example, in addition to the word "Recife" appearing multiple times, there is a drawing of a family of northeastern migrants, a minimalist rendering of the title of Gilberto Freyre's masterpiece *Casa-Grande & Senzala*, newspaper clippings about President Collor and other matters pertaining to national or global politics, a voter receipt with co-director Helder Aragão's name on it, and a number of references to popular culture in the United States. Following the montage, the image cuts to a New Year's Eve house party, where sexually liberated, drug- and alcohol-impaired young people celebrate the arrival of the 1990s. It is here that we first encounter Adriana, Bill, Farmácia, Francisco, and Luli. As the friends wrap up their night of partying while contemplating the sunrise and crashing waves at a nearby beach, Luli says, "With the year ending, let's get out of this place. Let's go somewhere where there is no sand, no beach, no sun. It doesn't even need to be Brazil. Actually, if I was super rich, I wouldn't even live in Brazil." The first episode ends with what plays both as a response to Luli and the ethos of the series. At another, albeit far more intimate house party, the group of friends meet EZK for the first time. Excitedly discussing his interest in a local band called Psicopasso, EZK puts on a tape cassette for his new friends. The song, which takes us to the closing credits, is actually Chico Science & Nação Zumbi's 1994 hit, "Cidade" (City). Over images of crabs—which are also present in the opening and symbolize survival in the mangroves—parts of Recife, and references to Brazil, Chico Science sings the following:

Ilusora de pessoas e outros lugares,	Illusory of people and other places,
A cidade e sua fama vai além dos mares.	The city and its fame go beyond the seas.
No meio da esperteza internacional,	In the midst of international cleverness,
A cidade até que não está tão mal.	The city is actually not so bad.
E a situação sempre mais ou menos,	And the situation always more or less,
Sempre uns com mais e outros com menos.	Always some with more and others with less.
A cidade não pára, a cidade só cresce	The city does not stop, the city only grows
O de cima sobe e o debaixo desce.	He who is at the top goes up and he who is at the bottom goes down.

So as to emphasize the importance of the lyrics, they also appear onscreen in white letters against a black backdrop. Once the song is complete, the image cuts to archival footage of Chico Science and Gilmar Bola Oito, a member of Nação Zumbi. Discussing the *manguebeats* movement, Chico Science concludes the episode by saying, "We started mixing music, experimenting, you know? Bringing together different types of music. And from that time and that experience, the rhythm that will one day take over the world exploded." Put differently, it is as if Chico Science is telling Luli: forget the negative things people are saying about Recife (and more broadly Brazil); forget the cultural hierarchy that places Recife in a subordinate position to that which comes from Europe and the United States. One need not leave Recife to make a mark or find something better. Rather, it is precisely the singular creativity of artists from Recife that will make its mark on Brazil and the world.

As I argued earlier, *1 contra todos* is in large part defined by its successful negotiation of global and local elements. Whereas that series draws on the enormously popular *Breaking Bad* and borrows from José Padilha's Brazilian blockbuster *Tropa de elite: O inimigo agora é outro* (2010), *Lama dos dias* plays more like a Brazilian art-house film. Even as the two works satisfy the quota requirements of the Pay-TV Law, one could argue that the former's international appeal and the latter's restricted regional focus on Recife both meet the objectives of their respective distribution channels: Fox and Canal Brasil. With a transnational reach, Fox has an interest in acquiring or producing content, Brazilian or otherwise, that will be of interest to numerous sectors of its culturally and linguistically diverse audience base. Canal Brasil, on the other hand, is available only in Brazil. What is more, unlike other international pay-television channels or even over-the-air channels like Globo or Record, Canal Brasil does not air non-Brazilian content. Instead, the channel's programming is largely comprised (70%) of Brazilian films.

More recently, however, Canal Brasil has increased its airing of fictional series. In addition to *Fim do mundo* and *Lama dos dias*, some of the recent productions included in the channel's programming grid are *Amor de 4* (dir. José Joffily), *Werner e os mortos* (dir. Cláudio Fagundes), *Angeli the Killer* (animated series, dir. César Cabral), and *Toda forma de amor* (dir. Bruno Barreto). Such an increase is in line with those comments made by Silveira regarding the growth of the production of series in Brazil—that is, in present-day Brazil one can earn a living by making television series. In a similar vein, Lacerda also recognizes the constitution of a new production and distribution reality coming about over the last decade. At the same time, Lacerda (Pinheiro, 2018) highlights the role of Brazilian or super Brazilian qualified channels (CABEQ or CEQ SB) in providing stability to the sector: "Just over five years ago, the independent television market in Brazil was still an almost unrealistic possibility, as it was virtually non-existent. But the emergence of previously non-existent resources would be of little worth, if it were not for qualified channels like CineBrasilTV, Curta!, Canal Brasil and the channels of the Box Brazil group, all of which embraced this new market, becoming responsible for the emergence of many producers, including producers outside of the Rio de Janeiro / São Paulo axis of production."

In the last line of his comment, Lacerda touches on an issue that has characterized Brazilian cultural production since the mid-nineteenth century and is also a core theme of *Lama dos dias*: the centralization of production in the country's two largest cities, Rio de Janeiro and São Paulo. Since its introduction to Brazil in 1950, television has largely been produced in and centered on portrayals of the two urban metropolises. In contrast, among others, Brazilian music can point to the regionally inflected Tropicalia movement and the popular genres of Axé (Bahia) and Sertanejo (Goiás, Mato Grosso do Sul, Paraná, etc.). At least since the 1930s—though one could also identify examples going all the way back to the colonial period—Brazilian literature has produced a number of consecrated authors from northeastern, northern, midwestern, and southern Brazil who write in and about their respective regions, though it is worth pointing out that they tend to be published in either Rio de Janeiro or São Paulo. The same could also be said of Brazilian film beginning with the Humberto Mauro–led *Ciclo de Catagueses* (Cataguases Cycle) in Minas Gerais in the 1920s to Glauber Rocha's *Cinema Novo* films set in Bahia of the 1960s to the more contemporary Casa de Cinema productions in Porto Alegre and the robust filmmaking in Pernambuco by such directors as Karim Aïnouz, Kleber Mendonça Filho, and Marcelo Gomes, among others. By comparison, prior to 2011, Brazilian television had never had any meaningful production that was not in some way connected to the production centers of Rio de Janeiro and São Paulo.

A work like *Lama dos dias*, as well as some of those discussed in the next chapter, however, highlights the ongoing geographic and production decentralization of the Brazilian mediascape. To be clear, this does not mean that the production of Brazilian series has suddenly in recent years become open to all. As shown in chapter 1, most production continues to be a costly endeavor, while also requiring a high level of technical expertise, factors that automatically exclude wide swaths of the population. What is more, as I will demonstrate in chapter 6, Globo continues to work hard to ensure it maintains its place as the industry leader. Nonetheless, the decentralization that in part characterizes such works does suggest that, when compared to the era that preceded it, the post-2011 mediascape is more open, more competitive, and more diverse than ever before.

In its exploration of such themes as art, counterculture, center/periphery, power, sexual liberation, and youth, *Lama dos dias* stands out for having been created and directed by Pernambucano artists, for shooting on location in Recife, and for employing a racially diverse cast of actors, nearly all of whom are from Northeastern Brazil. Lacerda's series also stands out for its aesthetic construction.[14] In addition to an excellent soundtrack that features original music and music from the period and a detailed *mise-en-scène* that portrays a region of Brazil and time period rarely seen in contemporary works of television, *Lama dos dias* experiments with the genre in the Brazilian context by recycling, repurposing, and incorporating three documentaries set and shot in Recife: Adelina Pontual, Cláudio Assis, and Marcelo Gomes's twelve-minute documentary, *Samydarsh: Os artistas de rua* (*Samydarsh: The Street Artists*, 1993), which provides a snapshot of street artists in Recife who during the early 1990s creatively employed any number of found objects to make music; Kátia Mesel's fifteen-minute documentary *Recife de dentro pra fora* (*Recife from Inside Out*, 1997), which constructs a social critique of Recife by drawing inspiration from João Cabral de Melo Neto's poem, "O cão sem plumas" and its focus on the city's Capibaribe River; and Paulo Caldas and Marcelo Luna's feature-length documentary, *O rap do Pequeno Príncipe contra as almas sebosas* (*The Little Prince's Rap against Greasy Souls*, 2000), which centers on the musician Helinho (o Pequeno Príncipe) to explore urban violence and socioeconomic inequality in Recife.

The intermixed presence of these documentaries serves three primary functions. First, the incorporation of scenes from the documentaries' respective portrayals of 1990s Recife helps create a narrative milieu that lends a heightened level of realism to the series' 1990s setting while also reinforcing the broader themes explored by the work—namely, Recife, creativity, and socioeconomic inequality. Second, at times, the incorporation of scenes from the different documentaries function as poetic brackets. During these moments, there is a pause in the narrative, and the viewer is presented with a lyrical, audiovisual contemplation of the gritty urban landscape and its heroic inhabitants. Third, and last, Lacerda's repurposing of the documentaries serves a meta function, insofar as it calls attention to not only Recife itself but to the creative directors who have been producing audiovisual works there since the early 1990s.

Indeed, each of these functions is present throughout the series' celebratory treatment of Recife's counterculture movement of the early

1990s, which, lacking resources, heroically pushes back against global and local forces that perpetuate working-class individuals' subjugation. As the series progresses, each of the main characters takes on a role in the burgeoning *manguebeats* movement. For example, Bill and Farmácia produce social commentary and musical criticism during their college radio show, *Cotonete* (Q Tip). Despite his mother's concerns about his new endeavor, EZK, a twenty-something black man who is tired of his mundane job with a Brazilian airline, throws himself into producing local bands—bands that, as he says, "speak our language; the language of the periphery." For EZK the best example of this is Psicopasso. For their part, the outcast members of Psicopasso, each of whom is black and from a marginalized community in Recife, desire nothing more than to earn a living expressing themselves by representing their community. As is the case throughout the series, the worlds of middle-class Recife (the group of college students) and lower-class Recife (EZK and the band) collide, resulting in amorous, creative, and intellectual exchanges. In one of many examples, Adriana (Isadora Gibson), Bill and Farmácia's friend from college, becomes the de facto stylist of Psicopasso. Her contact with the band eventually leads to a romantic relationship with Boyzinha, the group's lead singer. Such non-hetero-normative relationships are normalized by the series' nonjudgmental treatment of sexuality.

Francisco, an aspiring filmmaker, serves as the movement's unofficial documentarian. In one of his many conversations with Luli, he explains that what makes Brazilian filmmakers special is their unique ability to explore a dearth of technical resources by repurposing myriad objects to fit their creative needs. Francisco's understanding of filmmaking in Brazil evokes Cinema Novo's motto: *uma câmera na mão e uma ideia na cabeça* (a camera in the hand and an idea in the head). At the same time, it also remembers Oswald de Andrade's (1928) idea of artistic *antropofagia* and Robert Stam's (1997) considerations of an aesthetics of garbage in Brazilian cultural production.[15] In both cases, artists draw on whatever is available, whether high-brow European art or discarded trash, and through creative processes transform them into something uniquely Brazilian. Luli is both somewhat taken aback with and impressed by Francisco's belief and certainty surrounding the Brazilian arts. However, as evidenced by the example from the opening of the first episode when she expresses a desire to leave Brazil behind, Luli often takes on the role of the archetypal middle-/upper-middle-class Brazilian who locates all worthwhile culture as originating in Europe. Her conversations with her friends, but specifically with Francisco, reveal the symbolic stakes in play at both the level of the narrative and, more broadly, of Brazilian audiovisual production itself: to make music that is unique to and about Recife and to make films and series that are unique to and about Recife. Thus, when she asks him if he really believes in what he is saying—that is, if he really believes in Brazilian cinema—like Chico Science at the end of episode one and in the spirit of EZK's comment from earlier regarding local bands, Francisco provides a response that doubles down on the series' ethos: "Who said anything about Brazilian cinema? What I truly believe in is *cinema pernambucano*" (Pernambucano cinema).

Like Francisco, EZK, and Chico Science, the narratives of *1 contra todos* and *Lama dos dias* both relay an underlying belief in Brazil. Though they go about it in distinct ways, Silveira and Lacerda's respective series provide us with characters who, even in the face of doubt and perhaps its impossibility, support the idea of a better Brazil. Cadu, despite all the wrongs he has committed and the wrongs the system has committed against him, consistently seeks out a path to keep fighting for *um Brasil melhor* (a better Brazil). In the case of *Lama dos dias*, the vast majority of the characters believe in the power of their creativity and of Brazilian culture to transform "mud" into art and "Hellcife" into the birthplace of manguebeats, or, in the words of Chico Science, into "the rhythm that will take over the world."

3

The New Frontier

Internet Fiction

Since 2011, Internet access in Brazil has more than doubled. As with pay-television, albeit to an even greater degree, the increased presence of the Internet, whether through broadband or 3G or 4G, has further expanded the possibilities for distribution, production, and diverse portrayals of Brazil. Among the numerous new media celebrities and social media influencers who rose to fame outside of legacy television's structure, for example, are Whindersson Nunes and Felipe Neto.[1] Nunes, who is from Piauí, a small northeastern state, one of the poorest in Brazil, created his eponymous YouTube channel in January of 2013. Since that time, Nunes has posted over 350 videos that range from musical parodies to comedic commentaries on Piauí slang. At over thirty-six million subscribers and nearly three billion views, Nunes's channel is the second most subscribed channel in Brazil and the twenty-first most subscribed in the world (Top 50, 2019). Neto, who is from the northern zone of Rio de Janeiro, founded his YouTube channel in 2006. His comedically tinged, critical takes on celebrity quickly gained popularity, making his channel the first in Brazil to reach one million subscribers.[2] In 2011, Neto founded Paramaker studios, the first Brazilian YouTube Network. Before eventually selling the network to the French-based Webedia in 2015, among other channels, Paramaker was home to the wildly popular *Parafernalha*, a comedy troupe in the mold of Porta dos Fundos, the subject of chapters 4 and 5.

Though Nunes's and Neto's channels are among the most popular in the world, numerous others in Brazil have gained significant niche audiences. For example, Nátaly Neri's YouTube channel *Afros e afins* (*Afros and Things Related*), founded in 2015, focuses on fashion and beauty with an emphasis on disseminating "Do it Yourself" (DIY) knowledge. What distinguishes Neri's production from similarly focused channels is the centrality of her subjective position, which she explicitly declares in her self-introduction: "I am Nátaly Neri, a black woman and a feminist, who is passionate about thrifting, sewing, fashion, and DIY."[3] Over the first four years her channel appeared on YouTube, Neri's politically inclined work attracted nearly four hundred thousand subscribers and over eighteen million views. Also founded in 2015, Alexandra Gurgel's YouTube channel *Alexandrismos* (*Alexanderisms*), as the title makes clear, similarly emphasizes its creator's subjective position. Whereas Neri defines her position by her race and gender, Gurgel ties her subjectivity to issues pertaining to her physical appearance and society's questionable normalization of the female body: "*Alexandrismos* is a channel created by journalist Alexandra Gurgel, who, for years, endured body image issues. After an incessant search for self-knowledge, Gurgel hit play on YouTube, creating videos focused on body positive messages, self-esteem, hair, mental health, and relationships. In all the videos, Alexandra employs humor to promote a positive message, encouraging viewers to be who they are, regardless of their body shape, skin color, belief, or gender!"[4] Thus, in each of the examples, the YouTube stars' self-identification is both the point of departure *for* and more important *than* the topics dealt with in their videos. What is more, they each occupy historically obscured places within the Brazilian mediascape. As such, their work represents not only alternatives to the established, heterosexual, white norm but also serves as examples of a larger, ongoing challenge to that norm.

Along with the growing group of YouTube stars and Internet influencers, web series have emerged as an important aspect of the challenge to and the expansion of the Brazilian mediascape. Importantly, the openness and increased accessibility of the Internet and accompanying technology, has, in Brazil, provided minorities with never-before-seen artistic and geographic freedom, resulting in productions taking place outside of Rio de Janeiro and São Paulo and the creation of narratives that legacy television has historically had little interest investing in or showing. Some examples include *Esconderijo* (*Hiding Place*), a story of love between two females, Malu and Raquel; *O som do amor* (*The Sound of Love*), a musical comedy set in Salvador, Bahia; and *Punho Negro* (*Black Fist*), which tells the story of Tereza, a strong black woman who uses her super powers to combat the violence and racial injustices she encounters in her hometown of Salvador, Bahia. These—all of which are available on YouTube—along with the web series discussed below come nowhere near the enormous audiences that tune into TV Globo's *telenovelas*. Nonetheless, as Jean Aymar Christian (2018: 25) argues in *Open TV*, though "the market for indie scripted comedies and dramas [in the United States] is small, experimental, and fraught compared to that of higher-budget legacy series," such production "is rich with ideas, producing clear public benefit."

Perhaps the greatest public benefit is the proliferation of voices and the portrayal of historically underrepresented groups, ideas, places, and themes. With this in mind, the present chapter explores the expansion of Internet access in Brazil since 2011 and analyzes three critically acclaimed web series: *Septo* (*Septum*, YouTube, 2016), *Marcos: Uma websérie quase original* (*Marcos: An Almost Original Web series*, YouTube and Instagram, 2015–2016), and *3%* (YouTube and Netflix, 2011/2016–). *Septo* and *Marcos* are both award-winning series made exclusively for Internet distribution. Both come from recently formed production companies in cities far from the Rio-São Paulo axis of production: for *Septo*, Caboré Audiovisual, a small production company founded in 2013 and based in Natal, the capital of Rio Grande do Norte; and for *Marcos*, 1quarto, an upstart production company, comedy troupe, and mobile entertainment network, which began operating in 2013 out of Caxias do Sul, a mid-sized city in Rio Grande do Sul. *Septo* is a drama that follows the life of a young Olympic triathlete hopeful who begins to explore her newfound freedom and sexuality. *Marcos* is a parody of the Netflix original series *Narcos*. Though very different from one another in terms of genre, tone, length, and themes, both works are unique for representing regions of Brazil very rarely portrayed on the small screen during the Network Era. For its part, *3%* does away with both regional and national differences by situating its narrative in a post-apocalyptic world 107 years in the future. Additionally, whereas *Septo* and *Marcos* emerge out of the new Brazilian mediascape, the development of *3%* spans the pre and post-2011 eras. Moreover, the creators of *3%* employed the Internet as a means to market the series' pilot to television executives. Taken together, these three works reveal much about the reality of the new Brazilian mediascape and the importance of the Internet to the establishment of that era and of what is to follow.

The Rise of Internet Access

Today, Brazil is among the world leaders in terms of total Internet users and in the number of daily hours those users spend online.[5] Nonetheless, widespread access to the Internet in Brazil, whether via broadband or 3G or 4G technology, is a relatively recent phenomenon. Indeed, when commercial Internet first arrived in Brazil in 1996, fewer than 50,000 individuals, or .03 percent of the population, had access to the incipient technology (Carvalho, 2006: 132). A decade later, in 2005, household Internet penetration registered a paltry 13 percent (Lima, 2015; TIC Domicílios, 2005a). At the time, the primary point-of-entry was snail-paced modem dial-up, which accounted for 39 percent of all user access to the Internet. Faster technologies like broadband and wi-fi registered an unimpressive 8 percent and 6 percent of all Internet access. In that same year, personal computers were the devices most used (60%) to access the Internet (TIC Domicílios, 2005b). Mobile phones, on the other hand, constituted 21 percent of households' total Internet accesses (TIC Domicílios, 2005c). Five years later, in 2010, the number of households with some type of Internet access had doubled to slightly over 26 percent (TIC Domicílios, 2010). By comparison, already as early as 1998, 28 percent of households in the United States had some form of Internet access (Statista, 2013). Over the next seven years, however, household Internet access in Brazil grew to 61 percent, an increase of approximately 126 percent (TIC Domicílios, 2017a). Around the same time, 84 percent of all households in the United States had access to the Internet. What is more, approximately 92 percent of those households in the United States accessed the Internet through broadband services (Statista, 2013; Leichtman Research Group, 2018).

While Brazil is home to one of the largest Internet-user populations in the world and figures in the upper third in terms of global household penetration rates, the on-the-ground reality is still characterized by significant inequality. As Guillermo Orozco and Toby Miller have noted with regard to Latin America as a whole, the quality of broadband is poor when compared to that in places such as Sweden and Japan (2018: 63). Such far-reaching structural inequality, they correctly argue, not only "decreases the citizens' capacity to download and transmit to a great bandwidth"; it is further complicated by the fact that "access is unequally structured in terms of race, occupation, and region" (Orozco and Miller, 2018: 63–64).

Indeed, according to the 2018 Information and Communication Technologies (Tecnologias de Informação e Comunicação, TIC) report from the Regional Center for Studies on the Development of the Information Society (Centro Regional de Estudos para o Desenvolvimento da Sociedade, da Informação), access to the Internet in Brazil very much depends on where one lives and to which socioeconomic group one belongs. Not surprisingly, the southeastern (*sudeste*—e.g., São Paulo and Rio de Janeiro), midwest (*centro-oeste*—e.g., Brasília and Goiânia), and southern (*sul*—e.g., Curitiba and Porto Alegre) regions, the most economically powerful in Brazil, registered average household penetration rates of 69 percent, 68 percent, and 60 percent, respectively. The northern (*norte*—e.g., Belém and Manaus) and northeastern (*nordeste*—e.g., Pernambuco and Salvador) regions, the poorest in Brazil, had average household penetration rates of 48 percent and 49 percent. In somewhat similar fashion, the average penetration rate of urban areas is 65 percent, while rural areas—of which there are relatively more in the northern and northeastern regions—register nearly half that, at 34 percent (TIC Domicílios, 2018: 115). Unequal access is even greater when one considers class standing. For example, the average penetration rates among households belonging to Brazil's most well-to-do A and B Classes have consistently registered well above the national average, at 99 and 93 percent, respectively. Meanwhile, those households falling within Brazil's lowest-earning D and E Classes tracked far below the national average in 2017, at 30 percent (TIC Domicílios, 2018: 115).[6]

As already alluded to, in addition to issues regarding who and where, another important factor pertaining to Internet access is how. According to recent data, 88 percent and 81 percent of the A and B Classes used broadband as the primary source of connection to the Internet, numbers not far off the general average of the United States (92%) (TIC Domicílios, 2018: 118). Only 8 percent and 11 percent of these same two classes used a mobile connection, either through a modem or 3G or 4G, as their primary point-of-access (118). For the D and E Classes, however, these same categories register 34 percent (broadband) and 48 percent (mobile). Not surprisingly, the data also reveal that while 88 percent and 70 percent of the A and B Classes use *both* personal computers and cell phones to access the Internet, 53 percent of the C Class and 80 percent of the D and E Classes *exclusively* use cell phones to get online. Thus, as one would expect, the country's wealthier classes have more options when it comes to accessing the Internet. At the same time, these numbers suggest that the increase in Internet access among Brazil's C, D, and E Classes is occurring not by way of the personal computer but by the cell phone, a device owned by approximately 83 percent of all Brazilians over the age of ten. In fact, for the first time since data began to be collected in 2005, 49 percent of all Internet users in Brazil accessed the Internet exclusively through their cell phones (TIC Domicílios, 2018: 121, 125). But again, so as to not exaggerate the recent advances and prematurely discard the centrality of television to the lives of Latin Americans, Orozco and Miller point out that though the use of smart phones has exponentially increased in the last five years, only a minority of them are connected to high-quality broadband (to 3G, let alone 4G) (2018: 63).

While the Latin American reality highlighted by Orozco and Miller is certainly applicable to Brazil as well, over the last five-plus years one notes a clear shift not only in terms of smart phone growth but also in terms of a transition from second- (2G) to third- and fourth-generation (3G and 4G) technologies. According to data from the Agência Nacional de Telecomunicações (ANATEL, National Telecommunications Agency), in January of 2012—precisely the year in which the Pay-TV Law removed the barriers for foreign ownership of telecommunication companies—81.2 percent of all cell phone use was conducted on a pre-paid basis. What is more, 82.6 percent of all cell phones used 2G technology, with all other use coming via 3G. By October of 2018, monthly cell phone plans had climbed to 41.6 percent, meaning that pre-paid use had dropped to 58.4 percent. During that same year, 4G access passed 50 percent for the first time, reaching 53.9 percent by October. Conversely, only 10.9 percent of cell phone users relied on 2G technology by 2018 (Evolução do, 2018).

The numbers above provide some important insights regarding the presence of the Internet in Brazil. First, they reveal that the industry—not unlike what had occurred with the pay-television sector—experienced slow growth from its inception in 1996 to until around 2012. Second, the numbers, especially when juxtaposed with those from the United States, show that, despite the Internet's centrality to the constitution of contemporary global society, equal access granted to all is far from the norm. That is, not only does Internet access in Brazil lag far behind that of the United States; it also falls behind its neighbor to the north in qualitative terms. Though the Brazilian mediascape on the whole has witnessed significant increases in broadband and mobile Internet access—growth that has occurred alongside and in conjunction with a proliferation of screens from smart phones to tablets—as in the United States, television has not disappeared. Instead, television coexists with the emergence of alternative screens, which together renew and reimagine what television is and where and how it is consumed (Orozco and Miller, 2018: 60; Sanseverino and Gruszynski, 2018: 228). With this in mind, the two web series discussed below, and the genre in general, must be understood as simultaneously challenging and complementing more traditional fictional television content, namely through the diversity of their representations and geographical and production contexts. Ultimately, both works exemplify and contribute to the ongoing expansion and diversification of the Brazilian mediascape by, at the very least, augmenting the small screen possibilities for "who," "what," and "where."

Rio Grande(s): From *Norte* to *Sul*

In his exploration of the rise of web or "networked television," Christian emphasizes how the expansion of the Internet in the United States in the late 1990s and early 2000s "brought innovation to television by opening mass distribution to those excluded from legacy development processes, fostering new ways of creating and marketing series" (2018: 4). For decades, economic and production models employed by broadcast networks and cable television channels largely determined what was produced and how and where it was distributed and watched. However, Christian maintains that the rise of the Internet gave way to "open tv"—that which is networked and "occurs via Internet or web protocols," "is digital, on-demand, and peer-to-peer . . . eliminating the need for legacy network executives" (4). Along these lines, Christian contends that "open access to distribution gives producers a platform for creative expression and ownership, enables diverse storytelling for marginalized fan communities, and produces more dynamic ways of releasing, showcasing, and rewarding shows for brands, sponsors, distributors, and exhibitors" (5). In the recent past, such storytelling was difficult at best. As Michael D. Smith and Rahul Telang argue, for a long time, "signing a contract with a major publisher, label, or studio, was the only way to get access to the funding and production expertise necessary to create content, and to the scarce promotion and distribution channels necessary to distribute this content to an audience" (2018: 103).

Historically, in Brazil, access to production, talent, distribution, and audiences was concentrated largely in the hands of Globo. However, as is the case in the United States, the decreased costs of content creation, production facilities, and technology and the increase in digital distribution, financing, and capable below and above-the-line labor and talent have brought about a tide of change. Within this somewhat new reality, since around 2012, new media producers in Brazil increasingly practice "netcasting," wherein they create original web programming and web networks directed at niche audiences. Among the vast content creation, of particular importance are those works that "ring true to the realities or fantasies of a particular community, especially those for whom representations have been scant or inconsistent in the past" (Christian, 2018: 105). The Brazilian web series *Septo* is a particularly good example of such a work.

Septo is unique for three primary reasons. First, as already mentioned and will be discussed in greater detail below, the series was conceived of and shot in Rio Grande do Norte by individuals from that state. Second, the web series offers a progressive portrayal of female sexuality. Last, not only did the creators of *Septo* release the work exclusively on the Internet; they also raised a production budget of R$16,282 (slightly more than $5000 US) via Catarse, the first Brazilian crowdfunding website.

Each of these three unique characteristics was put on display when Pipa Dantas, the primary director and editor of the web series, created a *tudo ou nada* (all or nothing) crowdfunding page on Catarse's website in early January of 2016. Under the subheading *Equipe* (cast and crew), potential Catarse supporters are alerted to the fact that all of the twenty-five members of the web series' cast and crew hail from Rio Grande do Norte. What is more, the description makes it clear that *Septo*, if funded, would become the first fictional web series shot in its entirety in Rio Grande do Norte's capital city of Natal. From the earliest moments, then, the creators conceived of and marketed their idea as being rooted in and representative of a specific geographic location and culture. Within the context of Brazilian audiovisual production, especially as it pertains to television, geographic location and culture are frequently reduced to the country's two economic and cultural centers: São Paulo and Rio de Janeiro. Together, the two urban metropolises often function as stereotypical stand-ins for Brazil and Brazilian culture. Thus, the producers' emphasis on Rio Grande do Norte as both the creative source and object of the web series is in essence a political position-taking that recognizes and moves against a broader visual culture that subordinates—to varying degrees and with few exceptions—nearly every place outside of southeastern Brazil. At the same time, the position-taking seeks to appeal to individuals—either those from Rio Grande do Norte itself or those who believe in and support diversity in audiovisual narratives—to take part in and collectively transform the political act into reality.

The symbolic power of location in the rhetorical framing of *Septo*'s "pitch" is strengthened by its subsequent conflation with sexuality. Effectively alerting potential donors to their importance to the production while also placing them and the creators within a similarly informed ideological community—one made increasingly possible across vast timespaces by the Internet—the wording under the subheading *Projeto* (Project) uses the first-person plural (nós) to bring forth sexuality, the web series' other major theme. "*We know*," the opening reads, "that in Brazil there is a large LGBTQ + audience that wishes to be faithfully represented. Without being cheesy and while treating the relationship between two women in a realistic and natural way, each episode constructs an emotional narrative that moves the viewer. Considering that Rio Grande do Norte ranks as the third most dangerous state in Brazil for homosexuals, *we* want *Septo* to contribute in some way to advancing the discussion about LGBTQ + visibility" (Dantas, 2016, emphasis mine).[7] Whether invested in Natal, LGBTQ + issues, or both, contributing to the production of *Septo* functions as a statement on the part of the donor regarding the importance of representing groups often on the margins of Brazilian audiovisual production and, in broader terms, of Brazilian culture itself.

According to Catarse, *Septo* had a total of 189 donors, each of which gave anywhere from R$10 (slightly less than $3 US) to R$4000 plus (slightly more than $1,000 US). The overwhelming majority of the donations fell between the R$10 and R$100 levels, while only three donations were above the R$1000 threshold. Though nearly half of Brazil's twenty-six states were represented (twelve plus the Distrito Federal), 142 of the total number of donors were from Rio Grande do Norte, constituting approximately 70 percent of the final donation tally. The presence of geographical diversity among the donors combined with the particularly strong participation from those living in Rio Grande do Norte reveals a way in which the Internet creates the conditions for local regions to support and promote their own representation in the broader public sphere.

In fact, prior to 2011 and the subsequent expansion of the independent production sector fueled by the Pay-TV Law and the growth of Internet access, a work like *Septo* was very unlikely to ever be made. The primary reasons for this are twofold: first, leading up to 2012, the Internet was still not a widely accessible technology in Brazil; second, and related to the first, the state of distribution, production, and reception prior to 2012 was such that the crowdsourcing economic model—not to mention other possibilities—used by the creators of *Septo* was not a viable option. Production and creation, then, were both strongly tied to the reigning economic model of commercial television, which, as has been repeated throughout this book, had been perfected by TV Globo, thereby strengthening its hold over what was made and who could participate in production.

By September 28, 2016, however, the Brazilian mediascape was drastically different from the TV Globo-dominated Network Era. On that day, *Septo*'s first episode, "Obrigações" (Obligations) appeared on Brasileiríssimos, a website and YouTube channel dedicated to promoting Brazilian culture.[8] The remaining four episodes were released to the Brasileiríssimos YouTube channel over the next six weeks. At the time of this writing, together, the approximately eight-and-a-half-minute episodes have accumulated over 300,000 YouTube views. In May of 2017, *Septo* won the popular vote for the category of Best Web Series at the prestigious Buenos Aires Web Festival.

Septo's narrative arc is bracketed by the insertion of two iterations of the same scene—the first to open the web series, and the second to open the fifth and final episode. Together, they serve to foreshadow a before-and-after in Jéssica's life, symbolizing her eventual uncovering of a newfound identity and independence from her overbearing father. The web series' soundtrack, which lyrically locates Jéssica along her trajectory and musically reiterates her emotional states during that trajectory, further reinforces the life-altering developments—specifically discoveries regarding her health and sexuality—experienced by Jéssica.

The first of the two scenes in question appears at the outset of "Obrigações," when the viewer is presented with a number of out-of-focus and fragmented close-ups of a female's upper body. Through a series of slight jump-cuts, the camera moves as if it was blindly feeling about the whited-out space. Over the course of these quick shots, the camera momentarily settles on the female's neck, chin, and hair. While these shots are never in focus and therefore never allow us to see the female, neither in her entirety nor clearly, the camera does locate a photograph of a young girl standing alongside a woman wearing a racing swimsuit and cap. The young girl proudly displays a medal around her neck as the woman beside her reveals a toothy smile. Though more in focus than the previous shots, even this shot is fleeting, as it quickly gives way to more fragmented, whited-out shots of the female's chest, neck, and chin. These shots are then interrupted once again as the camera identifies, with a greater degree of clarity, a swim cap and goggles hanging from the white wall. Finally, in the last shots of this opening scene, the camera shifts quickly to an out-of-focus close-up of the female's hand, which guides pieces of her long brown hair as they fall lifelessly into the sink. It is here that two distinct sounds disrupt that of a buzzing noise, which, from the first moment, has been the one constant, connecting the seemingly disparate, fragmented shots together. Simultaneously, yet distinctly, we hear both an alarm clock and the female coughing. With the camera positioned looking down from directly above, the sound of the cough gives way to the appearance of blood, which stains the white sink. The sound of the alarm clock continues into the next shot where we encounter Jéssica sleeping alone in bed. After silencing the alarm, from a bird's-eye view the camera captures Jéssica, with a full head of hair, lying silently in bed.

The second of the two scenes in question appears at the outset of "Lugar nenhum, rota de ninguém" (Nowhere, nobody's route), *Septo's* final episode. Whereas in the first scene we never get a clear shot of the female, here a still somewhat jittery camera accompanied by a series of jump-cuts reveals an in-focus Jéssica with a freshly shaved head standing in front of the same bathroom mirror and sink. Establishing continuity between this and the opening scene from the first episode, the constant buzzing sound is present from the start. Though in that scene we only see Jéssica's hair falling into the sink, here the camera pulls back to show us the result, suggesting that this present moment is simply the continuation of the earlier moment. As with the first scene, this one ends with a cut to Jéssica once again being awoken by her alarm clock. However, rather than alone in bed, we see Jéssica lying next to Lua. The scene ends with Jéssica coughing blood into her hand.

During the period between the first and second scenes, much has happened to Jéssica. Avoiding—for the most part—the use of expository dialogue, *Septo* highlights the transformational developments in Jéssica's life by employing a sensorial mode—one that is manifested through *mise-en-scène*, cinematography, and the soundtrack. For example, throughout the first episode, Jéssica's understated, reluctant performance suggests, though never explicitly so, that she is struggling with her dedication to the sport. The reasons as to why are never given directly but instead are pieced together over time: (1) her motivation is external—that is, she has lost her mother, who was also a triathlete, and she wants to please her loving, yet overbearing father, who constantly makes it clear to Jéssica that she is just like her mother; (2) she is experiencing internal suffering—Jéssica is sick with cancer, and to complicate matters further, she is uncertain about her sexuality. Indeed, each of these two broad factors come into play at the end of episode one and the beginning of episode two when Jéssica, after a hard training session on the road, sets off to complete the day's training with a swim in the ocean. Overcome by her as yet unknown illness, Jéssica struggles to stay afloat. As she does so, "Quero descansar" (I Want to Rest), a song by the Canto dos Malditos Na Terra do Nunca, an indie rock band from Salvador, Bahia, ushers forth the closing credits. Jéssica, as the song suggests, is tired—of training, of feeling ill, and of being under the tight control of her father.

In the mold of traditional serial television, the uncertainty of what will happen to Jéssica at the end of episode one serves as a hook designed to draw the viewer back to see how it plays out. Indeed, at the outset of episode two, "Nós conseguimos" (We Did It), Lua, a thirty-something owner of a local NGO surf school, has saved Jéssica from drowning. Though initially only literal, by the end of the series, Lua also figuratively saves Jéssica from the demands of her father and her sport by encouraging her to explore and ultimately become her own person. This is first made clear when, shortly after pulling Jéssica from the ocean, Lua insists on giving her reluctant patient a lift to a medical clinic. On the way, as the two strangers sit in silence, "Amado" (Loved, or Loved One) by Simona Talma, an indie rock singer from Rio Grande do Norte, diegetically plays on the car radio. The lyrics, which speak of all-encompassing love, function to foreshadow the future relationship between the two women, while also signaling to Jéssica that she needs to open her eyes.[9]

At this point, however, Jéssica is still far from enacting any significant changes to her life. As soon as Lua leaves her at the clinic, Jéssica slips out a side door. However, because Jéssica had left something in the car, Lua returns to find the protagonist walking by herself down the street. Lua insists that Jéssica accept a car ride home. As during the earlier car ride, "Avec plaisir" (With Pleasure) by Luísa & os Alquimistas, another indie band from Rio Grande do Norte, plays on the car radio. The song's lyrics—"Enfeiticei você, *Desolé*, Eu sou bruxa, sim, *Avec Plaisir*" (I put a spell on you, I'm sorry, Yes, I am a witch, With pleasure)—reinforce the message from "Amado," suggesting even more forcefully that there is no turning back. Indeed, as symbolized by the nose ring (*septo*) she pulls down when not with her father, by the end of episode four Jéssica has distanced herself from following in her mother' footsteps. In the same episode, after telling her father she wants to start to be more herself, Jéssica informs Lua that she has never been with a woman and that she is no longer going to train. For the first and only time during the series, the episode does not end with "Quero descansar" aurally transitioning to the credits. Instead, "Move On" by Bian, a folk singer from Rio de Janeiro who gained popularity because of her beautiful singing voice and notoriety by coming out as gay, plays: "I forget what I wanted before, I saw you cross my way, and now I want more." In the last scene of episode five, an emotional Jéssica tells Lua simply, "I've decided" (Eu decidi). As the soundtrack has alluded to throughout the web series, Jéssica's transformation is now complete.

The first lesbian kiss on Brazilian television occurred on May 12, 2011, in the SBT *telenovela Amor e revolução (Love and Revolution)*, a full six decades after the inauguration of TV.[10] Nearly three years later, in 2014, the first lesbian kiss in a TV Globo *telenovela* took place, between Clara (Giovanna Antonelli) and Mariana (Tainá Müller) in Manoel Carlos's *Em família (In Family)*. The relative tardiness of such a moment is in large part due to a mediascape dominated by a single network whose ultimate objective is to capture the biggest possible audience to sell to advertisers. Such large-scale, high-budget commercial modes of production tend to marginalize content that might be considered controversial and potentially turn away viewers. Web series like *Septo*, however, forgo explicit attempts to please mass audiences, preferring instead to communicate with much smaller, often more receptive, and likeminded audiences. The relatively lower overhead, smaller production budgets, and the less regulated space of the Internet provide such web series with more creative freedom than would be possible in a prime-time *telenovela*. Thus, whereas the first lesbian kisses in Brazilian *telenovelas* represented a single—one might even say a somewhat muted—story among a number of more important plotlines, the central narrative motor in *Septo* is precisely the relationship between Jéssica and Lua. However, rather than function to call attention to what would on network Brazilian television come across as an anomaly, *Septo* normalizes the relationship by portraying it not as one between two women but as one between two regular human beings living out their lives.

Equally important is that the portrayal of Jéssica and Lua's relationship takes place in what is an at-moments beautiful, at-moments drab version of Natal, Rio Grande do Norte. Though TV Globo's *telenovelas* do portray different regions of Brazil, they are rarely shot on location, and when they are it almost never occurs in a work's entirety. Rather, the majority of *telenovela* productions takes place at the network's studios in Rio de Janeiro. Thus, the representations of such regions are predominately aestheticized, often idealized versions of the places themselves. In contrast, as discussed in the opening of this section, *Septo* is in every aspect a product of Natal: it was conceived, produced, and shot in Natal by a cast and crew who all live in the city or are from there.

The same could also be said of *Marcos: Uma websérie quase original* (2015–2016). *Marcos* does not explicitly engage in the identity politics that in part characterize *Septo*. Instead, operating through the comedic mode of parody, the web series' two seasons are void of any meaningful political position-taking. Nonetheless, *Marcos*, like *Septo*, was created, produced, and shot far from the entertainment capitals of Rio de Janeiro and São Paulo, in Caxias do Sul, the second largest city in the state of Rio Grande do Sul. As with the Colteivo Caboré Audiovisual, the independent production company behind *Septo*, *Marcos* was the work of 1quarto (1room), which was founded by a collective of graduates from the Federal University of Caxias do Sul. In addition to highlighting the geographical diversification occurring during the post-2011 era, *Marcos* further points to the diversification of distribution channels. Unlike *Septo* and *3%*—discussed in the next section—both of which utilized YouTube's platform, 1quarto initially conceived of *Marcos* as an Instagram web series, the first of its kind in Brazil. What is more, as mentioned earlier, the company describes itself as a mobile entertainment network.

Using Instagram's recently launched "stories" feature, 1quarto released the first of eight weekly episodes on December 9, 2015. Between July 14 and September 1, 2016, the group uploaded the same episodes to YouTube. Thus far on Instagram, the videos have accumulated a total of 49,952 views. On YouTube, the videos have accumulated an additional 8,209 views. Beginning on September 15, 2016, 1quarto released nine episodes over nine consecutive weeks of the second season of *Marcos: Uma websérie quase original* exclusively to YouTube. With the move from Instagram to YouTube, the group elected to produce more length-appropriate episodes. As such, on average, each episode comes in at one minute and forty-one seconds. The second season, which was screened at the Buenos Aires Web Fest and was an official selection at the Miami Web Fest and the Seattle Web Fest, where it won an award for Best Series, has accumulated 16,646 views on YouTube.

Limited by Instagram's stories time allowance, each episode from *Marcos*' first season runs for approximately fifteen seconds, with a total runtime of about two minutes and thirty seconds. The compactness of the web series results in individual episodes that play like snapshots of a day in the life of Marco (Diogo Severo), the work's protagonist. Lacking the more traditional hooks that are central to *Septo* and *3%*, it is only after having screened all the episodes that one can piece together a broader narrative. What is clear from the beginning, however, as indicated by the web series' promotional image and title page, *Marcos* is a playful medial transposition of the José Padilha–produced Netflix original series *Narcos*. While the web series' highly truncated narrative mimics in audiovisual terms the gritty aesthetics of realism that characterizes the Netflix series, it replaces the society-altering crime and violence committed by the calculated and ruthless drug lord Pablo Escobar and his cartel with petty crimes committed by Marco, a small-time smuggler from Caxias do Sul.

Unlike Pablo Escobar, whose reputation demands fear-driven loyalty from all in his universe, Marco is so inconsequential in his field that rival criminals incorrectly refer to him as Marcos, which he frustratingly feels the need to always correct with, "É Marco, porra!" (It's fucking Marco!). As such, if there is one overarching constant that characterizes the two seasons' seventeen episodes, it is Marco's oblivious incompetence, which consistently places the anti-hero in preposterous situations. For example, "Dívida" (Debt), the web series' first episode, smartly employs cinematography to maximize the restricted time frame within which the story unfolds. Despite sparse dialogue and limited action, the viewer learns immediately that Marco is the boss, though he's not very good at it. Shot in a single take, the episode opens in *medias res* with Marco and his colleague standing over a man, who, with a hood covering his face and his clasped hands on the back of his head, kneels before them. The three men all face the camera, so what we see is the head of the captured man in the lower third of the shot and the upper halves of Marco and his colleague extending upward through the upper two-thirds. Standing directly behind their prisoner, as Marco's colleague cocks their lone, shared gun—itself an early indication of the unpreparedness of the criminals—and points it at the man's head, only to hand it over to Marco, the camera rises up from the opening low-angle position. The upward movement to an eye-level angle of the two men removes the head of the kidnap victim from the shot. While Marco and his colleague continue their ridiculous back-and-forth about who should shoot the captured man, the camera slowly rotates to the right of screen until it is behind two men. Once the camera has completed its 180-degree turn, without any dialogue at all, it reveals the comedic punchline: Marco and his colleague watch the kidnapped man escape down the long country road.

Equally absurd, in "Suando Frio" (Cold Sweats), an armed Marco violently threatens to break down a door located in a darkly lit hallway. However, as we saw in the first episode, and as is characteristic of all eight episodes from the first season, the narrative twist is consistently that nothing is ever as it seems. Thus, rather than attempting to invade a residence as it appears, Marco, who declares he is nearly "shitting himself," is in reality desperately trying to gain access to an occupied bathroom. "Desova" (a slang term used among police officers when referring to the act of making a dead body disappear), the web series' fourth episode, opens with yet another low-angle shot from inside the trunk of a car, which Marco and his partner have opened. Though the point-of-view shot suggests the presence of a dead body, a cut to the next shot reveals Marco's partner throwing a bag into a trash can. Further deconstructing Marco's life of crime and playing up the unexpected situations, Marco admonishes his partner for throwing the recyclables in the trash, demanding that he responsibly deposit them in the appropriate nearby recycle bins. In reference to the film *Die Hard*, episode seven, "Duro de Matar" (Hard to Kill, or Die Hard), features Marco flailing a gun around a darkly lit living room and yelling at what seems to be a person lying on the floor. As Marco threatens to kill him, his irritated mother enters the room. Pushing Marco out of the way, she takes off her shoe and kills a cockroach, the revealed object of Marco's ire. In "Tiro certo" (Precise Shot), Marco climbs a tall building in downtown Caxias do Sul to take a selfie; in "Ambush," Marco ambushes his mother with a Mothers' Day surprise cake; and in "Craque" (Crack), Marco delivers not crack, as in the drug, but trading cards of Brazilian *craque* (very good) footballers.

Season two of *Marcos* similarly parodies Marco's unglamorous life of crime in Caxias do Sul. The central difference between this season and the first season is the distribution platform. No longer under Instagram's time constraints, the second season of *Marcos*, which premiered on YouTube, has an average episode run-time of nearly eight times the average length of episodes in the first season. Though the episodes are still relatively short, particularly when compared to a traditional television series or even when compared to *Septo*, the use of YouTube resulted in a significant expansion of Marco's narrative universe. Thus, whereas the first season lacks a temporal anchor and unfolds as a series of seemingly random, disconnected snapshots of Marco's life, the second weaves together a narrative that spans a period of three weeks.

The season's first episode, "Caça e Caçador" (The Hunt and the Hunter), begins with Marco and his girlfriend, Gislaine, having dinner at a nice restaurant. To the sound of Gislaine sobbing uncontrollably, an ever-confident Marco informs her that he is breaking up with her. Clóvis, Marco's associate, interrupts the couple's conversation to inform his boss "*tá na hora*" (it's time to go). In what follows, Marco and Clóvis drive through the dimly lit, quiet city streets of Caxias do Sul. As they do, the two engage in a nonsensical conversation about Brazilian and French pastries. Near the end of the episode, in-off, we hear a voice different from that of Clóvis's repeating, "Wake up boss, wake up." The shot then cuts from Marco and Clovis standing over and looking into the trunk of a car from where a bright light shines, to a daytime setting of Marco asleep in the passenger seat of his own car, where his other associate, Beto, pokes at him to wake up. With little hesitation, Marco aggressively grabs his gun from the glove compartment. Before exiting the car, Marco establishes both the episode's hook and the web series narrative motor, muttering aloud, "Now he's gonna pay." Who is going to pay, and why?

Moments into the second episode, the words "3 semanas atrás . . ." (3 weeks ago . . .) appear on screen. Everything that follows from the time this flashback is introduced falls within the three weeks leading up to the scene that brings the first episode to a close. That this is the case is made clear at the beginning of the ninth and final episode, which opens with the same scene from the earlier episode when Beto pokes at a sleeping Marco. During the flashback we learn that Marco has begun to sell pirated Blu-Ray DVDs of such titles as *Finding Dory*. The excitement derived from this new and potentially lucrative endeavor is undercut by the news that Clóvis is having an affair with Gislaine, Marco's ex-girlfriend. Betrayed, and his ego having taken a severe hit, Marco sets out to get back at Clóvis, who, along with his new boss, now sells drugs out of the trailer they stole from Marco. After rehearsing in the bathroom mirror the threats he plans to unload on Clóvis, Marco finally goes to confront his former associate. During the encounter, unseen gunshots are fired, though what exactly has happened is never shown. As if jokingly taking the viewer's position, a clearly shaken Marco, who has just made a harrowing escape, ends the episode and web series by declaring to Beto, "Não quero mais" (I don't want to do this anymore).

Faced with death, Marco realizes that he is not as tough or committed to a life of crime as the brazen declarations he frequently makes to his associates and mother seek to communicate. As a parody, 1quarto's portrayal of Marco is designed to stand in stark contrast to infamous crime lords like Pablo Escobar, whose violent transgressions attract the attention of news outlets, Hollywood executives, and global production and distribution companies such as Netflix. Marco, in his ignorant obliviousness, operates at the opposite end of the spectrum. His incompetent life of crime is such that he is not even able to realize successfully a plan that would draw interest from his local newspaper, let alone the audiovisual industry. Similarly, though operating with a degree of self-awareness lacking in its anti-hero, 1quarto recognizes its own upstart, decentered position. Desiring to break into the industry, though lacking in the varied forms of capital, members of 1quarto employ what has become a long-practiced tactic by transgressive newcomers—find the biggest, most successful example and make fun of it. The fact that the source of their parody was Netflix and one of its series and not TV Globo or one of its *telenovelas* speaks to the ways in which the field is continuously expanding, particularly for young Brazilians who, when compared to previous generations, are increasingly brought up in a mediascape characterized by its proliferation of viewing options.

As evidenced by *Septo* and *Marcos*, one result of the expansion of the

Brazilian mediascape since 2011 is the representation of places and cultures rarely seen on television. Thus, having peeled away the myriad ridiculous situations that make up *Marcos'* first and second seasons, what becomes clear is that they all unfold within the space of the southern city of Caxias do Sul. As with *Septo* and its portrayal of Natal and use of the distinctly *potiguar* accent, typical of natives of Rio Grande do Norte, from the other end of the geographic spectrum, *Marcos'* own visual and spoken lexicon provides spectators with a uniquely *gaucho* (natives of Rio Grande do Sul) version, not of the more well-known capital city of Porto Alegre, but instead of the rarely represented city of Caxias do Sul. Each of the two web series, then, through their distinct audiovisual constructions, spatiotemporal settings, narrative tones, themes, and modes of distribution, are specific niche representations of regions of Brazil, which, insofar as they exist within a mediascape long characterized by TV Globo and its *telenovelas*, function as alternative creative constructs of how to represent Brazil and what it means to be Brazilian.

3%: Streaming Global/Global Socioeconomic Inequality

3% is a post-apocalyptic drama set in a dystopian society inspired by Aldous Huxley's *Brave New World* and George Orwell's *1984*. The defining characteristic of this future society is the divide between the land-based *Continente* (Continent), home to a largely uneducated and highly impoverished population, and Maralto, an offshore community that houses a select and thriving group of former Continent inhabitants. In a nod to the current global social climate, the vast majority of the population of the Continent has been abandoned to a hopeless future. To borrow from Zygmunt Bauman (2004), the individuals that make up the landlocked population represent the "wasted lives" of late modernity and the onset of neoliberal capitalism. For Bauman, the global spread of modernity "has cancelled the division between 'centre' and 'periphery,' or more correctly between 'modern' (or 'developed') and 'premodern' (or 'underdeveloped' or 'backward') forms of life" (2004: 69). That is, in the contemporary global landscape, poverty and wealth simultaneously occupy the same spaces—independent of their geographic location and nearly always in an unequal manner. *3%*, however, presents a future world that is characterized precisely by the vast distance—real and symbolic—that separates the Continent (periphery) from the Maralto (center). The series' post-apocalyptic universe, then, harkens back to outdated notions of homogenous first- and third-world nations. The mechanism that produces and perpetuates the stark inequality that characterizes society in *3%* is the annual *Processo* (Process), a cut-throat selection competition designed to determine the 3 percent of hopeful twenty-year-old individuals who will "earn" the right to move to the uber-developed, technology-rich Maralto, where they will live happily ever after, far from the backward, underdeveloped reality that envelopes the Continent.

3% is known best for its release in November of 2016 as Netflix's first original series produced in Brazil. However, the roughly twenty-six-minute pilot of the web series was initially posted to YouTube in three approximately nine-minute parts on May 19–20, 2011.[11] Rather than the very specific, localized micro *Brazils* on display in *Septo* and *Marco*, the Netflix-produced version of *3%* takes a broader view, portraying a fictional society that has emerged out of an environmental disaster resulting from the failures of late capitalism. Despite the series' focus on the macro, like *Septo* and *Marco*, *3%* occupies a position that exists in contrast to TV Globo and to its own web pilot from 2011, which featured a disproportionately white cast. The Netflix series, however, reveals a notable shift in its representation, insofar as it replaces the homogeneous cast from the web pilot with one that more closely represents Brazil's diverse population.

More than five years before Netflix made the post-apocalyptic drama its first Brazilian original series, *3%*'s pilot was made available on YouTube. In May of 2011, user *serie3porcento* uploaded the first two installments accompanied by the following description and links to the *3%* Facebook and Twitter pages: "Brazilian sci-fi drama series pilot. We are looking for a TV network to support the whole season" (Aguilera, 2011). Of note is the explicit declaration by the web series' creators of their intention to transform the web pilot into a television series. Such an objective speaks to the context of the Brazilian audiovisual industry in 2009. It was during that year that Pedro Aguilera, Daina Giannecchini, Dani Libardi, and Jotagá Crema, creators of the YouTube video and all recent graduates of the University of São Paulo (ECA), applied for funding from the Ministry of Culture's FICTV competition to support their idea.[12] When the web pilot was completed in 2010, Globo and its vertical mode of production—which, as discussed in chapter 1, extended from television to film—still dominated the Brazilian mediascape. At the same time, due to its programming emphasis on imported content, the pay-television sector was not a viable option for incipient producers. Thus, working out of what was still a highly restricted field with limited options, rather than exploring the web series as a genre, the producers used the YouTube pilot to showcase and promote their work in hopes of breaking into the tightly controlled television industry.

In terms of narrative structure, there is in fact little in the web pilot that distinguishes the work from a more traditional dramatic television series. Following the title vignette, "Pilot—Ep. 1," as it is labeled, opens with a traveling close-up shot of a large, solid steel door sliding open to reveal a mass of individuals affrightedly awaiting instructions. As the scene unfolds, voiceover narration from Bruna (Júlia Ianina) informs the spectator of the central problem driving the narrative: "The world is divided in two sides: the good one and the bad one" (Aguilera, 2011).

After a series of events that establish that Bruna and the other characters are participating in a competition that represents their one chance to move from the "bad" to the "good" side, the first installment ends at the nine-minute mark with the revelation that Bruna—who, up until this point, the spectator believes to be the series' protagonist—has unexpectedly been eliminated from the competition. Not unlike what occurs immediately prior to one of a *telenovela*'s five commercial breaks, closing the episode in this way functions as a hook intended to draw the spectator back to watch the second episode. At the same time, considering the creators' broader objectives, this and the subsequent hooks, discussed below, also function to demonstrate to potential television executives that the young producers understand the narrative logic of proven television series and therefore have what it takes to create something successful for that medium. The second episode, which per YouTube's interactive characteristics can be initiated immediately by clicking on a link posted at the end of the first episode, provides the spectator with a recap, common in weekly serial dramas, as it picks up the narrative slightly before Bruna learns of her elimination.

Like the first, the second episode ends with a hook, leaving the spectator wondering how the interviewer will react to Fernando's (Thiago Balieiro) response to her question regarding why he wants to pass to the other side. Unlike the second, the third and final episode foregoes a recap, beginning instead with Fernando rejoining his fellow competitors after having passed the initial examination. As would be expected in Brazilian television drama, the biggest hook is reserved for the end of the web pilot.

Here, Bruna, who has not only been eliminated but murdered after she attacked a guard, takes up the central issue posed in her opening narration, telling the spectator in voiceover of what to expect as the rest of the narrative plays out: "They only choose 3 percent to go the other side. I did not make it" (Aguilera, 2011). Then, over the image of the three other main characters, Fernando, Rafael (José Geraldo Rodrigues), and Michele (Rita Batata), Bruna stimulates the spectator's curiosity by noting that one of the three will be successful (Aguilera, 2011).

While 3% plays mostly like a traditional network television series, and while its creators explicitly used YouTube as a means to get their series picked up by a network, the very fact they had the option of releasing it on a video-upload site indicates an opening of the Brazilian audiovisual field. Though by 2010 domestically produced web series in Brazil were still a relatively new phenomenon, the Internet, especially for the most affluent classes, was slowly emerging as an alternative space for the dissemination and consumption of audiovisual content.[13] Much had changed, however, by the time Netflix released the full season of 3% in late 2016. The gradual three-year implementation of the Pay-TV Law was complete, and for the first time since TV Globo came to reign over Brazilian television in the late 1960s, there were now a number of viewing options and robust production occurring outside of Globo's reach. The heightened competition resulting from an increase in distribution channels and designated spaces for the airing of Brazilian-produced content on those channels, the ever-growing presence of the Internet, and the proliferation of screens (e.g., mobile phones, tablets, laptops, etc.) had opened up production opportunities that previously did not exist.

Thus, when 3% did make it to television sets, as its creators had initially hoped, it was not at TV Globo but under the care of a massive streaming platform based in California, against which Globo was now competing (more on this in chapter 6). As Lotz argues, such shifts in industry logics have consequences for the creative and textual possibilities of a particular field (2017: 20). Specifically, Lotz contends that scripted television is the form most impacted by the nonlinearity of Internet-distributed television. Not surprisingly, then, the YouTube pilot, like the overwhelming majority of Brazilian television fiction pre-2011, featured a disproportionately white cast. However, within the context of the increasingly competitive new Brazilian mediascape and the possibilities it affords to producers and viewers alike, the creators of the Netflix series dramatically shifted its representation of Brazil: they replaced the homogeneous cast from the web pilot with one decidedly more diverse.

The Netflix version of *3%* does not follow TV Globo's long-established practice of emphasizing whiteness while casting actors of color for the few, select stereotypical roles—maid, chauffeur, drug dealer—historically reserved for such individuals (Araújo, 2000; Grijó and Sousa, 2012). Instead, for the most part, the Netflix series avoids character development based on predetermined professional and moral precedents tied to race. More specifically, among the numerous protagonists are four Afro-Brazilians (Michel Gomes, Vaneza Oliveira, Viviane Porto, and Zezé Motta), all of whom are portrayed as highly intelligent and driven individuals. Moreover, the cast of the first season features two actors of Japanese descent (Luana Tanaka and Daniel Uemura) and a protagonist in a wheelchair.[14] Two Japanese-Brazilian screenwriters, Cássio Koshikumo and Ivan Nakamura, are also key members of the writing staff.

In addition to the diverse cast and creative team, the series deconstructs the role of the white male heartthrob, present in virtually every Globo production, whether on television or on film. Indeed, the Netflix series can be read as a symbolic move away from the center—the white Brazilian elite—toward an understanding of Brazilian society characterized by racial, gender, and socioeconomic diversity. Marco Alvarez (Rafael Lozano) is an athletic, attractive, and charming twenty-year-old white man whose family has always secured a place in Maralto. The narrative initially frames Marco as one of the work's protagonists, a suggestion that strengthens over the first three episodes. However, in the pivotal fourth episode, Marco reveals himself to be dishonest, elitist, and violent. Consequently, Marco not only fails to complete the competition as his family members had before him, but his actions result in a seemingly violent death. The broader implication is that, in a competition and society centered on meritocracy, one's familial legacy, gender, and phenotype cannot be guarantees of either success or failure.

Such a positioning is reinforced in episode eight of the series' second season when Marco surprisingly reappears, though without his legs, which were lost in the aforementioned incident. In a society already characterized by a "survival of the fittest" ethos, Marco's limited physical abilities have rendered him a liability, at least in the eyes of the militia for whom he now works, performing the least desirable of tasks. Eventually, through cunning and violence, Marco rises up to lead the militia. His new role puts him in contact with Marcela (Laila Garin), the leader of Maralto's security forces. In yet another (*telenovela-esque*) twist, we learn that Marcela is actually Marco's mother. Rather than help her son, she makes it clear that in her eyes he is a failure and that his current situation is—following the overarching logic of Maralto and the *Processo* that provides entry to the utopian society—deserved.

In contrast, especially during the first season, the positions of power held by Nair and Aline—played by Afro-Brazilian actresses Zezé Motta and Viviane Porto—appear to support the idea that merit, not race, gender, or physical ability, is the key factor to both access to and success in Maralto. But even for those characters who are unsuccessful in their attempts to make it to Maralto, the series positions Afro-Brazilian characters like Fernando (Michel Gomes) and Joana Coelho (Vaneza Oliveira) as perhaps the smartest and most capable of all the competitors. By the end of the second season, Fernando and Joana, both inhabitants of the Continent, have risen to become two of the series' most important characters. For her part, Joana becomes the de facto leader of the *Causa* (the Cause), a group of Continent citizens that works to combat the inequalities perpetuated by Maralto and the Process. For his part, Fernando, along with Michele, his love interest, is set to become a founder of a new utopia, one inclusive of all humans, whether of the Continent or of the Maralto.

To be clear, the diversity and implicit critiques present in the Netflix version of *3%* are not necessarily the result of the opening up of the mediascape since 2011. An increasingly competitive mediascape does not guarantee more progressive productions, in the same way that the collective viewings of the Network Era did not guarantee national solidarity or less progressive representations. The post-2011 mediascape, however, has played a fundamental role *in creating the conditions* for such productions to emerge. Daina Giannecchini (Entrevista com a diretora, 2016), one of the creators and lead directors of both the YouTube and Netflix versions of *3%*, implies as much when she advocates for the construction of a new imaginary for Brazil, one in which "machismo and racism are no longer forces of oppression." One way for this to occur is through the fragmentation and expansion of the Brazilian mediascape.

Fragmentation takes place primarily through the proliferation of new fictional genres—in this case, the web series—produced to meet the demand of ever-expanding windows of distribution. Both the emergent content and channels of distribution attract small, niche audiences away from TV Globo's tens of millions of spectators accustomed to consuming the network's daily *telenovelas*. As Christian argues, "The rhetoric of the Internet challenging television has primarily involved opening up the medium to more producers and users. Broadband adoption and streaming technology encouraged a broader base of video producers, each working in a variety of genres, storytelling modes (serialized, non-serialized), and under a variety of business models, from web-grown networks, traditional TV networks and omnibus 'anyone can upload' sites like YouTube" (2012, 351).

The broadening of the Brazilian mediascape, then, results in a situation in which—just as TV Globo finds it increasingly difficult to reproduce its previously all but guaranteed audiences whose eyes are ever more diverted to different sources of content—individuals find themselves increasingly in contact with fictional representations of Brazil that contrast with the more conservative portrayals produced by TV Globo. As Appadurai argues, such a process has important consequences for the constitution of society as such (1996). He contends that the expansion of the mediascape allows for more individuals worldwide to "see their lives through the prisms of possible lives offered by mass media in all their forms" (1996: 53–54). It follows that the more diverse and inclusive such offerings are, the more expansive the possibilities are for individuals throughout the world. Along these lines, Appadurai notes that "the new power of the imagination in the fabrication of social lives is inescapably tied up with images, ideas, and opportunities that come from elsewhere, often moved around by the vehicles of mass media" (53–54). Similarly, the modifications to the field of audiovisual production since 2011 have expanded the Brazilian social imaginary, establishing a new space for the development of narratives not directly tied to TV Globo's hegemonic model. As evidenced by *Septo*, *Marcos*, and *3%* and the television series discussed in chapter 2, the growth of the Internet and pay-television sector has been a central aspect of this shift. Together, the two distribution sources and production spaces potentially combine to act on and in conjunction with ongoing transformations to society by further empowering and bolstering both the subjective and collective imaginations.

4

Entering Television through the *Porta dos Fundos*

Over the last three chapters, I have considered how the passage of the Pay-TV Law and the subsequent growth of the pay-television sector and the Internet propelled Brazilian television out of a five-decade Network Era. More specifically, the preceding discussion focuses on different transformations related to these two emergent areas, emphasizing the ways in which they have expanded the Brazilian mediascape—and by extension the Brazilian social imaginary—beyond TV Globo and its *telenovelas*' stronghold over the field and the imagined community. While it is evident that the developments unfolding within the new Brazilian mediascape have resulted in more diverse participation, production, and distribution, it is not yet clear how the expansion of the field and resulting fragmentation of audiences have impacted TV Globo's crown jewel: the *telenovela*. To this end, the first part of this chapter explores TV Globo's shrinking audience shares beginning in the early 1990s. By contrasting the network's struggles during the 1990s with those leading up to and immediately following 2011, a clearer picture of the waning Network Era and the nascent post-2011 mediascape emerges. So as to refine and complete this picture, the rest of the chapter centers on the rise and television and Internet production of Porta dos Fundos (Backdoor), situating the independent production company as a primary example of the new Brazilian mediascape and the creative, production, and distribution possibilities it affords.

The Beginnings of TV Globo's Audience Struggles

Following major audience hits like *Renascer* (*Reborn*, 1993) and *O Rei do Gado* (*The Cattle King*, 1996), as the twentieth century drew to a close, TV Globo's *telenovelas*' viewership found itself locked in a consistent decline.[1] In an attempt to understand the network's diminishing audiences and to provide both a quantitative and qualitative explanation as to why "*Rede Globo não é mais a campeã absoluta de audiência*" (TV Globo is no longer the undisputed ratings king), Sílvia H. Simões Borelli and Gabriel Priolli published *A deusa ferida*. Released in 2000, *A deusa ferida*—whose title translates to English as The Wounded Goddess and refers to TV Globo's deity-like status as Brazil's preeminent television network—situates the origins of TV Globo's audience struggles in the early 1990s. According to the authors (2000: 33), the downward trend was the result of reasons both internal and external to the broadcast network.

Internally, Borelli and Priolli (2000) pointed to the structuring influence of the aforementioned Globo Standard of Quality (see the Introduction), both as a business model and as an aesthetic orientation. In qualitative and discursive terms, Brazilian scholars, television critics, industry professionals, and government agents reduced the resulting difference between TV Globo–produced programming and other broadcast network–produced programming to the Rio de Janeiro–based network's successful implementation of the Globo Standard of Quality. However, Borelli and Priolli (2000: 161–62) maintained that the Globo Standard of Quality and the network's association between it and its large audiences eventually made it difficult for TV Globo to adjust quickly to changes in the field. Perhaps most significantly, the authors highlighted the general exhaustion of the *telenovela*. Borelli and Priolli (2000: 162–64) argued that the telenovela's long-term success during the prime-time hours had made TV Globo reluctant to experiment with the format, thereby leaving audiences with more of the same. Put differently, though industrial shifts were under way, they had not yet taken root to the degree that they would require the network's executives and decision-makers to reconceptualize a product that had proved to be one of the most successful in the world, at least in terms of audience share.

Externally, Borelli and Priolli (2000: 167–70) called attention to what they referred to as the rise of "new forms of watching" and "new modes for making television." At the time of *A deusa ferida*'s publication, the new forms of watching television highlighted by the scholars were the videocassette recorder and remote control. Increased access to these incipient technologies represented the first time in the history of Brazilian television that at least some viewers—namely, those who possessed the economic capital to purchase the technology—gained a degree of control of what, when, and how they watched television. The videocassette recorder made it possible for television audiences to tape their favorite programs and watch them outside of broadcast networks' linear programming schedules. Moreover, it afforded the viewer the opportunity to fast-forward through commercial breaks. Similarly, the remote control increased the possibility for channel-surfing, which further destabilized the certainty and power of advertisers' ability to hold the viewer's attention.

The new modes for making television identified by the authors were twofold. The first concerned the strengthening and diversification of the programming grids of broadcast networks such as SBT[2] and Rede Record.[3] During the 1990s, both of these São Paulo–based networks created successful, sensationalistic news programs (e.g., *Aqui agora*, SBT 1991) and popular variety shows (e.g., *O programa do Ratinho*, Rede Record 1997) that drew the attention of TV Globo's executives. Ultimately, Borelli and Priolli (2000: 119–20) argued that the dent these programs made in TV Globo's largely unchallenged audience share up to that point helped to increase overall program competition, as the Rio de Janeiro network sought to recapture its dominant numbers. The second change to the mode of making television centered on the implementation and slow growth of pay television (Borelli and Priolli, 2000: 167–71).

Transitioning into the Twenty-First Century

As is the case the world over, much has changed in the field of Brazilian television production in the nearly two decades since the publication of *A deusa ferida*. In fact, those internal and external reasons suggested by Borelli and Priolli for TV Globo's weakened position in the field have continuously become more present, challenging the network's dominance as never before. One important example has been the *telenovela* format, which has shown intensified signs of decline among audiences in recent years. The *telenovela*'s weakened position combined with significant transformations to the forms of watching and modes for making content have resulted in the growth of the production of series, which are increasingly made available on over-the-air networks, pay-television, and the Internet.

A look at the audience share of a small sample of TV Globo prime-time *telenovelas*[4] beginning in 2000 provides insight into how the format, with a few exceptions, has more recently found itself on a consistent downward path. In 2000, at the time of the publication of *A deusa ferida*, TV Globo aired *Laços de família* (*Family Ties*), written by Manoel Carlos. In its last chapter,[5] *Laços de família* achieved an audience share of 60 points, which left the *telenovela* with a 45 average over its 209 total chapters (Branco, 2003).[6] Though they began to fall off around 2008, audience shares for the fifteen *novelas das nove* (nine o'clock *telenovelas*) produced by TV Globo between 2000 and 2010 held relatively firm at an average of 44 points.[7]

From 2010 to the beginning of 2019, however, a clear shift in audience shares can be seen. In fact, not a single one of the fifteen *novelas das nove* produced by TV Globo during the period between 2010 and 2019 achieved an audience share of 40 points or above.[8] The largest audience share belonged to *Avenida Brasil* (*Brazil Avenue*, 2012) and *O outro lado do paraíso* (*The Other Side of Paradise*, 2017–2018), both of which registered averages of 39 points (Deodoro and Padiglione, 2012 and Pecolli, 2018). For the entire period, the total average audience share was slightly more than 33 points. Compared to the period between 2000 and 2009, this represented an overall decrease of slightly more than 24 percent.

Despite the decided decrease, a reader most familiar with the United States' increasingly fragmented mediascape will understand these numbers as representing a broadcast network success. For example, per the IBOPE metrics (see note 6), *A força do querer* (*The Edge of Desire*, 2017) and the already-mentioned *O outro lado do paraíso*, the two TV Globo *novelas das nove* that premiered in 2017, captured an approximate average of 7.8 and 8.4 million viewers in São Paulo (Peccoli, 2017, 2018). In Rio de Janeiro, the two productions drew an average of approximately 5.16 and 5.2 million viewers, respectively (Peccoli, 2017, 2018). Thus, in Brazil's two largest cities alone, these two *telenovelas* attracted an average of 11.5 and 12.4 million nightly viewers over their respective 172 chapters, each of which lasted for approximately fifty minutes and aired Monday through Saturday for about seven consecutive months. By comparison, in 2017 the most-watched program (excluding sporting events) in the United States was CBS's *The Big Bang Theory* (2008–). Since 2012, the sitcom has aired in twenty-four-episode seasons, with each weekly airing lasting eighteen to twenty-two minutes, excluding commercial breaks. During its eleventh season in 2017, the sitcom registered just over 18.5 million viewers nationwide. Therefore, without including the overall numbers, the two aforementioned *telenovelas* fare well in comparison to *The Big Bang Theory*. That comparison is even more favorable to Brazil when one takes into consideration that Brazil has approximately 120 million fewer inhabitants than the United States.

The juxtaposition made here between Brazil and the United States is intended to reveal the significant power TV Globo's *telenovelas* still wield over audiences that, while diminishing and increasingly not being reproduced, remain faithful to the network. Nonetheless, for the purposes of this book, what is important is not how Brazil's most-watched television fiction stacks up against that of the United States, but instead how the former, while still occupying a dominant position in the domestic market, compares to its own past and how that comparison reveals new and ongoing challenges to the network's hegemony. Indeed, the continuing decrease in TV Globo's audience share must be situated and understood within the context of the new Brazilian mediascape—an era defined by (1) increased competition from the Internet and global producers and distributors such as Netflix[9] and Amazon; (2) the fragmentation of audiences deriving from the proliferation of screens and access to content; and (3) the unprecedented growth of the pay-television sector. It is precisely within this context that one notes a substantial shift away from the Brazilian television of years earlier, particularly that which served as the focus for Borelli and Priolli's research in the late 1990s.

"O fantasma da TV paga" (The Ghost of Pay-Television), the sixth chapter of *A deusa ferida*, begins by addressing the apparent interconnectedness of TV Globo's declining ratings and the rise of the pay-television sector. However, Borelli and Priolli (2000) are quick to emphasize that, at the time of the book's publication, pay-television was still a recent phenomenon. Having quietly begun its operations in Brazil in 1990 and only introducing satellite transmission in 1997, the industry was indeed still very much in its infancy throughout the last decade of the twentieth century. In fact, it was so much so that Borelli and Priolli (2000: 169) argued that the biggest obstacle posed by pay-television to TV Globo was that it increased the quality of the transmission signal of all broadcast networks, which, unlike TV Globo, did not always have an unlimited national reach. Contrary, then, to what was being circulated in the media at the time, Borelli and Priolli correctly concluded that pay-television played a minor role in TV Globo's audience share decline and that an overemphasis on the incipient sector's impact on the audiovisual field as a whole would have been misleading in 2000. However, as discussed at length in chapter 1 and touched on in chapter 3, such has not been the case in the post-2011 era, during which, among other factors, rising pay-television and broadband Internet subscriptions have played a fundamental role in opening up the field to content consumption and production beyond TV Globo's hegemonic structure.

A Back Door to Television—From the Internet to Pay-Television and Back Again

In *We Now Disrupt This Broadcast: How Cable Transformed Television and the Internet Revolutionized It All*, Lotz fleshes out the interconnectedness of competitive norms and contexts through an analysis of the economic and creative logics undergirding a selection of innovative original programming produced for cable beginning in 1996 (2018: 48). Importantly, she identifies this year in particular as marking the end of the mass audience era in the United States (3, 4). Just as the upstart networks WB and UPN were "siphoning viewers from 'the Big Three,'" in 1996, cable channels were also increasingly attracting viewers, resulting in television's rapid transition "from a medium with programs for mass audiences to one that spoke to an array of niche tastes and interests." Specifically, with regard to original scripted series, the expansion of cable television toward the end of the twentieth century gave way to "a sector of television storytelling governed by different business practices and constraints" (47). The pioneer in this area was HBO, which created the series *OZ* (1997–2000), *Sex in the City* (1998–2005), and *The Sopranos* (1999–2007). In line with the channel's recently coined slogan, "It's not TV, it's HBO" (1996–2009), at the time the cinematic aesthetic and rarely depicted subject matter on display in these series represented a considerable departure from the storytelling norms of the Network Era. While the business and management practices of that era had long limited innovation, HBO's subscriber model eliminated the importance of advertiser support, ultimately enabling "audiences and those in the television industry to imagine television differently" (47).

The centrality Lotz gives to cable television as the harbinger of the Post-Network—or perhaps more aptly, "the *small screens* era"—can also be applied to Brazil, though not exactly in the same manner. As mentioned previously, unlike in the United States, pay-television was not first firmly established prior to the widespread transformations brought on by the advent and proliferation of the digital technologies and the Internet. Instead, in Brazil, the tectonic shifts to the mediascape are simultaneously deeply intertwined with the expansion of pay-television, the Internet, and digital technologies. As such, it would not be possible, as Lotz does, to simply identify pay-television series as the transformative motor driving the Brazilian mediascape toward a Post-Network Era. Rather, in order to gain a clear understanding of how this process is taking place in Brazil, one must simultaneously consider the impact of television and Internet fiction, which I attempted to do in chapters 2 and 3. Notwithstanding the importance of the series discussed in those chapters, perhaps there is no better example of this in the post-2011 Brazilian mediascape than the independent production company and YouTube sensation Porta dos Fundos (Backdoor).

In 2012, shortly after the Pay-TV Law was passed, a group of young friends working in the entertainment industry decided to leave their jobs and join forces to create their own production company.[10] Since that time, Porta dos Fundos has become the preeminent producer of fictional content for the Internet in Brazil. The group's success, however, has not been limited to the territorial confines of the South American giant; it has also turned itself into one of the most successful YouTube channels in the world. At the time of writing, the Porta dos Fundos YouTube channel has nearly sixteen million regular subscribers and its 1,000-plus videos have accumulated over five billion total views. In 2016, Porta dos Fundos was recognized as the most influential YouTube channel in the world (Zefr, 2016).

Even before Porta dos Fundos posted its first video on YouTube, the independent production company's future relationship with both the Internet and television had roots in the two companies that combined to create it: Antônio Tabet's website Kibe Loco and Ian SBF and Fábio Porchat's Fondo Filmes. Tabet first produced a print version of Kibe Loco in 1996 while still an undergraduate student at the Federal University of Rio de Janeiro (UFRJ). In the early 2000s, after graduating and taking a job as a marketing executive, Tabet began to produce an e-mail version he disseminated among colleagues and friends. By 2002, that version had transformed into the website Kibe Loco, which was modeled after the United States–based website College Humor—itself founded only three years prior by undergraduate students Josh Abramson and Ricky Van Veen. Like College Humor, Kibe Loco presented viewers with a fairly simple layout characterized by a steady stream of humoristic photos, headlines, and videos. Designed to entertain an eighteen to thirty-five-year-old target audience, the varied forms of content, often in a sophomoric sexual tone, poked fun at politics, economics, relationships, and social media, among other quotidian topics.

In 2005, Kibe Loco gained in notoriety when it became a ten-minute weekly segment on TV Globo's widely viewed Saturday afternoon variety show, *Caldeirão do Huck* (*Huck's Cauldron*, 2000–) (Carpanez, 2006).[11] Two years later, in 2007, Globo.com began to host the Kibe Loco blog. With more than 500,000 monthly accesses, Kibe Loco quickly became one of the most visited blogs in Brazil. In 2012, Tabet capitalized on the site's popularity by signing a contract with Globo's rival, Rede Record (O site de, 2012). Three years later, in April of 2015, Tabet transformed the blog-based brand into the *Show do Kibe*. Airing weekly at 12 PM on TBS, the *Show do Kibe* was a thirteen-episode deconstructed talk show featuring Tabet, who interviewed famous comedians and comedic actors, all of whom were unaware the camera was rolling (Kibe Loco desconstrói, 2015). Prior to the Kibe Loco brand's second experimentation with television, however, around the same time he signed the contract with Rede Record, Tabet partnered with SBF and Porchat's independent production company, Fondo Filmes, to found Porta dos Fundos.

SBF and Porchat established Fondo Filmes sometime in 2009. On August 1 of that same year, along with future Porta dos Fundos' founder and contributors, Gregório Duvivier, Clarice Falcão, Letícia Lima, and Rafael Infante, the independent production house created its own YouTube channel, which would serve as the company's content archive. Nearly all of the ninety videos in the archive are from 2010 or 2011. Though no new videos have been posted to the channel since July of 2013, it still has over sixty-five thousand active subscribers, and its videos have accumulated over twenty million views. In 2011, the production company founded a second YouTube channel, Anões em chamas (Little People in Flames). Currently, that channel has over 190 thousand subscribers, and its 200-plus videos have generated more than forty-five million views.

In general terms, the content from the two channels includes a mixture of brief narrative sketches, interviews, and animated videos. Though they do not consistently display the same high production quality as the Porta dos Fundos' later work—discussed in greater detail below—many of the videos present on these earlier channels contain the seeds of the acerbic, satiric tone, the controversial subject matter, and the use of parody that combine to characterize the former. Moreover, considering that many of the future Porta dos Fundos' collaborators take part in the Fondo Filmes and Anões em chamas channels, both in front of and behind the camera, those videos should be understood as experimental precursors in search of the formula that would later prove to be a resounding success on Porta dos Fundos' YouTube channel.

Two particularly good examples of the tone, subject matter, and humor that characterizes Porta dos Fundos work can be found in *Amanda* (2010) and *CSI: Nova Iguaçu* (2011), web series produced by Fondo Filmes and Anões em chamas. Before briefly examining these earlier productions and moving to a more in-depth discussion of work produced under the Porta dos Fundos brand, it is important to note that the central aim here is not to categorize, analyze, or theorize the Porta dos Fundos' production of humor—though such a study would be a welcome addition to the understanding of the contemporary Brazilian mediascape. Nor does what follows in the remainder of this chapter and in the next propose a definitive reading of the group's creative output. Instead, in establishing the broader context out of which Porta dos Fundos came to be one of Brazil's most successful independent production companies, I seek to emphasize the group's (and by extension the broader population's) increased access to emergent windows of distribution, namely, YouTube and pay-television channels. From this, I aim to highlight two broader points. First, when compared to broadcast network television, VOD sites like YouTube and pay-television channels like FX are not subject to the same regulations regarding content. As such, producers for these distribution windows have more creative freedoms than those same producers at a network like TV Globo. Related to the first, the second point is that, unlike established Brazilian broadcast networks, which employ an advertiser-supported economic model that results in programming designed to reach the largest possible audience, upstart independent production companies like Porta dos Fundos operating with modest budgets can experience relative success by engaging in a restricted mode of production, wherein content is directed toward a smaller, more tightly defined target-audience (Bourdieu, 1993).

Moreover, though I highlight some of Porta dos Fundos' videos and web series' use of humor as a tool for critiquing and challenging hegemonic norms as they pertain to such issues as religion, sexuality, and race, this is not to suggest that these particular instances—let alone the group's broader *oeuvre*—are always subversive or even understood as such. As Michael Billig notes: "one needs to be cautious about describing disciplinary humour as being unambiguously conservative, and rebellious humour as being objectively radical . . . At times, rebellious humour—or humour that is claimed and experienced as rebellious—can have conservative and disciplinary functions" (2005: 204, 2012). What is more, Porta dos Fundos comedic output is neither the first nor the only programming in the Brazilian context to employ satire, irony, and parody. Indeed, as have other broadcast networks, TV Globo has long produced works like *Casseta & Planeta* (1993–2010) and *Tá no Ar: A TV na TV* (2014–2019), which utilize these registers to poke fun at and criticize Brazilian society and television itself. That being said, the extent to which such programs can push beyond the socially accepted norms is limited by the fact that they are designed to appeal to a mass audience and that they must abide by restrictions both external (legislation, advertisers, interest groups, etc.) and internal (profits, budgets, talent, etc.). Such is certainly the case at TV Globo where, even when a program promotes certain progressive ideas, behaviors, or critiques, the network's (Bourdieu, 1993) *structuring* large-scale mode of production almost always results in a conservative hedging designed to avoid positions that might potentially isolate vast portions of its mass audience.

Porta dos Fundos' output, on the other hand, is irreverent, explicitly taking aim at sensitive topics and social issues. Again, returning to Billig (2005), the extent to which their "rebelliousness" registers as such is in no way guaranteed. Nonetheless, the ultimate takeaway here is that, leading up to the transformations that took root and expanded beginning in 2011, the sustained success of a small, independent production company like Porta dos Fundos was made almost impossible by the lack of distribution windows and the widespread dominance of Globo's media empire.

As I have attempted to demonstrate in previous chapters, since 2011 the proliferation of distribution windows, and the need to fill those windows with content, has resulted in a parallel media structure that exists outside of and competes with TV Globo. Within this new reality, the increased opportunities for production and consumption help create the conditions for alternative modes of production, while also spurring the siphoning off of TV Globo's *telenovela* audiences. Thus, in direct contrast with TV Globo's more conservative approach, Porta dos Fundos can elect to produce content that attempts to push the boundaries by displaying critical, and sometimes politically incorrect, ideas and behaviors. If viewers find the content on display in their videos offensive or off-putting, so be it. Porta dos Fundos' restricted mode of production is neither concerned with nor does it need a mass audience to achieve economic success and sustain the company's business practices, which was simply not plausible prior to 2011 (Bourdieu, 1993).

Amanda was directed, written, and edited by SBF and stars Letícia Lima[12] as Amanda. The nearly three-minute first episode begins with a still of the Anões em chamas logo and website.[13] To the sound of an upbeat instrumental, the image cuts to a comic-strip-like depiction of a series of women who happily, subserviently, and even seductively complete domestic tasks in a 1960s milieu that recalls that of *Mad Men* (AMC, 2007–2015). Reinforcing a passive, normative version of a domesticated female, the last shot of this opening vignette presents "Amanda" in pink cursive letters. Behind the cursive letters, there is in the background a black-and-white drawing of a Cary Grant–like figure embracing a housewife. Foreshadowing the satirical tone of the video, through the use of a speech balloon written in English, the figure declares, "The harder a wife works, the cuter she looks!" (SBF, 2010).

In the next shot, Amanda introduces herself and her show, which, as she tells us in a soft yet high-pitched voice, is directed at a female audience and aims to address their questions and concerns. As she does so, Amanda sits alongside a stuffed animal on her bed in a bedroom that evokes that of a teenage girl. She is dressed in a low-cut, revealing blouse and is conspicuously wearing lipstick and blush. Like the women from the opening vignette, then, the contrasts present in the figure of Amanda situate her as both a passive girl and a sexualized woman. The significance of these two characteristics and their implied absence of feminism, however, is, through the use of irony, deconstructed by Amanda's response to the question of the day, which derives from the host's interaction with her family's maid (*empregada doméstica*). Inquiring as to why she always wears a coat while working, Amanda informs the audience in a nonchalant manner of the maid's disturbing response: "Amanda, my husband kicks my ass every time he comes home drunk. What would you have me do, show up to work like Cheetara from *Thundercats* with dark spots all over my body?" Highlighting a socioeconomic disconnect and an overarching power structure that situates the working-class *empregada* in a subordinate position vis-à-vis her upper-middle-class employer, Amanda simply glosses over the seriousness of the violence experienced by the maid. That is, instead of addressing the reported domestic abuse, Amanda, who is seemingly more concerned with her Internet presence, tends to her virtual audience by posing the question of the day: "How does one avoid bruises, yellow hematomas, and blood-filled blisters?" (SBF, 2010).[14]

The absurdity of the question, which itself reveals Amanda's priorities and her lack of sociopolitical engagement, not only calls attention to the very real drama of abuse endured by her maid, whose name is, as if to further highlight Amanda's obtuseness, *Socorro* (Help), but also to the uptick in Internet personalities who position themselves as authorities on topics ranging from skincare and nutrition to sex and fashion. Along these lines, in what follows, the "expert" Amanda presents her audience at home with some "tricks" to finesse such "situations" while still looking sexy. She proposes "Os três Ps da Amanda" (Amanda's 3 Ps): *pomada* (creams), *palma* (palms), and *pancake* (foundation), each of which appears on screen written in the same cursive as the title sequence. Amanda proceeds to narrate in-off her absurd justifications, which include getting oiled up in preparation for a beating, situating oneself in such a way to receive the brute force of the palm of a hand while avoiding the dangerous finger bones, and cleverly using foundation to cover up the marks of abuse. In short, Amanda's dubious narration and the *mise-en-scène* within which it unfolds presents her as a vapid, sexual object who is politically alienated in terms of gender and class.

Nonetheless, as with future Porta dos Fundos productions, wherein white, upper-middle-class protagonists are frequently positioned as selfish, sexist, racist, and generally unaware of their regressive beliefs and attitudes, *mise-en-scène* and cinematography are employed to problematize and critique the characters' politically incorrect positions. In Amanda's case, her questionable subjectivity, which serves as the narrative motor, is undercut by an *Eisensteinian* montage of images of domestic violence, which function at a meta level to deconstruct her patriarchal position-taking. While Amanda shares her "tricks," a montage of black-and-white images fills the screen. Among others, the images, all of which implicitly or explicitly evoke domestic violence, portray aggressive men spanking terrified women; singers and former partners, Rihanna and Chris Brown happily together at a public event; a TMZ report that features a close-up of Rihanna's battered face following a beating from Chris Brown; and a man choking a woman. Again, whether the subversive message resonates with the viewer is debatable. What is not up for question, however, is that the meta-narrative made available via the editing situates Amanda as self-absorbed, politically alienated, and ignorant, thereby, at the very least, calling into question the advice she offers.

Another representative example from the earlier channels is the seven-part web-series *CSI: Nova Iguaçu*.[15] A co-production of Kibe Loco and Anões em chamas, the web series appeared on the latter's YouTube channel between September 2011 and January 2012. The web series, which was directed by SBF, parodies the hit spin-offs of CBS's successful franchise *Crime Scene Investigation*. In both *CSI: Miami* and *CSI: NY*, highly competent detectives solve extremely complex cases in two of the United States' most well-known and glamorous cities. In the Anões em chamas parody, however, two incompetent police detectives (Tabet and Gustavo Chagas) work murder cases in Nova Iguaçu, a medium-sized city of approximately 800,000 inhabitants located seventeen miles northwest of its much more famous neighbor, Rio de Janeiro. Like *Amanda*, *CSI: Nova Iguaçu* is built around highly confident characters who paradoxically lack self-awareness. Not only do the detectives of *CSI: Nova Iguaçu* frequently appear in Porta dos Fundos videos, as I will discuss in greater detail below, they more broadly represent the group's ongoing critique of societal structures controlled by incompetent, ignorant, and often racist men.

In every one of the roughly ninety-second videos, the two detectives repeatedly come across the same nameless victim (Gabriel Totoro), who each time has been murdered under different circumstances. Suspense is built through the use of dramatic instrumentals, cinematography, and editing that draws viewers' attention to clues through the use of shot-reverse-shot between the detectives and extreme close-ups of the objects they examine. Spoken lines are limited to a phrase or two, generally functioning to reveal the detectives' ineptitude. For example, in the second installment, the detectives encounter Totoro lying face up on a couch. Employing a close-up shot, the camera captures a conspicuous bloody gunshot wound to the victim's forehead. Despite the obviousness of the wound, Tabet's character picks up a discarded cigarette he encounters lying on the victim's chest. After examining the cigarette by sniffing and looking at it closely, the detective declares his findings to his partner: "It's a fucking gunshot wound!" (Essa porra é tiro!) (SBF, 2011a).

Similarly, in episode five, the detectives, outfitted in their characteristic black sunglasses and donning overly serious facial expressions, rapidly approach the crime scene in their unmarked police car. As they exit the vehicle, low-angle shots of the two establish the importance and power inherent to their chosen profession. At the locale of the crime, the detectives once again encounter Totoro, this time lying shirtless, face down with a red apple in his mouth. Close-up shots of the scene reveal a dead rat, a pair of scissors, and a grouping of candles. While looking down at the dead body, Tabet's character inquires: "What the fuck is all this for?" (Pra quê essa porra?). In accordance with the now-expected degree of ignorance and undercutting the officers' authority established through the opening cinematography, his partner responds matter-of-factly with a racialized stereotype: "Oshosi" (Oxóssi), the Yoruba spirit of the hunt, forest, and animals (SBF, 2011b).

On August 6 of the same year that Anões em chamas posted their last installment of the *CSI: Nova Iguaçu* series, the newly formed Porta dos Fundos released its first, and longest, video (fifteen minutes), "Porta dos Fundos Nº 1." Like the two examples discussed above, and as is the case with the overwhelming majority of the group's production since then, the "Porta dos Fundos Nº 1" employs satire and parody as a comedic mode to criticize Brazilian society and entertain its viewers. The video plays like a shorter version of *Saturday Night Live* (*SNL*). Presented by Totoro, who serves as the program's host, the work is a selection of short sketches that range from a white, middle-class executive who, due to dire financial circumstances, moonlights as a transvestite prostitute, to a new installment of the *CSI: Nova Iguaçu* web series. As with *SNL*, there is even a faux commercial promoting cocaine use for busy housewives: "Janaína é dona de casa e usa: cocaína... Cocaína. Porque a vida já é foda sem ela" (Janaína is a housewife and uses: cocaine ... Cocaine. Because without it, life's a bitch).

The video begins with Totoro introducing the program. Highlighting the forthcoming tone of the separate sketches, Totoro is ironically outfitted in a black tuxedo standing in front of a white background. Before he stumbles through the introduction, forcing the viewer to endure numerous takes, he says: "Hi, my name is César Menotti. You likely know me from the DVDs *Words of Love, Voice of the Heart*, or as the dead fat guy in *CSI: Nova Iguaçu*" (SBF, 2012). From the outset, the joke is on. By introducing himself as César Menotti, Totoro sheds light on the similar physical appearance he shares with the famous Brazilian country singer. However, he immediately deconstructs the bit by highlighting his uneventful role as the murder victim in the Anões em chamas web series. At the same time, the *CSI: Nova Iguaçu* reference suggests an already-existing audience. But the fifteen-minute video is not simply another release from Anões em chamas. Instead, as Totoro informs us, the sketches that follow his introduction form the launch of the new Porta dos Fundos YouTube channel.

As outlined above, Fondo Filmes and Anões em chamas–hosted videos were made by a number of future Porta dos Fundos collaborators. Additionally, many of those works contained the tonal and thematic seeds that would later come to define the videos produced by Porta dos Fundos. So, what distinguished the Porta dos Fundos channel from its precursors? A few characteristics deserve mentioning. The first is that in practical terms, the Porta dos Fundos channel replaced the other two as *the* primary brand and *the* site for the collaborators' production. The second is the qualitative jump with regard to production, which started with the *CSI: Nova Iguaçu* web series. In visual terms, all the uploaded videos have high-quality images, elaborate *mise-en-scènes*, and uniform, branded graphics presenting the title and Porta dos Fundos logo. In addition to the increasingly professional look of the group's videos, they all put into a practice a narrative formula that begins *in medias res*, effectively and efficiently placing the viewer in the heart of the plot. At what seems to be the end of the narrative, an instrumental cues the group's animated logo. However, the end of the narrative is not the end of the video. Viewers familiar with the group's work know that following the logo there is more: namely, an additional brief scene that serves as a comedic punctuation to the video. While this scene plays out, the credits roll along with links to subscribe to the channel and to watch other Porta dos Fundos videos.

Since the publication of "Porta dos Fundos Nº 1," at 11 AM every week on Monday, Thursday, and Saturday, the group has consistently released approximately two to five-minute videos. Their many sketches move freely between contemporary and historical time-spaces to present viewers with critical portrayals of local and global themes and issues, all of which vary in their degrees of seriousness and importance. In addition to their YouTube videos, Porta dos Fundos has experimented with varied audiovisual forms since its inception in 2012. For example, for the Internet or pay-television, the group has created the serial narrative comedies *Viral* (2014),[16] *Refém* (*Hostage*, 2014), *O Grande Gonzalez* (*The Great Gonzalez*, 2015), and *Borges* (2018–); an informal talk show about traveling called *Porta afora* (*Beyond the Door*, 2015–); and *Portaria* (*Lobby*, 2013), a now shuttered weekly program released every Sunday during which the Porta dos Fundos' cast members would comment on the best and worst moments from that week's videos.[17] The production company further diversified its content portfolio in 2016 when it released its first feature-length film, *Porta dos Fundos: Contrato vitalício* (*Porta dos Fundos: Lifetime Contract*).[18] Last, since 2015, members of the group have intermittently traveled throughout Brazil staging a Porta dos Fundos play, *Portátil* (*Portable*, 2015–).[19]

While the entirety of Porta dos Fundos' expansive and varied content deserves a detailed study, such an endeavor falls outside the scope of this book. Instead, of importance for this particular chapter is Porta dos Fundos' serial productions, specifically those that have appeared on both the Internet and pay-television. In 2014, around the same time Porta dos Fundos had transformed its YouTube channel into one of the most successful in the world, the independent production company and television executives from Fox Brasil began exploring the possibility of translating the former's Internet success to pay-television. The two parties eventually signed a contract in May 2014. Months later, on October 14 at 10 PM, Porta dos Fundos premiered on Fox Brasil. Oddly, very little in the Porta dos Fundos television version differed from what the group was doing on the Internet. In fact, the initial Fox Brasil run simply divided up all the group's YouTube videos into a total of twenty-six thirty-minute episodes. To provide broader continuity to the videos, as in the "Porta dos Fundos Nº 1," Totoro hosts the episodes wearing his signature ironic black tuxedo.

At 10 PM on March 18, 2015, Fox Brasil included *Refém* in its programming grid as an hour-long single airing. Initially released on YouTube on November 8, 2014, *Refém* is a web series of five approximately fifteen-minute episodes starring Aline Fanju and regular Porta dos Fundos' cast members Lima, Luis Lobianco, João Vicente de Castro, Porchat, Rafael Infante, and Tabet.[20] The series is a parody of the infamous Bus 174 hijacking that took place in Rio de Janeiro on June 12, 2000, and José Padilha's critically acclaimed documentary (*Ônibus 174*, 2002) about the day's events and the bus-hijacker Sandro's tragic life, which, as the documentary shows, was strongly impacted by his many encounters with Brazil's broken police force and public school and prison systems. Shedding light on the abundant urban violence in Brazil's most well-known city, the media's role in sensationalizing it, and the police force's incompetence in combatting it, the story revolves around an apparent bus-hijacking in downtown Rio de Janeiro. Rafael Infante's character, Rogério, is supposed to be on that very bus heading to São Paulo for business. Instead, the unfaithful husband is actually in a motel in Rio de Janeiro with his lover (Lima). Rogério's plan unravels when his wife Jordana (Fanju), who is at home watching the news, learns that his bus to São Paulo has been hijacked. In what follows, Rogério concocts a plan to save himself by finding a way onto the bus. However, via a series of intricate flashbacks weaved throughout the series, the viewer learns that the bus was never actually hijacked. Rather, overwhelmed by the 100-degree summer heat, the obese driver tries to fix the bus's faulty air-conditioning system. Unable to do so, he ends up suffering a heart attack, leaving the vehicle unattended in the middle of a busy street. That such an innocent occurrence set off blundering police protocols and sparked a media storm speaks to the very real urban violence that has come to be an inseparable part of the daily lives of millions of *cariocas*.[21]

What was gained by merely putting Porta dos Fundos' highly popular videos and web series on television? The answer to this question reveals some of the important ways in which the landscape of Brazilian television fiction has changed since 2011. Reports (Porta dos Fundos vai, 2014) announcing the contract between Fox Brasil and Porta dos Fundos noted that the independent production company was expected to produce a twelve-episode original series to air on Fox Brasil in 2015. Thus, while waiting for production of the new series to be completed, Fox Brasil attempted to draw at least a portion of Porta dos Fundos' large following to the network's programming grid. In addition, per the Pay-TV Law's quota system, the qualified space, international pay-television channel found in the Porta dos Fundos' content a quick and relatively inexpensive way to help it satisfy a portion of the mandated airing of locally produced content by a(n) (independent) Brazilian production company during prime-time hours. As far as Porta dos Fundos was concerned, the relationship with Fox Brasil provided the relatively new independent production company a place within television's long-established and economically viable structure. Along these lines, Fox Brasil aided Porta dos Fundos in the diversification of its portfolio, while also helping the group reach an audience perhaps unaware of their YouTube channel.

At 10 PM on November 2, 2015, Porta dos Fundos and Fox Brasil released the first thirty-minute installment of *O Grande Gonzalez*, a ten-episode serial comedy. Though the next chapter takes up *O Grande Gonzalez* in greater detail, it is worth mentioning here that the series was written and directed by SBF and stars Porta dos Fundos' cast member Luis Lobianco as Gonzalez, a magician who has been murdered by an unknown suspect while performing at a child's birthday party. Like *Refém*, but to an even greater degree, the series constructs a nonlinear narrative based on a series of flashbacks that reflect the accounts of each of the numerous suspects as (incompetent) police detectives Lucimar (Tabet) and Wagner (Castro) interrogate them. If there were doubts surrounding the independent production company's first foray into television in 2014, the serial comedy put those to bed. Although well below its nearly sixteen million YouTube subscribers, the series attracted over one million viewers, increasing Fox Brasil's prime-time audience share by 43 percent and elevating the network to second place among pay-television networks and fifth overall for the time slot (Estreia de O Grande, 2015). In addition to its commercial success, a number of critics (Carvalho B, 2015) hailed the series for its originality as it transitioned from the "small, small screen" to the "small screen."

On March 13, 2018, Porta dos Fundos released *Borges*, its second serial comedy. The series, which aired Tuesdays at 9:30 PM on Comedy Central, consists of ten thirty-minute episodes. Unlike the group's YouTube sketches, but similar to its other television productions, each episode has a beginning, middle, and end, attending to Comedy Central's (and more broadly, non-premium pay-television's) existing advertising structure. The majority of the series takes place within the offices of Borges, a small company whose business centers on importing goods. The series begins with the company on the verge of bankruptcy after its principal owner, Borges (Lobianco), has stolen from the business and cheated his partners, Erasmo (Tabet), Pablo (Rafael Portugal), Rosana (Thati Lopes), and Sônia (Karina Ramil). Concerned that their many creditors and former employees may think they had something to do with Borges's illicit practices, the remaining partners decide to communicate their innocence and dire situation by making a video for the Internet. Surprisingly, the poorly conceived video ends up being the solution to their problem when they realize that its accumulated views has earned them some revenue. As a result, the four partners decide to turn Borges into an independent production company producing videos for the Internet to pay back their outstanding debts.

In the episodes that follow, the newly founded production company's work functions as a parody of Porta dos Fundos itself. For example, in episode two, "Religião" (Religion), one of Borges's early videos offends a religious group, which threatens the company with yet another lawsuit. In 2017, the Dom Bosco Center, a recently formed Catholic association located in Rio de Janeiro, had sued Porta dos Fundos for moral damages to the tune of five million *reais*: one *real* for every YouTube view at the time of filing. The video in question, "Céu Católico" (Catholic Heaven), makes fun of the arbitrariness of Biblical redemption through the polemical presence of a repented Adolpho Hitler in heaven. Claiming freedom of speech and citing its many other videos that have taken aim at evangelical Christianity, Spiritism, and Umbanda as evidence that the group in no way targets Catholicism, Porta dos Fundos requested the case be dismissed and that Dom Bosco pay its legal fees (Porta dos Fundos quer, 2018).[22]

Another example of *Borges* parodying Porta dos Fundos is from episode three. In "Tapicrepe," (Tapioca Crepe), the company makes a video critiquing the poor customer service of a local restaurant chain. However, rather than negatively affecting the chain, as was the intention, the video goes viral, exponentially bumping the restaurant's sales. Similarly, in 2013, Porta dos Fundos published a video titled "Spoleto." Portraying employees as rude and overly aggressive, the video employs humor to criticize the customer service of Spoleto, a well-known Italian fast-food restaurant with hundreds of locations spread throughout Brazil. As in the "Tapicrepe" episode, rather than bringing a lawsuit against the independent production company, Spoleto executives realized the marketing power behind the video and decided to partner with Porta dos Fundos to make a second and third video, "Spoleto 2: O retorno" (Spoleto 2: The Return) and "Spoleto 3" (Levin, 2012). Together, the videos have accumulated more than twenty-four million views.

It was Porta dos Fundos' success, evidenced by such numbers and by their prolific production, that first drew the attention of Fox Brasil executives. Toward the end of 2014, leading up to their first series, the group brought on former Fox/Discovery Brasil and Endemol Brasil executive Juliana Algañaraz as a partner and CEO. Algañaraz would remain in the role for only eight months. However, as Karoline Grubert Bezerra Portela notes, the agreement between the two parties was important for pushing the company to further emphasize production across different platforms and for diverse audiences (2017: 26). By the time the group released *Borges* on Comedy Central, it had gone from creating satirical sketches and parodies exclusively for YouTube to owning an expansive portfolio that included various formats spanning the Internet, television, and film. Once again, the group's success attracted the attention of a global media company. Needing to fulfill the Pay-TV Law's quotas for its channels in Brazil and interested in adding more content to its own transnational portfolio, Viacom purchased a majority stake in Porta dos Fundos on April 19, 2017.

As with their fictional counterparts from *Borges*, the friend-owned start-up operation based in Rio de Janeiro had found a formula for success that, in a few short years, had won over audiences in both Brazil and abroad. The group's success—however increasingly intertwined in the global mediascape and its continued attempts at striking a balance among global flows of capital and modes of distribution and local cultural and linguistic specificities—is best understood as stemming simultaneously from its aesthetic and cultural proximity to TV Globo and from the way in which it distinguishes its content from that of the Rio de Janeiro network. In terms of their formal composition, for example, the group's sketches and series are of a very high quality. The *mise-en-scène*, cinematography, editing, and sound of Porta dos Fundos' Internet sketches combine to establish a polished aesthetic very similar to TV Globo's Standard of Quality.

Though many Brazilian YouTube channels—like those of aforementioned Nunes and Neto and the wildly popular Kondzilla—have since caught up in technical terms, the company's high production value stood out from other comedic sketches in Portuguese on the Internet while also putting them on par with comparable productions coming from websites like Funny or Die. In this way, albeit to a much lesser extent, Porta dos Fundos' foray into television mirrors TV Globo's rise to dominance in the late 1960s. At that time, TV Globo had established an aesthetic that was on par with that which was being exported into Brazil by Hollywood. In addition, however, to the distinct aesthetic mark of the network's programming, TV Globo cemented its success by also focusing on representing local themes. Johnson's discussion of the development of the Brazilian film industry is helpful here for fleshing out the cultural logic behind TV Globo's early gains (1987). He argues that the dominance of North American cinema in Brazil created a situation in which Brazilian audiences began to see imported films as superior to Brazilian films. As a result, Brazilian audiences became leery of films that did not conform to the technical quality characteristic of Hollywood films, "even if produced locally" (1987: 11).

Thus, it was TV Globo's representations of Brazil and Brazilians—which were comparable to American television and produced in the mode of the 1940s Hollywood Studio system—that allowed domestic audiences to see themselves on television through a formal composition they had widely come to accept as superior to anything produced locally. As such, the result was that TV Globo gave its audience something other domestic broadcast networks, Brazilian films, and Hollywood films could not: locally produced content with a production value that was on par with that which was considered to be the best. In a manner similar to TV Globo's appropriation of the Hollywood aesthetic, and its application to the local context, Porta dos Fundos' refined aesthetic depictions of segments of Brazilian society co-opt TV Globo's aesthetic. Consequently, the presentation of Porta dos Fundos' work in a TV Globoesque aesthetic makes it both familiar and attractive to the large audiences who have been reared on TV Globo's television fiction and, consequently, have come to expect a base-level of audiovisual quality. At the same time, the aesthetic distinguishes the Porta dos Fundos channels from the vast majority of the seemingly endless number of YouTube channels that also produce fictional content.

Nonetheless, Porta dos Fundos differs from TV Globo in important ways that allow the independent production to transcend the rigidity of the Globo Standard of Quality singled out in *A deusa ferida* as negatively affecting TV Globo's audience share. Namely, as with the web series discussed in chapter 3, Porta dos Fundos' brief satirical sketches, small budgets, and their distribution outside of the more content-restrictive broadcast network channels free the group to portray themes and issues in ways that would never be possible for TV Globo. In addition to those already mentioned, some examples include the following: religion—Jesus Christ interacting with a human resources department to discover his professional skills and potential job possibilities ("Setor de

RH—Jesus"/"Human Resources Sector—Jesus," 2012); urban poverty—a tour guide takes a group of foreign tourists on a safari-like "expedition" through a *favela* in Rio de Janeiro ("Pobre"/"Poor," 2014); European colonization—indigenous Brazilians trying to gauge how long the Portuguese explorer, Pedro Álvares Cabral, would stick around following his "discovery" of the northeastern coast of Brazil ("Descobrimento"/"The Discovery of Brazil," 2016); political corruption—a politician explaining to a congressional inquiry how he was "forced" to remodel his home with public funds ("Reforma," 2016); homosexuality—a deconstruction of the disparaging and extremely offensive term *viado* (faggot; "Viado"/"Faggot," 2014); and racism—a white police officer insisting on a line of questioning that presumes the perpetrator of a robbery to be a black man, despite the victim assuring the officer that it was a white man who robbed him ("Negro," 2014).

Thus, while TV Globo's *telenovelas* frequently deal with similar issues, Porta dos Fundos' aggressive and irreverent positioning, couched in sarcastic and colloquial language, distinguishes its brand from that of the broadcast network, thereby attracting younger viewers versed in digital and social media and interested in alternative discourses that challenge the status quo. Clearly, each of the examples I have cited, and the satirical tone through which they are communicated, could never appear on TV Globo for fear of antagonizing sectors of its enormous audiences and thereby potentially losing advertising revenue, not to mention government restrictions regarding over-the-air content. The opening-up, then, of the pay-television industry, which forced global players such as Fox and Viacom to air content created by Brazilian independent production companies like Porta dos Fundos, and the impact the expansion of the sector had on the growth of the Internet provide more individuals the opportunity to produce or participate in the production of programming for diverse, fragmented audiences that runs counter to that which has traditionally come from dominant, more conservative sources such as TV Globo. The next chapter's discussion of the TV Globo series *Mister Brau* (2015–) and the Porta dos Fundos' *O Grande Gonzalez* (2015) expands on the structural shifts discussed thus far by emphasizing an example in which those shifts affect the broader representation of a theme.

Blackness in the Post-2011 Mediascape

In his influential work *Communications, Culture, and Hegemony*, Jesús Martín-Barbero (1993) contends that the characteristic melodrama of the Latin American contemporary *telenovela* provides a language for the popular forms of hope. Martín-Barbero argues that the melodramatic *telenovela* serves as a mediating link between past and present popular culture, allowing the people as a mass to recognize themselves as authors of their own history (1993: 240). While Martín-Barbero's argument is convincing, especially at the level of the nation or of Latin America as a whole, within the Brazilian context the "*estética sueca*" (Swedish aesthetic) or "vast sea of whiteness" that broadly has historically characterized television fiction suggests that a significant portion of the "people as a mass" is capable of recognizing itself only insofar as it does not take into consideration matters of race (Araújo, 2000; Joyce, 2012: 15).

That this is the case is made especially clear in Joel Zito Araújo's *A negação do Brasil: O negro na telenovela brasileira* (*The Negation of Brazil: The Afro-Brazilian and the Brazilian Telenovela*, 2000). In his seminal study, whose title makes explicit a symbolic covering up and erasure of the Brazilian racial reality, Araújo provides the reader with a comprehensive analysis of the portrayals of Afro-Brazilians in *telenovelas* between 1963 and 1997. Araújo considers the roles (or lack thereof) available to Afro-Brazilians in each of the respective decades. The conclusions reached regarding the different decades are then placed in a broader comparative context, resulting in both a synchronic and diachronic understanding of the ways in which Brazilian television's primary symbolic good has long underrepresented and misrepresented Afro-Brazilians. In this way, Araújo's research highlights a decades-long hegemonic process wherein Brazilian television fiction, supported by and often aligned with the dominant legal, political, and economic structures, engages in an unequal "social intercourse" with audiences to negotiate (or negate) a meaning of Brazil (Bakhtin, 1991: 199). Along these lines, Muniz Sodré (2015) argues that the Brazilian elite—whether economic, intellectual, mediatic, or political—interact to such a degree that the group takes on a familial nature. The media, as the representative of the collective Brazilian elite, Sodré contends, works to solidify an outdated understanding of the people, "without committing to truly public causes or to affirming the diversity of the Brazilian population" (2015: 277). In terms of diversity, Araújo observes that "the representation of black actors has experienced slight changes since the 1960s, when they were exclusively offered roles portraying subaltern characters" (2008: 980). In the 1970s, a small number of black actors secured roles as characters who were upwardly mobile. None, however, was ever given a role as the protagonist of a *telenovela*. Beginning in the 1980s, Araújo points to evidence of a slow, progressive opening of more, and more diverse, roles to Afro-Brazilian actors (2000, 2008). Despite this, however, the author is quick to highlight that over 30 percent of all TV Globo *telenovelas* by the end of the 1990s did not include even one Afro-Brazilian actor, and another third barely passed the threshold of 10 percent of the cast comprised of Afro-Brazilian actors.

Lest one conclude that the passage of time since the publication of Araújo's works has rendered his findings obsolete, Wesley Pereira Grijó and Adam Henrique Freire Sousa's (2012) more recent study of the same topic in *telenovelas* during the first decade of the twenty-first century found that little had changed. Similarly, and even more recently, a quantitative analysis of race and gender in TV Globo's *telenovelas* from 1995 to 2014 from the Federal University of Rio de Janeiro's Grupo de Estudos Multidisciplinares da Ação Afirmativa (Multidisciplinary Studies of Affirmative Action Research Group, GEMAA), found that, on average, white actors and actresses played 90 percent of the central characters while black and *pardo* (brown) actors and actresses played a paltry 10 percent of those roles (Campos, Candido, and Feres Jr., 2014). Such unequal representation in Brazil's most accessible, widely consumed, and exported symbolic good is striking, particularly when one considers that, according to the most recent census from 2010, blacks and browns (*pardos*) make up 50.8 percent of the country's total population.[1] A shift in focus, however, from the *telenovela*, which has been thoroughly covered by a number of excellent studies, to an examination of the series, an emerging and understudied area of Brazilian television fiction, reveals developments that have the potential to significantly alter the way Brazil is portrayed on the small screen.

Race and the underrepresentation of Afro-Brazilians are interrelated and central topics of "Em algum lugar do futuro" (Somewhere in the Future), the nineteenth episode of the critically acclaimed series *Cidade dos homens* (*City of Men*, TV Globo and O2 Filmes, 2002–2005, 2017–2018).[2] Aesthetically and discursively progressive, the 2005 finale exploded the fictional confines of the coming-of-age tales of Laranjinha (Darlan Cunha) and Acerola (Douglas Silva), the series' young, impoverished black protagonists. In doing so, the episode presented the viewer with an uncharacteristic metacritique that laid bare the lack of opportunities available in the predominately white Brazilian television industry for Cunha and Silva, both of whom search for new roles as their participation in the series comes to an end. Using the *Cidade dos homens*' episode from 2005 as a point of departure, this chapter analyzes representations of race in two contemporary Brazilian serial comedies: *Mister Brau* (*Mr. Brown*, TV Globo, 2015–) and *O Grande Gonzalez* (*The Great Gonzalez*, Fox Brasil and Porta dos Fundos, 2015).

Though touted as the first serial comedy in the history of Brazilian television to feature an affluent Afro-Brazilian couple and though at times it offers a progressive representation of black Brazilians, *Mister Brau* perpetuates racial stereotypes, employing its black protagonist to promote an outdated ideology of racial democracy and racial mixing as the answer to Brazil's racial and socioeconomic inequality.[3] In contrast, I contend that *O Grande Gonzalez*, despite a cast nearly devoid of black Brazilians, constructs a critique of the systemic racism directed at and experienced by black Brazilians. The analysis of the two series' distinct portrayals of blackness is not in any way intended to be exhaustive. Instead, it is an argument in favor of studies of representation that include fictional works of television outside of or in addition to TV Globo's *telenovelas*. More specifically, it is a call for scholars to consider the varied matters of representation within the context of the structural shifts occurring during the post-2011 mediascape, accounting for how such shifts have played (or perhaps not) a central role in expanding production beyond the hegemonic confines of TV Globo's vertical production model, resulting in the emergence of new voices and the possibility for more critical contemplations of race and other pressing social issues.

Blackness Outside of *City of Men*: The Marginalization of Cunha and Silva

Cidade dos homens began its first of six seasons with a four-episode run in October 2002. The series follows the lives of Laranjinha and Acerola as they labor to survive from their marginalized position in one of Rio de Janeiro's South Zone *favelas*. Though the tone is one of optimism and perseverance, over the course of the series, Laranjinha's and Acerola's normal adolescent activities unfold in the context of an often violent, impoverished space where they face explicit racism, lack of parental figures, the allure of the drug trade, and teenage pregnancy. As the "Em algum lugar do futuro" episode suggests, however, the real struggle has only just begun for Darlan Cunha and Douglas Silva, the actors playing Laranjinha and Acerola.

In "Em algum lugar do futuro," Laranjinha and Acerola—no longer the cute ten-year-old boys upon whose lives the premise of the series was initially based—are now in their late teens. At this late stage in the series, despite their age, they have, for all intents and purposes, become men. The episode opens with a young black boy selling pirated CDs on a busy city sidewalk. When his friend, another young black boy, approaches to greet him we learn that their names are Laranjinha and Acerola. (The viewer familiar with the series will recognize this particular plotline's similarity to the fourth episode, "Uólace e João Vitor"). Beginning the episode in this manner challenges the spectator to question what is going on: "Who are these boys? Where are the original Laranjinha and Acerola?" Things become even more confusing when both Darlan and Douglas appear separately, approaching the two new characters to inquire about the CDs for sale. Oddly, yet foreshadowing what is soon to be their reality, it seems as though the series' protagonists have suddenly been relegated to nameless extras.

Following a transition to the off-screen space, actress, presenter, and director Regina Casé (playing a version of herself) yells out "Cut!" Casé's on-camera presence along with the various mechanisms of set-production that appear in the shot make it clear that the scene just witnessed is a part of an updated version of *Cidade dos homens*. The two unknown boys, then, are the actors cast to play new iterations of the Laranjinha and Acerola characters. The implications here are twofold. First, and most important, the continued fictionalization of Laranjinha and Acerola's lives in the *favela* suggest that the hardships and numerous forms of inequality structured in power and violence they endure each episode are not exceptions to the rule but part of a larger social reality that perpetuates itself. Second—and this is only made clear after having completed the episode—if the Brazilian television industry continues to negate and exclude blackness, the young black actors playing Laranjinha and Acerola will, like Darlan and Douglas, one day find themselves without a place in the industry. In other words, we are dealing with a vicious cycle of negation.

Dejected, as they watch themselves being replaced and almost immediately forgotten, Darlan and Douglas enter a TV Globo van that whisks them away from the on-location shoot. On the ride home, Douglas asks the visibly troubled Darlan what he thinks will happen to the characters Laranjinha and Acerola as the continuation of the series unfolds. Darlan's reply—that he is "more concerned with what will happen to Darlan and Douglas"—serves as the episode's narrative motor. In what follows, the episode interweaves parodies of auditions, archival footage, voiceover commentary, interviews, and animated depictions of possible futures for Darlan and Douglas. These varied aesthetic and narrative devices function as a means of reflection on the actors' personal coming-of-age tales, fondly recalling their well-deserved fame and critical acclaim, first for their supporting roles in *Cidade de Deus* (*City of God*, 2002), then as the protagonists of *Cidade dos homens*, both the television series and the homonymous 2007 feature-length film directed by Paulo Morelli. At the same time, the devices serve to contemplate and critique the unjustly uncertain futures of the two young men as they attempt to secure new roles in other productions.

On their way home in the TV Globo van, the driver picks up Letícia Spiller, a well-known white Brazilian actress who has an audition at TV Globo's Projac Studios. After Darlan and Douglas share their respective professional trajectories with Spiller, which are intermixed with archival flashbacks, she tells the now out-of-work actors that, like them, she too was a child actor and is also currently unemployed. Although problematic and oversimplified, the broad professional parallels established among the three actors serve an important function in the episode's development. Following Spiller's advice, rather than going home, Darlan and Douglas decide to accompany the actress to Projac Studios, where they too will audition for roles.

In the boys' first audition, despite doing very well, the director tells Cunha and Silva that they are too young for the parts. The same director, however, informs Spiller, their audition partner, that she has secured a role in the upcoming *telenovela*. Though Spiller's success and their rejection evokes the unsettling findings of the studies mentioned above, because Cunha and Silva are indeed clearly too young for the roles, age, not race, serves as a logical justification for their failure to be selected. Nonetheless, the boys' subsequent auditions and interactions with industry professionals unveil the systemic racism present in Brazilian television.

In response to their first failed audition, the two actors decide to try for a more "age-appropriate" role. The part in question is for that of a sixteen-year-old boy whose concerned parents long for him to get out of the house and make friends. Darlan goes first. Though visibly startled by witnessing a black actor coming out of the bedroom into the living room, the white actors playing the parents do not initially give up on the scene. Before long, however, they interrupt the audition to tell Darlan he cannot play their son. Surprised, he responds, "Why not? It says here, an attractive sixteen-year-old boy. That's me." While the two actors agree that that is true, they point out that Darlan does not "look like them." That is, they are white and he is black. Clearly upset, Darlan goes to the dressing room, where he informs Douglas that the audition went horribly and that the son needs to be white, though he wonders aloud, "Why couldn't the son be black?"

The answer to Darlan's powerful question is implied during the actors' subsequent, improvised audition. Discouraged, but not defeated, the resilient teenagers get a gig as extras on the upbeat family sitcom *Grande família* (TV Globo, 1972–1975, 2001–2014). In the middle of the scene, Darlan interrupts the dialogue between the sitcom regulars Tuco Silva (Lúcio Mauro Filho) and Beiçola (Marcus Oliveira) to ask them about a possible part on the show. During the exchange between the actors, Mauro Filho, no longer in scene and now playing a fictionalized version of himself, mockingly asks the two if they have looked for work on *Linha direta*, a news program that produces sensationalistic portrayals of everyday urban crime and violence. Darlan perceives Mauro Filho's malice and implicit racism and indignantly asks, "So do you mean to say that two black men can only be on television if they are stealing!?" In his paternalistic reply, Mauro Filho—like the two white actors from the previous audition—becomes the overseer of race, informing Darlan that he, unlike his friend Douglas, is not even black. Douglas declares that Mauro Filho's comments are discriminatory and forcefully demands to know how many black people work on *Grande família*.

The message from this scene is clear: returning to Darlan's earlier rhetorical question, the actor playing the son cannot be black because, in the broadest terms, the television fiction produced by TV Globo is predominantly white. Or, to return to Araújo (2000: 38, 40), Brazilian television's portrayals of a white Brazil, fueled by the elite's push for the Europeanization and North Americanization of the country—a position-taking that has roots in nineteenth-century positivism—continuously reaffirm "the symbolic victory of the ideology of whiteness." The episode suggests that challenges to this distorted reality carry with them severe consequences. In fact, in an exchange that evokes Brazil's past of slavery, when Douglas raises the objection to the discrimination both he and Darlan have suffered, the white Mauro Filho silences the two teenagers by literally chasing them off the lot. In doing so, Mauro Filho figuratively expels the boys from the center (TV Globo's Projac Studios) and visibility (mainstream broadcast network television) and sends them back to the marginalized position from which they began: the favela and, by extension, its limited, often stereotypical televisual representations.

Of course, "Em algum lugar do futuro" is itself a TV Globo co-production that criticizes the broadcast network's representation of race. Importantly, that this is the case demonstrates TV Globo's capacity to be self-critical. Indeed, neither the network nor the broader media group that controls it is a monolith. However, while the "Em algum lugar do futuro" critique is progressive and needed, a few points must be made. First, O2 Filmes, one of the largest independent production companies in Brazil, produced the series with a relatively high degree of autonomy. In large part, this autonomy derived from Meirelles's decision to shoot most of the series on location, far from TV Globo's Projac Studios, a privilege likely afforded to Meirelles due to his symbolic capital, which was at an all-time high for having just been nominated for an Oscar for *Cidade de*

Deus. Additionally, Meirelles employed a number of nonprofessional or unknown actors who had first appeared in his Oscar-nominated film. The use of such actors further reduced TV Globo's influence, both literally and symbolically, while also allowing Meirelles to recreate *Cidade de Deus'* neo-realist pop aesthetic (Bentes, 2005).

Thus, in what was an uncommon practice for TV Globo, the series did not fall within the network's vertical production practices. And this brings us to the second point: the role that TV Globo did play, according to Suzana Schwertner (2007: 58), actually functioned to marginalize the series in relative terms. More specifically, TV Globo's minimal and sporadic marketing and inconsistent air days and late time slots—always after 10:30 PM and on several occasions even after 11 PM—limited the series' uneven political message. Schwertner's argument needs more explanation. It is true that the series, as with nearly all TV Globo fiction that is not a *telenovela*, airs during post-prime-time hours. Nonetheless, Schwertner's point is that the overwhelming importance—both in economic and symbolic terms—the industrially produced *telenovela* has within the TV Globo structure ultimately results in more experimentally progressive works relegated to airings that receive less attention. This could be said, for example, of all of Luiz Fernando Carvalho's shorter format mini and microseries, which, as I have argued, represent some of the most aesthetically progressive television in the world (Carter, 2018). Along these lines, the last episode's forward-looking metacritique, despite airing on TV Globo, was constrained or, to evoke Hall, "policed" by the network and therefore not seen by as many spectators as it might otherwise have been (1993: 107).[4]

Looking Back from "Somewhere in the Future": *Mister Brau*'s Longing for a Racial Democracy

Despite this, there was reason for hope. The "Em algum lugar do futuro" episode dealt explicitly with Brazilian television's generalized marginalization and misrepresentation of Brazilians of color, issues raised only years earlier in Araújo's book. However, nearly ten years later, another highly touted TV Globo series had not progressed to meet the challenge presented by *Cidade dos homens'* finale. Rather, it had regressed to an emphasis on Brazil as a racial democracy. Indeed, that emphasis was one of the central ideologies highlighted by Araújo (2000, 2008) as structuring Brazilian television's characteristic whiteness and underrepresentation of individuals of color. Brazilian television fiction's employment of the idea of the nation as a racial democracy, Araújo argues, was designed to project the notion that the mixed-race country had risen above the problem of race (2008: 979). In 2015, TV Globo and Jorge Furtado, a co-screenwriter of the "Em algum lugar do futuro" series' finale, teamed up to create the thirteen-episode first season of *Mister Brau*.[5] The serial comedy centers on the relationship between Brazilian music superstar Mister Brau (Lázaro Ramos) and his wife, manager, and backup dancer Michele Brau (Táis Araújo), and their socioeconomic ascension to the predominately white Brazilian elite.[6] *Mister Brau*'s interrelated focus on class and race was indicative of an already ongoing effort on the part of TV Globo to capture the aforementioned large and growing C Class, a sizeable portion of which is composed of black or brown Brazilians (La Pastina, Straubhaar, and Sifuentes, 2014: 107; Rêgo, 2014: 93).

Part of the significance of *Mister Brau*, and the attention paid to it, stems precisely from Brazilian television's role as a cultural mirror and from the historical absence of blacks reflected in that mirror (Subervi-Velez and Oliveira, 1991: 80; Araújo, 2000: 229–230; Sovik, 2004: 318; Joyce, 2012: 15; Mitchell, 2013: 178; La Pastina, Straubhaar, and Sifuentes, 2014: 104–108). In an interview leading up to *Mister Brau*'s premier, series creator Jorge Furtado (Mesquita, 2015) explicitly commented on this representational lacuna: "Brazil's population is 52% black or brown, and this percentage is not represented in Brazilian television and film. With a black population of 13%, the United States has more black protagonists in film and television series." Furtado goes on to say, "We are a racist country; we abolished slavery very late. This division of the country is important, and we need to talk about it in order to get past it" (Mesquita, 2015). By putting similar words in the mouths of his characters, Furtado reiterates his own understanding of race and racism in Brazil, both implicitly and explicitly, throughout *Mister Brau*. However, despite Furtado's promising comments, *Mister Brau*'s narrative ultimately expunges the problem of race, arguing for its dissolution through the discursive implementation of the idea of a racially mixed and therefore racially egalitarian Brazilian population. In doing so, despite the centrality of its Afro-Brazilian protagonists, the series paradoxically situates itself in the broader context of

TV Globo's *telenovela* production, which has a long history of erasing the importance of race by promoting Brazil as a racial democracy (Silva, 1999; Araújo, 2000; Grijó and Sousa, 2012).

Before the series formally introduces Mister Brau and Michele, the narrative picks up *in medias res*. At three in the morning, the two characters stand in front of a large house in one of Rio de Janeiro's most affluent communities located in the Western Zone. Admiring the beautiful home, Mister Brau asks Michele, "So, let's go in?" to which she responds, "Are you crazy?!" (*Mister Brau*, 2015). Despite Michele's insistence to the contrary, Mister Brau runs around to the side of the house, informing her that he will find a way inside. Shortly thereafter, Mister Brau appears at the front door with the keys, letting his wife into the house.

Once inside, the couple navigates through the space, which appears to be under construction or being moved into. Commenting on the home's grandeur and how they have always dreamed of owning a house like this, the couple finds their way to the backyard, where they eventually strip down to their underwear and jump into the pool. Soon, their playful shouts awake their white neighbor, Andréia (Fernanda de Freitas). Alarmed, Andréia shakes Henrique (George Sauma), her equally white husband, from his slumber to inform him of a possible break-in next door. Calm, collected, and rational, Henrique asks his wife, "How do you know they did not buy the house?" Undeterred, Andréia goes to the balcony off their bedroom, where, through her binoculars, she sees Mister Brau in the pool. Focusing on his nude, black body as it emerges from the water, Andréia definitively declares, "It's a thief!" In the next shot, responding to Andréia's phone call, neighborhood security descends on the backyard to apprehend the "trespassers." Andréia's behavior can only be understood as racist. In fact, Andréia appears to have put into practice one of Achille Mbembe's many eloquent definitions of race and racism. In the spirit of the great Frantz Fanon, Mbembe argues that, when taken to its limit, race or racism "reassures itself by hating, deploying dread, and practicing altruicide: the constitution of the Other not as similar to oneself but as a menacing object from which one must be protected or escape, or which must simply be destroyed if it cannot be subdued" (2017: 10). The need for protection against the *intruders* or for their ultimate destruction disappears only when it is revealed that Mister Brau and Michele are actually wealthy, famous entertainers as well as the owners of the recently sold house. This new knowledge sets off a problematic transition in which Mr. Brau's black body moves from symbolizing a threat to the "white" space to the justification of the body's presence in that space as a result of its connection to fame and fortune. In short, the Black Man, represented by Mister Brau, is, in Mbembe's words, a "figure, an 'object,' invented by Whites and as such 'fixed' by their gaze, gestures, and attitudes" (2017: 43). Along these lines, the scene in question highlights the two opposite poles of the social spectrum invented by white Brazilians for Brazilians of color: violent trespasser or entertainer.

While there are other important moments throughout the series, this scene is arguably the work's most powerful and progressive. So often portrayed as criminals thirsty for violence, prisoners, slaves, favela dwellers, or hired help, black Brazilians like Mister Brau and Michele are not supposed to be in affluent neighborhoods like the one represented in the series. According to a symbolic, ancestral archive of television images, if in such a space, they are expected to be working as maids or doormen, or in similar subaltern professions reserved for Brazilians of color (Rial, 1999; Silva, 1999: 348; Araújo, 2000: 97, 150, 168; Grijó and Sousa, 2012: 190–191, 193; Rosas-Montero, 2014: 68). Nonetheless, Mister Brau's and Michelle's socioeconomic ascension seems to lend support to the idea that "*Black men can succeed*" (Rosas-Montero, 2014: 68). However, as Rosas-Montero (68) contends, such is only the case if "he plays by the [white man's] rules." Otherwise, Mister Brau and Michele's presence (and by extension, all Black Brazilians) implies a rupturing of social norms: a breaking of the law.

Along these lines, the opening scene of *Mister Brau* activates the viewer's familiarity with a broader social imaginary, established in part by sensationalistic journalism, oversimplified representations of people of color, or what Teresa Caldeira (2000) refers to as the "talk of crime," and a history of slavery and racism.[7] The scene, then, at the very least, challenges the viewer to recognize the problematic, socially constructed notions of race in Brazil. In this way, Andréia's explicitly racist behavior toward Mister Brau and Michele serves as a mirror for the viewer. The "misunderstanding" is seemingly resolved when Henrique informs his wife that she needs to open her mind, be more modern, and realize that the country and world have changed. In what reads like a message intended for both his wife and the viewer, the enlightened Henrique further emphasizes his point by asking his racist wife, "Did you know that the GDP of Brazil's favelas is equal to that of Uruguay?" "Enough with all the prejudice!" he concludes.

It is difficult to argue with Henrique's message. The problem, however, is not the message itself but how the series suggests overcoming racial prejudice in Brazil. Primarily through the figure of Mister Brau and his words, the series puts forth the thesis that racist attitudes in Brazil stem from a generalized misrecognition of the country's racial composition. Broadly speaking, racial mixing has characterized Brazil and its development since the Portuguese reached the territory's northeastern shore in 1500. Consequently, Brazilians are multiracial and multicultural, and to focus exclusively on one's skin color is to misunderstand that the majority of Brazilians have traces of European, African, and Indigenous descent. Such a position is an explicit reference to the idea of Brazil as a racial democracy.[8] Though he did not coin the term, in his seminal study, *Casa-grande & senzala* (1933) (*The Masters and the Slaves*, 1946), Brazilian anthropologist and sociologist Gilberto Freyre made famous the idea of racial democracy, arguing that "every Brazilian, even the light skinned fair haired one carries about him on his soul, when not on soul and body alike, the shadow or at least the birthmark of the aborigine or the negro, in our affections, our excessive mimicry, our Catholicism which so delights the senses, our music, our gait, our speech, our cradle songs, in everything that is a sincere expression of our lives, we almost all of us bear the mark of that influence" (Freyre, 1946: 278). As Eakin shows (2017), the *Freyean* mythology of racial mixing would play a central role in defining what it meant to be Brazilian in the twentieth century. As with other academics in Brazil and around the world, Eakin points to the waning power of racial democracy's reign toward the end of the twentieth century. Nonetheless, a series like *Mister Brau* demonstrates that the idea is still alive and well.

Mister Brau's support for the concept that Brazil is a racial democracy is most clearly demonstrated in the series' second episode, which establishes a metaphorical relationship between an adhesive bandage and Brazil's need to heal its deep racial divide. While playing music with some friends during a party in his backyard, Michele approaches to draw her husband's attention to his bleeding finger. When Mister Brau stops to get an adhesive bandage, his friend Lima (Luís Miranda) notices that the box containing the bandages states that the light-colored product is "skin-colored." The obvious absurdity of such an absolutist and limiting description propels Mister Brau—whose very name is a *Brazilianization* of the English word "brown"—into a didactic lesson on Brazil's current racial composition, one that clearly recalls Furtado's comments from the interview cited earlier. With the music paused and the entire party listening attentively—a clear cue to the audience at home that it too should pay close attention—Mister Brau indignantly declares, "What do you mean 'skin-colored'!? Brazil's population is 52 percent black [*negros*]!" Lima emphatically responds, "Exactly! We are the majority! Skin color in Brazil should be understood as dark!" Mister Brau, however, undercuts this powerful, albeit formulaic and didactic exchange when he responds to his friend—and, by extension, to the partygoers and those watching at home—with a conservative, middle-of-the-road suggestion that conjures up the myth of racial democracy. He concludes, "No! There should be a number of different colors—a number of skin colors!" Drawing the camera's attention to the partygoers' different skin colors, he continues, "Look here, each skin color is a different color."

Having evoked Brazil's past of miscegenation, Mister Brau brings the scene to a close by explicitly declaring his support for a multicultural, racially democratic Brazil: "Everybody is different. The world is not black and white, right? There should be many colors. There should be a multicolored adhesive bandage. There should be . . . No! There must be. There will be! We will have one!" To the crowd's enthusiastic cheers, Mister Brau calls them—and more broadly, Brazil as a whole—to arms. "Let's make one!" he emphatically proclaims. Of course, the "one" in Mister Brau's proclamation refers to an adhesive bandage, but the subtext positions the bandage as a metaphor for the nation's racial divide. A deep open wound, caused by centuries of slavery and racial inequality, has yet to scar. Healing, the series suggests, can only come through a curative that is both multicultural and racial, one that necessarily represents Brazil's diverse racial composition.

After throwing himself into developing and marketing his own "Braudaid," Mister Brau learns to his dismay that multicolored adhesive bandages have been commercialized for at least fifteen years in the United States. The result of his potential copyright infringement and—at the level of the subtext—his appropriation and importation of a global North ideology for understanding race in the unique Brazilian context—one of the major tenets behind Freyre's conceptualization of race in Brazil—forces Mister Brau to clarify his position in front of an arbitrator. During the meeting, Mister Brau explains that his intention with the creation of "Braudaid" was—unlike the already existing (American) product—never to confuse itself with the skin color of its user. Instead, he says, "Our intention, my intention, was to always mix the different colors. Mixing is always more healthful."

Mister Brau's comments represent a form of popular culture undermining the current racial discourse in Brazil, which, in at least academic circles, by the 1970s had moved toward the binary black/white model from the United States as an attempt to assert forcefully the importance race plays in systemically perpetuating socioeconomic inequality in the country (Telles, 2004: 47–61). In place of such a binary model, Mister Brau suggests its opposite—that is, a return to the ideal of a racial democracy within which racial mixing is one of the defining characteristics of Brazil and race is erased as a deciding factor in one's socioeconomic position. In essence, *Mister Brau*'s bandage metaphor advocates for a discourse that fits into a long tradition of hegemonic race theories in Brazil. Though this has certainly changed for the better in more recent years, with race becoming an increasingly central topic to Brazilian society, Larry Crook and Randal Johnson have noted that the "importance of race in the structuring and perpetuation of social inequalities" has tended to be neglected (1999: 3).

This problematic position is further heightened by the way in which the series declares affluent white male Brazilians innocent of racism. For example, despite his explicit sexualization of Michele, Henrique, as mentioned earlier, stands in stark contrast to his wife's racist comments. Whereas Andréia reveals blatantly prejudiced behavior and ideas about race, Henrique frequently speaks out against racism, even when the perpetrator is his own wife. Henrique's white, well-to-do father-in-law who owns the law firm where Henrique works similarly sexualizes a woman of color, but quickly admonishes his daughter when she makes racist comments in his presence. By explicitly positioning these men in contrast to the racist Andréia, the series not only acquits them of participating in racist behavior but locates such behavior within another misrepresented and relatively powerless minority, white Brazilian women. Such a dynamic paves the way for apparently benevolent white males like Henrique to step in and take control. Indeed, the two men come to agreement almost immediately, when Mister Brau reveals—in an example of his characteristic happy-go-lucky ignorance and superficiality—that he has a manicurist, a hair stylist, and a masseuse, but not an attorney. Overly eager for Henrique to come on board, Mister Brau naively offers his neighbor such a high percentage of his own earnings that it makes Henrique blush with joy.

In short, the series' construction of gender and racial dynamics establishes white women as the locus of racism. In contrast, white men are portrayed as open-minded, intelligent, and racially and socially malleable individuals. Despite their intelligence, wit, and hard work, black women are ultimately reduced to hypersexualized objects for white men like Henrique and his father-in-law to enjoy (Mitchell, 2013: 177). Black men, exemplified by Mister Brau, are brainless individuals who at their best are clownish figures entertaining the masses. This last point is particularly important, since *Mister Brau* has been praised specifically for featuring affluent black Brazilians. One of the takeaways from this rare portrayal of a well-to-do man of color, however, is that successful black men, unlike their wealthy white counterparts, achieve their respective economic status through the limited possibilities available to them, namely, playing soccer or working as entertainers. Thus, while *Mister Brau*'s representation of blackness and racism in Brazil appears, on the surface, to be progressive, it actually embodies a form of veiled racism that, consciously or unconsciously, has long characterized Brazilian television fiction, both in terms of its production and symbolic output. Though writing in 2005 about the United States, Darnell M. Hunt's observations regarding the audiovisual industry in that country are also apt for describing *Mister Brau* and another recent TV Globo series, *Subúrbia* (*Periphery*, 2012): "Against a backdrop of increasing racial diversity a white-controlled industry continues to channel blackness in ways that affirm whiteness, while at the same time promoting the fiction of an America beyond race" (Hunt, 2005: 300). Similarly, some recent *telenovelas* have embodied certain advances, depicting the black Brazilian as having left the kitchen and the favela to become a boss, a doctor, or a model. With the opening up of the field, such advances are likely to continue and even increase; however, one cannot overlook that these are still only exceptions to the rule that have historically situated Brazilians of color as occupying socially inferior positions (Grijó and Sousa, 2012: 203).

A View of Blackness through the *Porta dos Fundos*

In *Watching Race: Television and the Struggle for "Blackness,"* Herman Gray recognizes and mostly agrees with the widely accepted notion in critical television studies of race "that television representations of blackness work largely to legitimate and secure the terms of the dominant cultural and social order by circulating within and remaining structured by them" (1995: 10). However, Gray is also careful to recognize the possibility of representations that run counter to those that support and structure the hegemonic discourse: "There are alternative (and occasional oppositional) moments in American commercial television representations of race, especially in its fragmented and contradictory character . . . In some cases," he continues, "television representations of blackness explode and reveal the deeply rooted terms of this hierarchy" (10).

Within the Brazilian context, such representations are becoming increasingly possible, in large part due to the growth of the pay-television sector and the Pay-Television Law's requirement for domestically produced content, which has fueled the emergence of new channels, producers, and narrative formats. As discussed in the previous chapter, one important example arising out of this new context is the independent production company Porta dos Fundos. Since its creation, Porta dos Fundos has produced a number of videos that have served as an "oppositional" voice on matters regarding racism and racial inequality. Indeed, in its YouTube videos "Negro" (2014), "Redução" (Reduction, 2015), and "Amiguinho" (Little Friend, 2015), for example, and its serial comedy *O Grande Gonzalez* (2015),[9] Porta dos Fundos uses satire to construct representations of racism that, to cite Gray once more, "explode and reveal the deeply rooted terms" (10) of the socially constructed racial hierarchy. Such explicitly confrontational representations were far from the norm in the TV Globo–dominated mediascape prior to 2011.

On August 4, 2014, Porta dos Fundos released "Negro." The satirical sketch revolves around a thirty-something white man (João Vicente de Castro) who has hurriedly entered a police station to report he has just been robbed on the street in front of the building. Calmly sitting behind his desk, the white Sergeant Peçanha (Antônio Tabet)—a recurring Porta dos Fundos character who parodies the violent, corrupt, and racist Brazilian police force—immediately falls into a series of questions about the assailant: "Was he black [*negro*]? A nigger [*preto*]? A super big creole guy [*creolão*]? A big black guy [*negão*]?" (SBF, 2014).[10] Shocked by Peçanha's unapologetic racism, the victim continuously insists that the assailant was a white man. Undeterred, Peçanha asks if the man accompanying the assailant was "*um preto*" (a nigger). Again, the man takes a deep breath before telling the sergeant that the assailant was alone. Nonetheless, Peçanha presses on with his line of questioning, descending into more and more ridiculous racial stereotypes, ranging from the assailant's clothing—"Was he wearing a shirt with 'Olodum' written on it?" (a reference to the Afro-Brazilian percussion and cultural group based in Salvador, Bahia)—to his hair: "And his hair, was it Rastafarian, dreadlocks, or black power?" When he finally accepts that the assailant was white, Peçanha simply and confidently assures the victim, "Don't worry then, he'll return your stolen goods."

But Peçanha does not stop there. If he was unable to get his guy in "Negro," in "Redução," Peçanha employs the police force's systemic racism to do whatever it takes, even arresting a newborn baby. The sketch begins with a uniformed Peçanha entering a hospital hallway where an Afro-Brazilian man (Gustavo Chagas) stands admiringly holding his newborn baby. Approaching the unexpecting father, Peçanha inquires: "Where's the criminal?" "Who!?" the clearly taken-aback father asks. "José Pires Chagas!" Peçanha says, before requesting the newborn's identity and proof of employment. Peçanha then goes on to ask if the baby is poor and Afro-Brazilian, answers he himself deduces by taking a closer look at the "suspect." Following a series of increasingly absurd questions regarding race, class, and criminality, Peçanha tells the unassuming father: "With all due respect, you are fucked. Statistically speaking, soon I will have to arrest your boy. So, considering the reality, one shouldn't leave for tomorrow what one can do today" (SBF, 2015a). And with that, Peçanha arrests the baby, snatching him from his powerless father's arms.

How can there be such explicit racism if, as Mister Brau suggests, Brazil is home to widespread racial mixing? This is precisely the question Porta dos Fundos addresses in the video "Amiguinho." The video's description sarcastically states: "We all know that Brazil is a racial democracy. Just look through your surveillance cameras or through the bars of your gated communities and you will see that everybody gets along and is happy. How can there be racism if the favela is so close to the rest of the city? Black people in Brazil have as many rights as anyone else. That is, as long as they stay in the places that others have assigned to them. Anything outside of that only creates problems" (SBF, 2015b).[11] "Amiguinho" begins with two white parents (Clarice Falcão and Porchat) in a meeting with the headmaster of their child's elite private school. The parents plead with the principal to reconsider the expulsion of João, who has blown up a bathroom pipe with a homemade bomb. In a twist, though it seems that the parents are advocating for their own son, it turns out that they have no connection at all to João. Rather, they want João to be reinstated because he is the school's only black student. According to the parents, it is extremely difficult to find a reputable private school in Brazil with a matriculating black student. For them, it is not at all important that black students receive the same education as their children or that their children learn in a diverse environment; what is important is maintaining a progressive, liberal image. That is, the parents desperately need someone like João because his presence at the school and potential visits to their home allow them to negate any future claims of racism. In fact, their need for João is such that they offer to resolve the "issue" with money. Knowing nothing of João's life or family, the parents assume that because he is black he is poor and lives in a *favela*. The principal, however, reveals that João's parents are actually quite wealthy and live in one of the most expensive neighborhoods in Rio de Janeiro—news that the "concerned" parents readily recognize cannot get out for fear it would ruin the power of their "token black friend."

Unlike *Mister Brau*, the Porta dos Fundos' sketches more accurately locate the primary source of racism in Brazil within white men and the structures—that is, the economy, education, police force, and politics—they traditionally oversee. The independent production company revived this critique in the ten-episode serial comedy *O Grande Gonzalez*. Not long after *Mister Brau* premiered on TV Globo in September 2015, the first thirty-minute installment of *O Grande Gonzalez* aired at 10 PM on November 2, 2015. In addition to differing in their aesthetic and narrative complexities, one thing that immediately stands out between *Mister Brau* and *O Grande Gonzalez* is that, while the former's cast features a number of Afro-Brazilian actors, the latter's is almost exclusively white. However, it is precisely the absence of black characters that heightens *O Grande Gonzalez*'s critique of race and racism in Brazil.

Written and directed by SBF, the series stars Porta dos Fundos' cast member Luis Lobianco as Gonzalez. Gonzalez, who goes by the stage name The Great Gonzalez, is a debt-ridden, mediocre magician who is supposed to have been mysteriously murdered while performing at a child's birthday party in an upper-middle-class neighborhood in Rio de Janeiro. Other members of Porta dos Fundos' largely white recurring cast (Castro, Duvivier, Falcão, Infante, Porchat, Tabet, and Totoro) feature in the "whodunit" narrative. From the police station where they are interrogated by detectives Lucimar (Tabet) and Wagner (Castro), each episode pieces together a specific suspect's account of the day's events. The result is a series of subjective flashbacks that when woven together over the course of the ten episodes function to establish an overarching theory, only to deconstruct that theory as more evidence is introduced.

By the tenth and final episode "A reconstituição" (The Reenactment), the viewer has been presented with each suspect's account of the day of the alleged murder. Nonetheless, clarity is still lacking. Thus, in order to put all the parts together and sum everything up one last time, the police detectives decide to take all the suspects back to the crime scene to reenact the events from the day in question. Finally, with the reenactment complete, the suspects (and viewers) eagerly await Lucimar to reveal the name of the murderer. To their (and our) surprise, however, Lucimar informs the suspects and those present that The Great Gonzalez drowned in his water tank due to an allergic reaction to shrimp. Immediately, Rebecca (Falcão), one of the suspects, seeks clarification: "So you're saying that nobody here is responsible for his death." "Not so fast!" Lucimar responds. "Actually, none of this would have happened," he continues while pointing to a middle-aged black female who appears from offscreen in handcuffs, "if the cook hadn't taken the shrimp out of the water Gonzalez used to fill up his tank." Camilo, Rebecca's husband, asks, "My God, so it was the cook?" The absurd conclusion, emphasized by a montage of a series of exchanged looks of disbelief among the suspects, becomes even more so when Lucimar responds with: "Not just her. We found a whole criminal faction here, all of whom were responsible for the murder of The Great Gonzalez." As Lucimar says these words in response to Camilo's question, the camera cuts to the detective, who is now standing alongside a black cook, chauffeur, maid, and gardener, each of whom is in handcuffs. Ironically, it is the clown Rômulo (Porchat) who speaks for the entire shocked group when he sensibly, albeit hesitantly, asks Lucimar, "And you . . . maybe you want to share your theory as to why they are guilty?" (SBF, 2015c). Lucimar remains silent as he looks toward the "criminal faction." The subsequent point-of-perspective shot reveals the black, handcuffed characters, thus suggesting that no response is necessary—that their very existence is all the evidence needed.

Though the opening scene from *Mister Brau* similarly calls out racism in Brazil, following episodes, as laid out above, deconstruct that racism while also locating it in another marginalized minority. In contrast, the critique of racism and social injustices played out in the *O Grande Gonzalez* scene is strengthened even further by the scene that opens episode six, "A Madrastra" (The Stepmother). Appearing right in the middle of the series, the beginning of "A Madrastra" stands out for being the perhaps most absurd moment among the many that help to establish the series' outlandish tone. Despite the absurdity, it is, along with the scene discussed above, the most important in the series. Indeed, when considered together, the two scenes point to a spectrum of structuring power in Brazilian society that places the white elite on the side of impunity and the impoverished black community on the side of punishment.

"A Madrastra" begins in a large, industrial kitchen. The head chef declares he is going to take a bathroom break. As he exits the kitchen, for no apparent reason, the rest of his team follows in suit. Left behind is a pastry chef, who, standing before a birthday cake, mechanically, as if reciting lines, states: "It is good that someone stays behind to finish this huge and very delicate cake that I can't get right because I am stubborn and didn't listen to Mrs. Fernandes; because if I had listened to Mrs. Fernandes this cake would be much tastier." The pastry chef then sighs deeply and grabs a large kitchen knife before continuing: "Well, first I will put away this huge knife so nobody gets hurt while I finish decorating this huge, delicious, and very expensive cake." As he utters these words, he braces to ice the cake. However, a bit of frosting squirts forth from his piping device onto the floor. The pastry chef steps on the frosting, unrealistically causing him to slip all over the kitchen until he eventually makes his way to the spot approximately ten feet away where he had hung the very large kitchen knife. Somehow, despite the knife hanging loosely from a utensil rack, the pastry chef manages to accidentally stab himself in the upper back. Still flailing about, the same knife accidentally stabs him another twenty times before he dies. All the while, with the same mechanistic delivery as before, the pastry chef mentions aloud how the absurd incident was nothing more than a random accident he himself had caused. In fact, prior to the final stab wound, he even goes so far as to wipe down his fingerprints, which, according to what we have just witnessed, would have necessarily been all over the kitchen.

Up until this point, it is not at all clear what is happening. In fact, unless one paid close attention to episode five, one would not even know that Mrs. Fernandes was Rebecca's surname from a previous marriage. Though it is suggested in the title ("the stepmother")—Rebecca is the stepmother to Camilo's son, the birthday boy—that the episode centers on Rebecca's possible involvement in The Great Gonzalez's death is only revealed when the scene cuts from the dead pastry chef to Rebecca's interrogation. There, shrugging her shoulders, Rebecca ends her retelling of the events to Lucimar and Wagner with a simple "That's it." Incredulous, Lucimar seeks clarification: "While you were in the bathroom with two waiters, the chef, with whom you had had an argument, accidentally stabbed himself twenty-one times with a kitchen knife?" To which Rebecca responds: "That is what happened. That is, what I can affirm is that the jury agreed with my *opinion* of the facts and said that the prosecution did not have enough evidence."

Put simply, despite the obvious impossibility of Rebecca's account, she is let free. At the same time, even in possession of clear evidence showing that The Great Gonzalez's death was an accident and that none of the arrested had anything to do with it, the black cook, chauffeur, maid, and gardener all go to jail. As such, the series employs these two seemingly disparate scenes to unmask a social reality characterized by harsh injustices, which, for their part, contrary to what we see in *Mister Brau*, are definitively the result of race. In fact, one potential interpretation of the series is that it is a rereading of Roberto DaMatta's (1979) conceptualization of the *indivíduo/pessoa* (individual/person) binary proposed by the anthropologist in *Carnavais, malandros e heróis* (*Carnavals, Rogues, and Heroes*).

In this important study of Brazilian culture, DaMatta argues, "The person deserves solidarity and differential treatment. The individual, on the contrary, is the subject of the law, an abstract focus for whom rules and repression were made . . . In terms of the dialectic of the individual and the person, we have a hierarchical universe made up of a small number of people, who command the life and destiny of a multitude of individuals, who must obey the law" (1979: 218, 231).[12] João Cezar de Castro Rocha sums up the anthropologist's point nicely, concluding that in DaMatta's "vocabulary, everyone in Brazil aspires to the status of 'person' in detriment to the condition of the 'individual'" (2005: 13–14).

O Grande Gonzalez clearly situates Rebecca as a "person"—she has bent the law (or perhaps, the law has bent before her) to ensure her freedom—and the nameless, working class, black characters as "individuals"—they must bow to the law, which has left them with no recourse. In DaMatta's conceptualization of the two structuring categories of Brazilian society, race does not appear as a major factor. However, in the Porta dos Fundos' series, insofar as the two scenes discussed here simultaneously exist to contrast and inform one another, race appears as *the* deciding factor. As such, the series, supported by the three sketches, suggests that "persons" in Brazilian society are, with rare exceptions, white; individuals, on the other hand, also with rare exceptions, are black.

Given the documented under/misrepresentation of blacks on Brazilian television, the comparison between *Mister Brau* and the Porta dos Fundos' YouTube videos and television series reveals that it is not sufficient merely to put people of color on-screen, especially if the portrayals perpetuate outdated ideologies and long-established stereotypes of marginalized racial minorities, as in the TV Globo–produced serial comedy. Along these lines, Stuart Hall has argued that invisibility is replaced by "a kind of carefully regulated, segregated visibility" (1993: 107). *Mister Brau*'s black protagonists' symbolic movement from invisibility to "segregated visibility" is made palatable by his conservative position-takings regarding race and racism in Brazil. Of course, one could argue that *O Grande Gonzalez* does the same. However, as I have demonstrated in this chapter, whereas the TV Globo series clears Brazil's most powerful group—white men—of engaging in racist attitudes, *O Grande Gonzalez* and the group's other videos locate the country's systemic racism precisely within that powerful group. What is more, the often *uncritical* humor in a program like *Mister Brau* positions the black subject as a caricature who need not be taken seriously while, at the same time, promoting the internalization of the racial hierarchy "with minimum conflict and without the need for segregation" (Telles, 2004: 222). This reality is compounded further by the fact that TV Globo (Social Mission) brands itself as the author of what it means to be Brazilian, while also declaring that its mission is to contribute to the education of its hundreds of millions of viewers.

Ultimately, of interest here are those changes to the Brazilian mediascape that have given way to new modes of distribution, economic models, formats, and emerging voices who seek out conflict and make light of racial segregation; those that critically challenge established power structures such as TV Globo; or those that employ strategies that, as Hall contends, "can make a difference and can shift the dispositions of power" (1993: 107). Porta dos Fundos' meteoric rise as a producer of content for both the Internet and pay-television represents one among a number of emergent challengers to the established power structure, while also exemplifying a broader, ongoing shift to the Brazilian mediascape. As an independent production company founded shortly after the implementation of the Pay-TV Law and during a period of strong growth for the pay-television sector and Internet, Porta dos Fundos has maximized the relatively less-regulated space of the Internet and the Pay-TV Law's content stipulations for pay-television to position itself as a critically progressive voice on important social issues in Brazil. Whereas *Mister Brau*'s adoption of the hegemonic discourse of racial democracy via racial mixing results in the work's cooption into what Antônio Candido has referred to as the "polo da ordem" (realm of order) (1970: 76–84), Porta dos Fundos' satirical YouTube videos and serial comedy *O Grande Gonzalez* lay bare, for its tens of millions of viewers, the fact that in Brazil, "whites continue to enjoy the privilege of racial status," while black Brazilians are represented as violent criminals or, in exceptional cases, as entertainers and athletes (Telles, 2004: 238). In doing so, the narratives created by Porta dos Fundos remain unresolved and thus echo as a continuous critique of the status quo.

In the end, the fundamental difference between *Mister Brau* and *O Grande Gonzalez* can be summed up by their competing visions. The former introduces a multicolored adhesive bandage that merely covers—but cannot heal—the still-festering wound of racial prejudice in Brazilian history and society with the comfortable and comforting ideology of racial democracy, long a characteristic of TV Globo fiction. Even though *Mister Brau* is at times progressive in its portrayal of race in Brazil, such a position ultimately advocates for the maintenance of the status quo, which, in terms of Brazilian audiovisual production, is Globo itself. This is not to say that Globo is a monolith, that in its enormous structure it does not produce and air diverse portrayals of Brazil. Instead, the point here is that in its enormity and search for the largest possible audiences, the media conglomerate, especially as it pertains to its over-the-air production, has conservative tendencies, which all too often fail to speak truth to the country's most powerful. The latter, however, calls out the white Brazilian elite, and by extension the very creators themselves, for its (and their) role in creating and perpetuating racial and socioeconomic inequality. Put simply, *O Grande Gonzalez* employs a comedic surgical intervention, which, from a position of opposition to TV Globo, does not pretend to offer a cure but at least cuts open the wound, exposing the infection within.

6

Globo *Plays* Series

In the new Brazilian mediascape, the rise of pay-television and the Internet have lured millions of spectators away from TV Globo's *telenovelas*, thereby weakening the network's hegemonic stronghold over audiences, advertising, and production and contributing to the broadening of the country's social imaginary. Nonetheless, while the significant shifts occurring within the post-2011 era have left TV Globo less powerful, the network has remained—to borrow Lotz's description of broadcast networks in the United States around 2010—"something like a three-hundred-pound gorilla (reduced from [its] eight-hundred-pound glory days) being attacked by a disorganized pack of dogs" (2018: 82). Indeed, in this new moment in the history of Brazilian television, the game has changed; broadcast networks like Record and SBT, both of which have mounted at best marginally successful challenges to TV Globo over the years, no longer present the greatest threat to the media conglomerate's dominant position. Instead, like TV Globo, the two networks—and increasingly, pay-television channels as well—find themselves faced with the interconnected rise of streaming services and audiences that watch linear television at significantly decreased rates.

In *Streaming, Sharing, Stealing: Big Data and the Future of Entertainment*, Smith and Telang (2016: 12) ask: "Is technology changing overall market power in the entertainment industries?" According to the authors, particularly when viewed from a historical perspective, the answer "appears" to be no (12). However, they complicate the matter further by asking: "But what if the entertainment industries are facing *multiple* changes? What if advances in computing and communications technologies have introduced a set of concurrent changes that together are fundamentally altering the nature of scarcity—and therefore the nature of market power and economic profit—in the entertainment industries?" (13). Smith and Telang maintain that when one considers the relatively recent rise of "digital distribution and its unlimited capacity," "low-cost production technologies," the "introduction of new powerful distributors," and the "development of advanced computing and storage facilities," it is evident that a shift in power is already under way (13–14). Though as it pertains to film and television, Smith and Telang focus primarily on Netflix's disruption of the United States market, a similar phenomenon is afoot in Brazil, where fragmented audiences increasingly explore myriad content available on pay-television, YouTube, and global streaming sites. As they do so, it becomes more and more clear that Globo can only hope to situate itself not *as* but *among* the industry leaders, most of which are located outside of Brazil.

It would, however, be a mistake to conclude that the broadcast network and media conglomerate will concede its over five-decade dominance without a fight. Rather, as television critic Tony Goes recently reported in the *Folha de São Paulo*, Globo has been "quietly" ("*sem muito alarde*") preparing to take on Netflix. With this in mind, the present chapter explores Globo's entrance into the streaming market as Brazil's first "studio portal" (Lotz, 2017: 62), emphasizing its significance in a mediascape increasingly informed by factors both local (e.g., Law 12.485/11 and augmented access to content from players outside of Globo's network of production and distribution) and global (growth of Netflix and other streaming services). Operating out of a Network-Era model characterized by commercial breaks and fixed, linear viewing, Globo largely built its unmatched success on the production and distribution of *telenovelas*. More recently, however, the media conglomerate has focused its attention on the production and distribution of series, which have become a central feature of its streaming service, Globo Play. Added to the already discussed upsurge in pay-television and web series in previous chapters, the hike in production of series by the largest producer of *telenovelas* in the world represents, I argue, a watershed moment for both the Brazilian mediascape and the nation as an imagined community. Exploring these issues further, the remainder of the chapter focuses on two Globo original series: *Supermax* (2016) and *Assédio* (*Harassment*, 2018). In addition to considering the varied aesthetics and representations of these works, the discussion delves into their respective production contexts and distribution rollouts. Together, the two Globo original series exemplify the media conglomerate's broader efforts to reposition itself within a field ever focused on the production of series for audiences that are becoming more and more accustomed to nonlinear viewing across a multiplication of screens.

Globo Goes Over the Top

In an article published in the Brazilian newspaper *O Estadão* in October 2018, Pedro Rocha reports that "following a global trend, Brazil will finish 2018 with a record number [seven] of original series produced exclusively for large streaming services that operate in the country." Leading up to 2018's banner year, only one original Brazilian series had been made exclusively for a streaming platform—the already discussed *3%*, released by Netflix in 2016.[1] However, rather than understand 2018's uptick in production as an anomaly, citing Erik Barmark, vice president of International Original Content, Rocha reports that not only does Netflix intend to produce and release at least ten original Brazilian series per year going forward, but the company has a team in place to ensure those productions meet the needs and desires of Brazil's diverse audience, particularly those populations living outside of Rio de Janeiro and São Paulo. In addition to mentioning the relatively small yet increased presence of streaming services like Amazon and Hulu, Rocha highlights Globo's production of *Além da Ilha* (*Beyond the Island*, 2018) and *Assédio*, both original series released exclusively to the company's streaming service, Globo Play.

So as to understand how and why the production of such a relatively small number of series garnered the attention it did, the discussion of Globo Play, the focus of this chapter, must be preceded by a brief consideration of Netflix Brasil. Four years before Globo Play began operating in November 2015, Netflix rolled out its standard-setting streaming service to Brazilians on September 5, 2011, at a monthly subscription rate of R$14.90 (approximately $9 US at the time). Early on, Netflix faced a number of issues in the Brazilian market. Chief among them were a catalogue lacking in recent titles and local productions and broadband speeds and costs. Initially, subscribers in Brazil had access to 609 films and 5,545 episodes of series (Martins, 2012). By September of 2012, at which point Netflix had a total of one million subscribers in all of Latin America, those numbers had ballooned to 1,539 and 23,138. When Reed Hastings visited Brazil in 2012 to commemorate Netflix Brasil's one-year anniversary, the company CEO noted that the increase in the subscriber base allowed the upstart streaming service to purchase the rights to more titles. Those titles, including such critically acclaimed films and blockbuster hits as *The Artist* (2011) and *Hunger Games* (2012), in turn attracted more subscribers, which further allowed the streaming service to purchase the rights to more film and television works. Nonetheless, even with a growing catalogue and recently signed agreements with Brazilian networks Band and TV Cultura, Internet speeds and costs remained a serious barrier to Netflix's desired growth. Addressing these barriers, Hastings highlighted the costly prices of unlimited broadband plans, which were largely restricted to high-earning households. The vast majority of broadband subscribers—a number that was less than five million households at the end of 2011—could only afford plans that were limited to 20G and 40G download speeds, which directly affected the viewing experience, often resulting in a lower-quality image and buffering (Petró, 2012).

Despite the early obstacles, at the start of 2019 Netflix Brasil had over eight million subscribers. In addition to representing about 6 percent of the company's total base, Brazil factors as its second largest market in terms of subscribers, trailing only the United States. In Brazil, Netflix has quietly become an industry leader. According to Ricardo Feltrin (2018), Netflix Brasil's estimated revenues of R$1.4 billion (slightly more than $360 million US) in 2018 represent 50 percent more than those revenues of SBT, one of Brazil's largest broadcast television networks (2018). What is more, having already surpassed the country's second largest pay-television provider, Sky (5.4 million subscribers), Netflix Brasil is poised to overtake Net Claro, which is currently the market leader with 8.7 million subscribers (Feltrin, 2018).

Propelled by new competitors and unprecedented growth in the pay-television and telecommunications sectors, the domestic mediascape had become more competitive than ever before when Globo finally entered the streaming market in 2015. At the end of that year, Netflix Brasil had approximately three million subscribers, a number that more than doubled over the next year alone (Base de usuários, 2017). At the same time, the pay-television sector had reached a near all-time high with 19.1 million subscribing households (Dados do Setor, 2018).[2] Like Netflix Brasil and the pay-television sector, Internet access was experiencing significant growth in Brazil. For example, when the lights turned out on 2015, broadband subscriptions had climbed to never before seen heights, reaching 8.2 million households, while Internet access via 3 and 4G technology pushed to then record highs, accounting for 70 percent of all mobile Internet access (Dados do Setor, 2018; Evolução do, 2018). Even without accounting for Globo's traditional competitors such as Record, SBT, and Band, it is clear that Brazilians had more entertainment options than at any other point since the inception of television in 1950. More precisely, audiences previously glued to Globo's *telenovelas* found themselves increasingly lured to new content, which was in turn increasingly detached from linear viewing.

Perhaps rightfully so, and certainly not unlike the manner in which legacy media companies in the United States apprehensively reacted to the onset of what would become foundational shifts to the industry in that country, Globo was reluctant to alter its business practices, which had proven a resounding success for more than fifty years. Nonetheless, by 2015, the company was left with little choice. In a sense, the game the media company had dominated for decades had new rules and a new generation of competitors. Even so, Globo did not go full stop when rolling out its streaming service. Instead, Globo Play initially served three primary functions: (1) to create an on-demand archive of Globo classics, including its extremely popular *telenovelas*; (2) to allow audiences to catch up on television programming missed that day or week; and (3) to stream live events, such as soccer (*futebol*) and volleyball matches (Capoano, 2016: 10–12). Thus, closer to Hulu's model than to that of Netflix, the latter two functions of Globo Play were still deeply embedded in a linear mode of program viewing created for commercial broadcast television. In a 2016 interview with *Variety* about the recent launch of Globo Play, Globo CEO Carlos Henrique Schroder emphasized the centrality of the company's traditional practices: "TV will continue to play an extremely important role in people's lives. It works like a thermometer of the population; it brings everyone onto the same wavelength, at the same time. Some of the TV genres that contribute to this are *telenovelas*, reality shows, journalism and sporting events. All of them have an important element of being able to generate concurrent social conversation in real time" (Hopewell, 2016). At the same time, Schroder revealed that even this would soon change: "Globo Play is a platform that prepares Globo for the future of video content distribution. In upcoming years, there will be more and more multiplatform content consumption, which will demand increasing flexibility in television viewing" (Hopewell, 2016). Just over a year after Globo Play began its operations, audiences appeared to be realizing Schroder's prediction. As Vieira and Murta highlight, in roughly a year, largely exercising the free option, which provided registered users access to clips and videos, the Globo Play platform had accounted for ten million downloads of the app and 6.3 billion minutes of streamed content (2017: 41). What is more, Vieira and Murta note that as audiences increasingly connected to Globo Play, whether through smart phones, smart TVs, tablets, web browsers, or ancillary devices like Chrome Cast and Roku, Globo accumulates data (41). More intricate and precise than the focus-group and audience-metric data that characterized TV Globo's measurement practices in the Network-Era, the data stemming from the company's streaming service provides Globo a better understanding of its audiences' viewing behaviors as well as the flexibility to experiment with the distribution of content.

The negotiation of legacy and new media was at the core of the rollouts of two Globo series, *Supermax* (2016) and *Carcereiros* (*Inmates*, 2017). Though both original works premiered on Globo Play, they were never conceived of as series made exclusively for the streaming platform. Instead, the two series eventually aired on TV Globo. Thus, the introduction of *Supermax* and *Carcereiros* to viewers occupied a middle ground that hesitantly explored the media conglomerate's foray into streaming while still holding tight to its Network-Era bread and butter. More specifically, the releases of *Supermax* and *Carcereiros* functioned to promote Globo's new service and to gauge Globo Play viewers' behavior, before eventually landing where the heavy advertising dollars were: on broadcast network television. Over the next year, however, Globo pivoted from the strategic hedging that characterized the release of these two works to a more determined effort to grow its streaming service.

The pivot itself began with a maneuver by Globo never before seen. Since its debut in 1988, every Monday at 10 PM TV Globo has included in its programming grid *Tela Quente*, the airing of a contemporary film. However, on August 27, 2018, for the first time in the session's thirty-year history, TV Globo used the *Tela Quente* timeslot to present its audience with the first two episodes of *The Good Doctor* (ABC, 2017–), which were edited to play as a feature-length film.[3] The airing was an audience success, recording the highest ratings for the *Tela Quente* time slot since 2012 (Aposta da Globo dá certo, 2018). Surprisingly, despite clear interest in the series, no other episodes would be aired on TV Globo. Instead, the remaining sixteen episodes from the first season could only be viewed on Globo Play. Thus, in just two short years, Globo had altered its strategy from one that used its newly minted streaming service to promote its over-the-air programming to one that employed its television programming grid as a means to publicize Globo Play.

The exclusive release of *The Good Doctor* in late 2018 was only the beginning of Globo's plan to secure a place for itself among streaming leaders in Brazil. Around the time Globo rolled out the North American series, the company raised the streaming service's monthly fee from R$15,90 to R$18,90 (approximately $4.75 US), slightly lower than Netflix's least expensive option (R$19,90). Despite the increase in price, according to CEO João Mesquita, during the four days following the airing of *The Good Doctor*, Globo Play experienced the most sales in its brief history (Guaraldo, 2018). Nonetheless, Globo Play reports that even with twenty million Brazilians accessing the streaming service, the majority continues to use the free option to watch primarily clips of *telenovelas* and the news (Guaraldo, 2018). While many of the platform's new subscribers were spurred to action by their desire to watch *The Good Doctor*, their continued subscriptions would be secured only if, once there, they were to find other titles of interest. Thus, in addition to Globo Play's already-existing vast catalogue of TV Globo *telenovelas*, miniseries, specials, and films (both domestic and foreign), the company was prepared to further seduce subscribers and would-be subscribers with such exclusive series as *A Million Little Things* (ABC, 2018–), *Charmed* (CW, 2018–), and *Killing Eve* (BBC, 2018–). Intent on growing its subscriber base to twenty million and doubling accesses to forty million, Globo Play announced it would exclusively offer one hundred foreign series by the end of 2019 (Guaraldo, 2018). The streaming service also announced that it would continue to produce and release exclusive Brazilian original series like the dramas *Ilha de Ferro* (*Iron Island*, 2018) and *Aruanas* (2019) and the sitcom *Shippados* (2019).

As we have documented thus far, Globo's about-face was a response to a more competitive marketplace, particularly one disrupted by the growth of the pay-television and telecommunication sectors and the Internet. Along these lines, Eduardo Schaeffer, the recently hired director of Globo's newly formed *Unidade de Inteligência Digital* (Digital Intelligence Unit), has stated that Globo's competitors are now tech companies and the new economic models and strategies they employ (Sá, 2018b). This of course does not mean that network television will disappear. Instead, as Lotz has argued, tech-driven new media have had a revolutionary impact on legacy media by introducing into the landscape "a new mechanism of distribution that allows evolution of legacy companies and the creation of a sector—maybe sectors—of internet-distributed television" (Lotz, 2017: 2). Though recognizing that many similarities persist between broadcast network and cable television and Internet-distributed television, Lotz contends that technological affordances of Internet-distributed television—chief among them, the delivery of "personally selected content from an industrially curated library"—and "the varied protocols they allow, encourage an industrial operation and viewer experience that is quite different from norms developed for previous mechanisms of television distribution" (4).

Perhaps more than any other development, nonlinearity has been the most distinctive change to television distribution, production, and viewing norms offered by Internet-distributed television. In broad terms, capacity constraint (what can be on television at any given time is limited to the number of hours in the day and the number of channels in existence) and time specificity (what is on television is on at a particular time of the day) characterize linear television. As a result, Lotz astutely notes that people "watched television" or tuned in to "see what was on," rather than selecting a specific program among myriad available options (2017: 23). Within a context in large part defined by space limitations, the guiding economic logic behind linear television is to select and air content that is likely to attract the largest possible audience, which would then be sold products via the thirty-second commercial advertisements. Such reasoning is itself a construct, insofar as content could be selected and aired for a variety of other reasons. For reasons Lotz notes, for example: "It was the best developed, it brought the most underrepresented voice, or it indicated the highest aspirations for the conventions of the medium" (24). Nonetheless, even as the market became more competitive and networks and content creators began to address niche audiences, "the primary strategy remained selecting the content likely to attract the most audience members—just perhaps the most women, children, or sports fans depending on the target of the channel" (24).

Nonlinear television, on the other hand, eliminates time specificity and greatly reduces capacity constraint. As such, "portals," which are the channel equivalents of Internet-distributed television, have been freed from the spatiotemporal constraints of time-fixed programming grids. Instead, their main task is curation, which is directly tied to their respective search algorithms and interfaces (Lotz, 2017: 8–9). What portals actually include in their curated catalogs is largely the result of a two-headed strategy that considers the audience and content acquisition (24). In terms of the former strategy, the major divergence here from broadcast network television is the emphasis put on niche audiences. While not dissimilar from pay-television's targeting of niche audiences, Lotz maintains that rather than providing audiences with niche programming that is on at a specific time, as is the case with pay-television, the nonlinearity of Internet-distributed television allows for portals to develop deeper, more robust catalogs of the niche content a particular subscriber might be interested in consuming (24–26). What is more, because portals have largely foregone the ad-supported model in favor of a subscriber model, they must have a little something for everyone—what Lotz refers to as a "conglomerated niche strategy"—for if not, subscribers can potentially cancel their subscription and take their dollars elsewhere (26). So as to meet the demands of a broad client base that is the sum of a plethora of niche audiences, portals must acquire or produce enough diverse, enticing, and exclusive content and, through their particular algorithm, get that content in front of the right eyes to attract and maintain the myriad niche audiences (26).

But in order for a streaming platform's search algorithm and interface to yield the data needed to offer curated, personalized content, it is necessary that the portal attract subscribers. In Brazil, where audiences have long become accustomed to receiving free, over-the-air domestically produced content characterized by high production values, it is not an easy task to convince viewers to pay for content, especially if that content is similar to what they already get for free (Straubhaar, 1984). They must be persuaded that a streaming service, be it Netflix or Globo Play, provides some type of added value. Along these lines, in the words of Smith and Telang, "selection" and "satisfaction" are key to any portal's success (2016). As seen with the example of *The Good Doctor* release, Globo believes, at least for the time being, that the most efficient and productive way of communicating the added value of Globo Play is, perhaps somewhat ironically, through its broadcast network. Indeed, for Mesquita, this, along with the fact that it is a local—that is, Brazilian—media company, is precisely what gives Globo Play a leg up on its competitors. Thus, even as it seemingly enacts a shift away from linear to nonlinear viewing, the interconnectedness of its varied operations (e.g., broadcast network, pay-television, film production, etc.) and its position as the leading Brazilian media company remain guiding lights for the group's overarching strategy. Regarding the former, Mesquita highlights a simple fact: "Netflix doesn't have a TV Globo at its disposal" (Guaraldo, 2018). In the same interview, Mesquita goes on to suggest that the *Tela Quente* was an experiment with a larger plan in mind: "I'm not saying that it is going to happen, but just imagine that we created something called a 'Globo Play Session,' a weekly airing on TV Globo designed to present some product from the Globo Play catalogue? . . . We still have the biggest showroom in Brazil" (Guaraldo, 2018). In essence, Mesquita is emphasizing that the *new media* Globo Play has something *new media* Netflix—its latest and perhaps most formidable competitor—does not: a *legacy media* broadcast network in the form of TV Globo. Directly tied to Globo Play's legacy media base is the importance TV Globo has historically placed on itself as the source for symbolically constructing and representing Brazil. Along these lines, implicitly recognizing the importance of "cultural proximity" and viewers' preference for culturally proximate or locally produced content (Straubhaar, 1991, 2003), Mesquita points to the other factor that distinguishes Globo Play from all would-be non-Brazilian competitors: its Brazilianness (*brasilidade*) (Sá, 2018a).

Though Globo entered the streaming market tentatively and relatively late, the media conglomerate was careful to hold on to its most important asset: its enormous catalogue of content produced in-house. Indeed, since Netflix arrived in Brazil in 2011, Globo has refused to license its content to other media companies (Sá, 2018b). This fact is important for two reasons. First, as already mentioned, the move from linear to non-linear television has made way for the on-demand access to an endless catalogue. Insofar as it allows for the offering of content without having to intermittently negotiate distribution contracts, rights ownership becomes a desirable objective, if not a necessary condition for media companies. Second, owning the rights to its content permits Globo to enter the world of Internet-distributed television already leveraging an impressive collection of exclusive content. Any viewer interested in past TV Globo *telenovelas*, miniseries, or specials can access them only by subscribing to the company's streaming service, a factor that could weigh heavily in those cases in which one must decide, for financial reasons or otherwise, between competing streaming services and Globo Play.

Prior to Globo's entrance into Internet-distributed television, it dominated broadcast network television through its vertically integrated "studio-television network." In terms of channels and production, if not also in terms of audience share, Globo similarly sat atop the pay-television sector. As the group transitions to Internet-distributed television, it is evident that it is positioning itself to continue to be Brazil's premiere source of entertainment by becoming the country's top studio portal. In addition to leveraging its library of content on Globo Play, Globo recently launched over-the-top film and soccer (*futebol*) streaming services. Traditionally included in premium pay-television subscription packages, Globo elected to allow interested individuals to bypass pay-television operators and subscribe directly to Telecine Play—a Globo partnership with Disney, Fox, and Universal featuring a substantial catalogue of films—and Premiere, which, like NBA League Pass, gives exclusive access to the Brazilian Soccer Championship (*Campeonato Brasileiro*).

In broad terms, while allowing for the entrance of a few new competitors like Netflix and Amazon, as has been the case in the United States, Globo's maneuvering suggests that the Brazilian mediascape will continue to feature the media conglomerate as *one* of the primary driving forces behind what audiences watch. This is partly because, as Ramon Lobato argues in *Netflix Nations*, similar to what intellectual probing bore out in earlier discussions surrounding transnational flows of television content, "audiences still want television in their own language, with familiar faces, and culturally relevant stories" (2019: 182). This does not, however, mean that, like the previous fifty years, the next fifty will usher in a period of dominance by Globo. Instead, even as the media conglomerate continues to be a leader in the field, barring government intervention, over the next decade a number of factors will converge to make the Brazilian mediascape even more competitive. First among these will be the continued growth of the Internet, which will gain in both access and speed. Second, not only will the existing portals like Netflix, Amazon, and Globo Play further solidify their positions within the field; they will almost certainly be joined by at least a few more competitors.[4] Third, and related to the first two factors, the increased capacity offered by Internet-distributed television and the need for niche content to fill out the catalogues of streaming services will result in greater demand for the development and production of scripted series, both domestic and foreign. What is more, the substitution of ad-supported content for subscriber-supported content will potentially shift creative allegiances away from corporations and products to the viewer. As such, especially when compared to the period leading up to 2011, one can expect not only a significant uptick in the domestic production of series but more series that speak directly to the diversity that comprises a particular portal's actual or desired subscribing base.

The discussion that follows focuses on the series *Supermax* (2016) and *Assédio* (*Harassment*, 2018). Though Globo has produced other series[5] that are currently available on Globo Play, I have chosen these two because of what their respective production and distribution tell us about Globo's streaming service and how it has developed during the short period between the series' releases. What follows is not an exhaustive account of over-the-top television in Brazil. Nonetheless, by emphasizing the role of Globo, a discussion of the two series does reveal the characteristics of Brazil's ongoing shift from linear to nonlinear television; from broadcast network television to Internet-distributed television; from studio network to studio portal; from the large-scale production *telenovela* to the niche series. As these shifts play out, what we find is not a simple process of replacement or substitution of earlier norms but instead the constitution of an audiovisual experience informed by the combination of legacy and new media models. A primary result of the ongoing legacy/new media dialectic has been Globo's expansion to the production of series alongside its large-scale production of *telenovelas*.

Maxing Out in *Supermax*

Supermax is an example of an early Globo response to some of the widespread transformations to television in Brazil discussed throughout this book. More specifically, the 2016 series is instructive for two primary reasons: its creative process and its distribution. Showrunners[6] José Alvarenga Jr., Marçal Aquino, and Fernando Bonassi conceived of *Supermax* sometime in 2015. Alvarenga, who has spent his entire career at TV Globo, is best known for directing such network sitcoms as *Os normais* (*The Normal Ones*, 2001–2003), *A diarista* (*The Housekeeper*, 2003–2007), and *Divã* (*Divan*, 2011). Both Aquino and Bonassi are best known for their work as authors and screenwriters. Though already a celebrated writer, Aquino rose to even greater prominence when, while still in the process of completing the novela *O invasor* (*The Trespasser*), director Beto Brant convinced him to develop the work into a screenplay for *O invasor* (2002), which would eventually be considered one of the best Brazilian films of all time. Aquino also wrote or co-wrote screenplays for *Os matadores* (*The*

Killers, Dir. Beto Brant, 1997), *Nina* (Dir. Heitor Dhalia, 2004), *O cheiro do ralo* (*The Smell from the Sewage Drain*, Dir. Heitor Dhalia, 2007), and *Eu receberia as piores notícias dos seus lindos lábios* (*I'd Receive the Worst News from Your Beautiful Lips*, Dir. Beto Brant, 2011). Similarly, in 1996, for her debut feature-length film, Tata Amaral adapted Bonassi's first novel, *Um céu de estrelas* (*A Starry Sky*, 1991). In addition to continuing to publish literary fiction, Bonassi went on to write or co-write the screenplays for *Os matadores*, *Castelo Rá-Tim-Bum!* (Dir. Cao Hamburger, 2000) and *Carandiru* (Dir. Héctor Babenco, 2003), to name a few.

The fact that Globo brought in two well-known writers to work with Alvarenga is not in and of itself unique. Rather, as Igor Sacramento (2008) has demonstrated, and as I (2018) have argued with regard to Luiz Fernando Carvalho's work, TV Globo's broadcast network programming has long been open to Brazil's artistic elite for at least an occasional production/paycheck. It is also not unique that these three individuals collaborated on a television series. Prior to *Supermax*, from 2009 to 2011, Aquino and Bonassi created the TV Globo series *Força Tarefa* (*Task-Force*). During the police drama's three-season run, Alvarenga served as the general director. Three years later, the trio teamed up to create *O caçador* (*The Hunter*, 2014), a fourteen-episode crime drama starring Cauã Reymond that aired on TV Globo between April 11 and July 11, 2014. Instead, what makes the creation of *Supermax* different from nearly all other Brazilian television fiction leading up to the series' 2016 debut is its adoption of the "writers' room" model, so commonly associated with television fiction in the United States.

In addition to Aquino and Bonassi, Raphael Draccon, Carolina Kotscho, Braúlio Mantovani, Raphael Montes, Dennison Ramalho, and Juliana Rojas rounded out the writing team. Though from different artistic points of departure, the writers all have experience working with dramas built around suspense. For example, both best-selling authors whose work is available in multiple languages throughout the world, Draccon writes fantasy fiction, while Montes publishes police dramas.[7] Conversely, Kotscho, Ramalho, Rojas, and Mantovani's respective careers are more clearly aligned with the Brazilian film industry.[8] Kotscho, for example, was the co-screenwriter (along with Patrícia Andrade) for Breno Silveira's already-mentioned box-office hit *2 filhos de Francisco* and (along with Julie Sayes and Matthew Chapman) for Bruno Barreto's *Flores raras* (*Reaching for the Moon*, 2012). The least experienced of the group, Ramalho received attention for co-writing (along with Marins) *Encarnação do demônio* (*Embodiment of Evil*, 2008), a horror film directed by José Mojica Marins.[9] Throughout her career, Rojas has co-directed, co-written, and edited a number of films with fellow Brazilian director Marco Dutra.[10] Mantovani, arguably the most famous and celebrated of the group, wrote, among others, the screenplays for *Cidade de Deus* (*City of God*, Dir. Fernando Meirelles, 2002), *O ano em que meus pais sairam de férias* (*The Year My Parents Went on Vacation*, Dir. Cao Hamburger, 2006), *Tropa de Elite* (*Elite Squad*, Dir. José Padilha, 2007), and *Tropa de Elite: O inimigo agora é outro* (*Elite Squad: The Enemy Within*, Dir. José Padilha, 2010), four of the most commercially successful and critically acclaimed Brazilian films of the twenty-first century.

Together, the group of eight authors, screenwriters, and directors plotted, debated, and drafted each of *Supermax*'s twelve episodes. However, prior to the constitution of the writers' room, Alvarenga notes that he, Aquino, and Bonassi had written rough drafts of nearly all of the episodes when they decided that they simply did not understand the genre sufficiently to be able to pull off their desired outcome. In response, the three creators invited the other writers. As Alvarenga describes it, they did not ask the writers to develop and draft specific episodes. Rather, they began by going back to the drawing board, breaking down the twelve episodes one by one. As they discussed the individual episodes and their place within the broader narrative, the room was guided by the overarching logic that the best idea would win out (Russo, 2016). The implication is that the nonhierarchical process afforded the participants a great degree of creative freedom and input, or, as Mantovani understands it, a childlike space where all were free to suggest whatever came to mind (Russo, 2016.).

The second factor that makes *Supermax* an illustrative example of how Globo is responding to the post-2011 mediascape is its distribution. Globo's rollout of *Supermax* was characterized by a significant amount of hedging on the part of the media conglomerate. That is, just as the company wanted to capitalize on the advertising revenue associated with its lucrative broadcast network business, it also understood the need to respond to audiences' increased interest in access to nonlinear content. According to various industry reports, *Supermax* was initially slated to air on TV Globo in 2015. However, due to an economic recession and decreased rates for advertising spots, Globo pushed the series' debut to 2016. As mentioned in the opening of this chapter, by that time Netflix was experiencing significant growth, which did not go unnoticed by Globo.

Writing for the *Folha de São Paulo*, on September 16, 2016, Gabriela Sá Pessoa published an article whose headline read, "Globo follows Netflix's tactics, debuting the series *Supermax* online today" (Globo segue tática da Netflix e estreia série *Supermax* hoje on-line). But the truth is, Globo did not entirely follow Netflix's tactics. Instead of simply making all of *Supermax*'s twelve episodes available to Globo Play subscribers, the company released only the first eleven episodes on its streaming platform. Additionally, on September 20, 2016, only four days after the Globo Play premiere, the first episode of *Supermax* debuted on TV Globo in the 11 PM slot, with the remaining episodes airing each Tuesday over the next eleven weeks. In theory, Globo's hybrid distribution of *Supermax* would appeal to those segments of the population that were already no longer tuning into the broadcast network's programming grid—that is, those individuals who found themselves increasingly attracted to streaming platforms and Internet content. At the same time, aware that a significant portion of its over-the-air audience lacked the economic capital to subscribe to Globo Play (or other streaming platforms), the weekly releases of the prestige series would ensure that those individuals had a reason to keep their television sets tuned in to TV Globo. In the words of Amauri Soares, director of programming, "With *Supermax*, we are achieving something extraordinary, which is to bring together the best of the on-demand, binge-watching experience with the best of the collective over-the-air experience" (Sá Pessoa, 2016).

What made sense in theory did not play out in practice. First, the Globo Play viewer, if so inclined to binge-watch the first eleven episodes upon their release to over-the-top service on September 16, would have to wait until December 13 to screen the last episode. Clearly, according to this logic, Globo placed a much greater importance on its over-the-air programming and the lucrative advertising revenue that has long propelled that business to dizzying streams of profit for the Marinho family. Nonetheless, the plan backfired, as the series was an absolute flop in terms of audience share and critical reception. In fact, after opening with a low but respectable 14.9 points—roughly the equivalent of one million households in the city of São Paulo—audience ratings plummeted to 9 points, a record low for the time slot (Stycer, 2016).

Supermax's lack of success lies in Globo's and the creators' failed attempt to be all things to all people. Like its hybrid distribution, the series' narrative was constructed with the objective of attracting both a niche *and* a mass audience. This is most clearly evident in the two overarching genres that structure *Supermax*'s narrative: horror and terror and reality television. Within the context of Brazilian television (and film to a slightly lesser degree), the horror and terror genre is virtually nonexistent. Nonetheless, Globo believed there was a demand for such content, particularly from millennials and members of Generation Z. As such, with network ratings dropping at a steady rate and with the understanding that the decline was in large part due to TV Globo's difficulty in reproducing its audiences, especially among the younger demographics that were and are increasingly attracted to nonlinear content, Globo saw *Supermax* as a work that would appeal to its lost generation. Considering *Supermax*'s hybrid distribution, a series only appealing to a younger demographic would likely turn away the larger television viewing audience. There needed to be something more.

Whereas the horror and terror genre is at best underproduced in Brazil, reality television, namely *Big Brother Brasil*, trails only the *telenovela* in terms of audience interest and loyalty.[11] In what appears to be a balancing act, Alvarenga, Aquino, Bonassi, and their writing team created a horror and terror story that was structured by a *Big Brother*esque reality show, complete with *Big Brother Brasil* host Pedro Bial.[12] Twelve contestants, five women and seven men, gather at an abandoned maximum-security prison (Supermax) in the Brazilian Amazon, where they engage in weekly competitions to win R$2 million. Through the candidates' respective video applications to the reality show and a series of flashbacks, the audience learns that each contestant has engaged in what is at best questionable to at worst abhorrent behavior, ranging from accidental homicide to political corruption to premeditated murder.

In the days following the opening challenge to determine the competition's first leader, host Pedro Bial does not, as promised, check back in with the participants. What they do not yet know is that Bial and the production team have all been murdered by Baal, a demonic force who lives in the tunnels of the abandoned prison along with a collection of female zombie-like creatures that make up his cult. Determined to grow his tribe, Baal, a former evangelical pastor named Nonato who was infected years earlier by an unknown virus during the construction of the prison, seeks to capture and impregnate the competition's women with his offspring.

Over time, the participants realize that the reality show is over and that *in reality*, with no one watching at home, they are competing solely for a chance to escape Baal with their lives.

In a neo-baroque turn toward excessive accumulation, or perhaps even more apt, in a grotesque audiovisual application of Oswald de Andrade's call for artistic *antropofagia* (cannibalism), the series expands endlessly in generic and narrative terms, incorporating elements that range from the crime drama and *telenovela* to intertextual references to mega-hits or cult favorites like *Lost*, *True Detective*, and the *Walking Dead*. Not only, then, are the mode of production (the adoption of the writers' room model) and distribution (Globo Play and TV Globo) hybrid forms that combine the local and global, but so too are the artistic elements that make up the narrative. Hybridization is also employed on a symbolic level. In what reads as a metacritique of the contemporary field of broadcast network television, the participants, who frequently look directly into the many cameras strategically placed throughout the prison to address the audience at home and who also explicitly comment on competing in a reality show on Brazil's largest broadcast network, slowly come to grips with the fact that the audience is no longer watching. Just as they do, the first physical signs of an unknown virus appear on contestant Cecília's (Vânia de Britto) body. Shortly thereafter, when she morphs into a flesh-eating zombie, her colleagues are forced to stab her to death and burn her body. The message is clear: if one is not attentive, strange, exogenous forces are ready to take over.

Of course, in the post-2011 mediascape, such is also the case with Brazilian television. To simply continue to make *telenovelas* in a mediascape increasingly defined by nonlinear content, a proliferation of screens, and bingeable series is to become irrelevant. Aquino and Alvarenga both hint at this as a driving force behind the creation of *Supermax*. According to Aquino, "These are new times we are living in . . . It is difficult to listen to the public, yet fascinating at the same time" (Sá Pessoa, 2016). For his part, Alvarenga recognizes that in these new times audiences demand works like the Netflix series *Stranger Things* (Sá Pessoa, 2016). Considering the creators' comments and the reality of the post-2011 mediascape, *Supermax*, through its production, distribution, creation, and symbolism, reveals a strategy for how to survive the ongoing transformations to the field: adapt. Indeed, by the end of the last episode, ten of the twelve participants have died. The exceptions are Padre Inácio (Leonardo José) and

Sérgio (Erom Cordeiro). Though the former is the only participant to escape the prison, he is unable to fight off the virus, which causes him to transform into a new, more powerful version of Baal. The latter, on the other hand, remains alive, albeit trapped alone inside the prison. For subsequent seasons, which are likely to never materialize, we are left to imagine a pending battle similar to that faced by Brazilian television: Baal—the local/global hybrid force—is coming for Sérgio—Brazilian television's traditional yet weakened and imprisoned hero.

Assédio—The Brazilian Series at Its Best

Almost exactly two years after the first eleven episodes of *Supermax* were made available to subscribers of Globo Play, on September 21, 2018, all ten episodes of *Assédio* were released to the streaming platform. However, unlike what happened with the Alvarenga-led series in 2016, the Globo/O2 Filmes co-production did not immediately find its way to post-prime-time television. Rather, Globo employed a strategy similar to that of *The Good Doctor*'s rollout, whose first two episodes, as discussed in the opening of this chapter, were presented over the air, with the remainder available exclusively on Globo Play. Nearly three weeks after the series' debut, the *Folha de São Paulo* reported that the first episode of *Assédio* would air on October 15, 2018, during the aforementioned *Tela Quente* session. The report went on to state that Globo executives had decided to invest in their streaming platform and that the series was central to its plans for success (Globo quer emplacar, 2018).

Clearly, the respective distribution strategies of *Supermax* and of *Assédio* represent a significant shift in how Globo views its streaming platform. Whereas the distribution of *Supermax* leaned more heavily toward legacy media—it was initially set to debut on television in 2015 but did not due to low advertising rates resulting from the economic recession—*Assédio*'s rollout emphasizes Globo's new media. In both cases, however, legacy and new media intermix in an attempt to maximize viewership, independent of whether the priority lies with Globo's broadcast network viewership or the company's focus on growing its streaming business. Thus, in the case of *Assédio*, its airing during TV Globo's traditional *Tela Quente* session was intended primarily to promote the series on Globo Play. That this is the case is further evidenced by the fact that, despite securing an audience share of nearly 25 points (compare that to *Supermax*'s high of 14.9, record low of 9, and overall average of 11 for a similar time slot), Globo stood firm by not airing the remaining nine episodes, essentially forcing interested viewers to subscribe to the streaming platform (Falcheti, 2018).[13]

Beyond its distribution, like *Supermax*, *Assédio* stands out in the field of Brazilian television fiction. However, whereas the 2016 series was a commercial and critical failure that reproduced many of the field's hegemonic norms and stereotypes regarding race, gender, and sexuality, not to mention the failed neo-baroque accumulation of genres and plotlines, *Assédio* represents some of the best Brazilian television of the last twenty years, both in terms of its audiovisual construction and its nuanced portrayal of power, gender, and race in Brazil.[14] *Assédio* is a loose adaptation of Vicente Viladarga's *A clínica: A farsa e os crimes de Roger Abdelmassih* (*The Clinic: The Farse and Crimes of Dr. Roger Abdelmassih*, 2016), an investigative look at the rise and fall of Dr. Abdelmassih, an extremely successful fertility doctor accused and convicted of raping and sexually assaulting more than thirty of his female patients over the course of his career. In what is far from a common occurrence in either Brazilian film or television, a pair of women wrote and directed the adaptation. Maria Camargo, fresh off her work on Luiz Fernando Carvalho's TV Globo microseries *Dois irmãos* (*Two Brothers*, 2017), an adaptation of Milton Hatoum's homonymous novel from 2000, wrote the adapted screenplay. Amora Mautner, a longtime TV Globo employee who garnered attention for her direction of the wildly successful *telenovela Avenida Brasil* (2012), directed the series.[15]

Assédio employs Dr. Abdelmassih's deplorable story to construct a biting critique of the reigning patriarchal and misogynistic behavior that structure such Brazilian institutions as the legal system, the media, medicine, and science. The series' critique, however, is not restricted to Brazilian society. Rather, insofar as its production and distribution unfold within the transnational context of the #metoo movement, the narrative explodes the geographical boundaries of Brazil, inserting itself into a broader discussion regarding the longstanding, normalized mistreatment of women throughout the world. Indeed, in the broadest sense, *Assédio*'s narrative functions as one large #metoo statement.

Camargo and Maunter structure the series' first seven episodes around video testimonies from Stela (Adriana Esteves), Eugênia (Paula Possani), Maria José (Hermila Guedes), Vera (Fernanda D'umbra), Daiane (Jéssica

Ellen), and Eva (name used by Stela to denounce Dr. Sadala), each of whom relate the abuse they suffered at the hands of Dr. Sadala (the fictional version of Dr. Abdelmassih, played by Antônio Calloni) to Mira Simões (Elisa Volpatto), a journalist who has dedicated a significant portion of her career to uncovering Abdelmassih's crimes. The series opens with Stela's testimony, which, as with the others, takes place in Mira's apartment in 2009. Sitting with her back to the camera, the out-of-focus victim is brought to tears as she speaks with disgust and horror about the abuse she endured.

As is characteristic throughout the series, the narrative cuts from the video testimonies to subjective flashbacks of the abuse. In Stela's case, the narrative jumps backward to 1994, when she and her husband, Homero (Leonardo Netto), first met with Dr. Sadala to discuss fertility options. Sitting at the desk in his modern, yet sterile, white office, where a collage of baby photos is prominently highlighted on the wall directly behind him, Dr. Sadala matter-of-factly asks the couple, "Do you have faith?" Here, for the first time, we are introduced to Dr. Sadala and the central psychological trait that defines the understanding he has of himself: that he is a direct extension of God. This is made clear in the next scene, which shifts from Stela's flashback to a Sadala interview from 2009. In a setup that evokes an El Greco or Caravaggio painting, Dr. Sadala's face is softly lit so as to stand out against the mostly blacked-out image. Providing the sensation that he is speaking directly to the viewer, Sadala intently looks at an implied interlocutor and says in a slow, elongated drawl, "God. God knows who speaks truth."

From Sadala's macabre monologue, which we later learn to be a conversation with Artur, a publicist brought in by Sadala and his associates to "fix" the accusations made against him, the next shot cuts to 2007, where the doctor, his wife, and his mother prepare to enter a gala in honor of his illustrious career. In this moment, the narration has shifted to an omniscient perspective, allowing the viewer intimate access to Sadala and others at the party. For what follows in the remainder of the series, the gala is important, serving two narrative purposes. The first is to introduce the viewer to some of the key characters, all of whom, with the exception of Mira, work to enable and even glorify Sadala and by extension the patriarchal structure he represents and from which they benefit. The second is to foreshadow Sadala's forthcoming downfall. Because the beginning of that downfall in large part is the result of Stela's bravery to speak out against Sadala, the rest of the episode oscillates back and forth between the gala in 2007 and Stela's experience in 1994.

The two moments converge when Stela appears at the gala to confront the feted doctor. Before she is able to get to him, however, she is overwhelmed and passes out in the middle of the ballroom. Just as the camera captures from a high-angle shot the vulnerable Stela lying on the floor, Sadala's voice enters in-off to further render her powerless. In a narrative that evokes those commonly employed by powerful men to delegitimize their victims by highlighting the idea of female hysteria, Sadala says in a grave, serious tone: "When a woman wants something, she will go to much greater depths than a man will. When a woman believes in the dream of having a baby, she gives it her all." At this point, with soft, yet tense orchestral music providing continuity, the shot of Stela in 2007 cuts to an out-of-focus Sadala during his 2009 meeting with Artur. Still looking at the nonvisible interlocutor, Sadala concludes his defense by explaining why someone like Stela would accuse him of such a serious crime: "When a woman can't get pregnant, it is very hard on her; it is very difficult for her to move on."

But such a discourse has no place in *Assédio*, which aims to speak truth to power by unmasking the abhorrent abuse and systemic violence that too often push women to suffer in silence. Functioning as a direct response to Sadala's comments, the next scene cuts back to Stela's subjective flashback. By now, Stela and her husband have scraped together all the money they could to cover the expensive fertility treatment. Full of hope and "faith," Stela has given herself over fully to Sadala's expertise and track record of success. Rupturing that faith, in what follows the viewer watches in disbelief as Dr. Sadala rapes a drugged Stela who lies helplessly on an examination table in the doctor's clinic. The scene immediately following the rape, the episode's last, takes the viewer back to Stela's video testimony, which opened the series. The reader will recall that in that scene Stela sat, out of focus, with her back to the camera. Here, however, Stela is in focus, facing the camera. She goes on to give a powerful account of how what Sadala did affected her life, noting that the pain was not merely physical but also psychological. The episode concludes with a visibly emotional Stela, quietly uttering, "I lost everything."

If not "everything," all the female victims in *Assédio*, and by extension their partners and family members, have at the very least been robbed of their happiness, overall well-being, and ability to trust others. However, it is precisely from the state of loss and vulnerability that the victims, who find power in their newfound knowledge of their shared experience, rise up together to unmask a tangled web of systemic sexual abuse. Thus, Stela is just one of the many examples in the series of women speaking out against Dr. Sadala and the institutionalized sexual violence he symbolizes. Nonetheless, in every instance, the women face structures that seek to silence their voices. Stela, for example, is sent to a psychiatric ward for her "crazy," unstable behavior. Exercising the authoritative voice of his position, Dr. Sadala tells his victim/patient, Eugênia, whom he has just sexually assaulted, that she must not get worked up lest she run the risk of losing the baby *he gave her*.

In a similar vein, yet employing a logic more explicitly defined by stereotypes regarding class and geography, Dr. Sadala coldly lays out for Maria José, a working-class woman from northeastern Brazil, the subaltern position she occupies in Brazilian society: "Oh, Maria José, look closely at your face; who is going to believe you?" Sure enough, when Maria José reluctantly informs her sister of Dr. Sadala's crime against her, she asks if Maria José is certain it was not her fault—if she had not somehow led the doctor on. Like Maria José, Daiana's class and race are factors used to remind the victim of her lack of power. When Dr. Sadala sexually assaults Daiana, a working-class black woman employed at Sadala's clinic, she storms out of the building. Desperate to reclaim control of the situation and uphold their position of power, Dr. Sadala's lawyers present Daiana with a choice: keep quiet or lose her job and pension. After a meeting with Dr. Sadala, Daiana's own out-of-work husband encourages her to keep silent and take the money. However, in one of the series' most powerful scenes, Daiana, whom the system has unfairly placed in the extremely difficult position of having to choose between keeping an unwanted job to provide for her children or speaking out against injustice on the behalf of other victims of sexual assault, boldly declares: "Why can't I speak? Why can't I declare to the world what happened to me? What's stopping me? Nothing! . . . For me, there is only the truth, and I am not afraid of it!"

Daiana's statement encapsulates the ethos of *Assédio*: women *and* men must speak out against sexual assault; remaining silent is not an option.[16] As the examples demonstrate, this message is put on display through the depictions of women of different classes, races, and regions of Brazil who are forced to take on the institutions that structure Brazilian society and in doing so normalize behaviors and practices that ultimately work to maintain women in positions subordinate to men. That the series' fictional portrayal of Dr. Sadala's heinous crimes is but a starting point toward a broader conversation—one brought largely to the attention of the global social imaginary by the #metoo movement—is emphasized at the very end of each of the ten episodes. After the last credits have faded to black and the accompanying somber violin goes silent, the following phrase unfolds onto the screen in bold, white letters: "When violence screams, scream. Report it. Call 180" (*Quando a violência grita, grite. Denuncie. Ligue 180*). Viewers, then, are both made aware of and encouraged to report violence to Brazil's Hotline for Assistance to Women in Situations of Violence (*Central de atendimento à mulher em situação de violência*).[17]

As outlined in the beginning of this chapter, in the two years that separate the releases of *Supermax* and *Assédio*, Globo made a stronger commitment to growing the company's streaming platform. However, this does not mean that the hybrid strategy utilized for the *Supermax* rollout was suddenly discarded. Rather, as Globo experiments with responses to Netflix's encroachment on its hegemonic position within the field, it is clear that the media conglomerate sees its broadcast network business not only as a lucrative source of revenue but as a tool its foreign competitors lack. At the same time, as the Brazilian mediascape continues to evolve and grow in such a way that leads to more competition and therefore a decrease in TV Globo's over-the-air audiences, it seems clear that the media conglomerate is going to have to take a page out of its own book and repeat what it did in the late 1960s when it first rose to prominence. As touched on in chapter 4, at that time, the upstart network hit on a formula that provided domestic television audiences with locally produced content that aimed to represent Brazil. Even if that Brazil was more often than not an idealized, largely middle-class, white version and consequently either excluded altogether or simply misrepresented sizeable portions of the country's population, it was always closer to the local reality than that which was imported from Hollywood. Nonetheless, that in and of itself was not sufficient. The other aspect of Globo's successful formula was the consistently high production values of their output. *Assédio* is a prime example of both. With it, Globo takes a dramatic series, a genre nearly synonymous with twenty-first-century television in the United States, and produces a very high-level Brazilian version capable of competing with almost any similar product on Netflix or any other streaming platform. Thus, as it did with its *telenovelas*, if Globo is going to challenge Netflix and other portals, it will have to give Brazilians what they seem to increasingly want: locally produced *series* that are on par with the local and global series produced for pay-television, the Internet, and emergent over-the-top services.

Conclusion

On March 30, 2018, while seeking election to Brazil's highest office for a third time, Lula threatened to sue Netflix for *The Mechanism*'s depiction of his alleged role in the Car Wash corruption scandal (Ex-presidente, 2018). The news made headlines all over the world. *Aljazeera* and the *New York Times*, for example, both highlighted the California-based company's role in stirring the pot in Brazil: "Netflix series on Brazil's corruption exposes political divisions" and "Latest Uproar in Brazil's Raw Political Debate: A Netflix Series." Just over a week after announcing his legal threat against Netflix, the former president turned himself over to federal authorities in Curitiba, where he began serving a twelve-year sentence for corruption and money laundering. Since that time, as he had leading up to his incarceration, Lula has maintained his innocence while also criticizing the corrupt, partisan politics he believes landed him in jail in the first place.

A year into his prison sentence, Netflix's presence was still hovering over Lula's legal issues. To call attention to his imprisonment and ongoing political tensions in Brazil, supporters around the world participated in the *Jornada Lula livre* (Free Lula March). Days before the event, organizers of the *Jornada* released a promotional video titled "O sistema" (The System). A brief parody of *The Mechanism*, the video presents the viewer with a quick-hitting barrage of shots depicting rural and urban Brazil, politicians engaging in corruption and other illicit behavior, TV Globo's nightly news, and the quotidian toiling of seemingly hopeless laborers and students. As in the Netflix series, wherein investigator Marco Ruffo (Selton Mello) continuously refers to the rampant corruption in Brazil as an ever-spreading cancer, in "The System," voiceover narration informs the viewer of the many ills that destroy the nation from within: "That's right, friend, when the system gets together to accumulate power, it is those of us down at the bottom who suffer ... The media, the judiciary and financial systems, the protected; a country without hope, a country without law, without shame, where Globo accuses, the judiciary condemns and the people are left to pay the bill." Emphasizing the point further, over images of Lula and Marielle Franco—the recently assassinated human rights activist and Rio de Janeiro City Council member—the narrator calls the viewer to arms: "The system is fucked. They don't forgive anybody who stands against it; they pursue, accuse, and condemn. It is time to give the system what it deserves."

The video's message is clear: a select few thrive in Brazil while everyone else, especially the minorities and the poor, suffers. But that is only part of it. The choice of Netflix's *The Mechanism* as the source of the video's parody suggests that exogenous factors embedded in neoliberal politics and global flows of capital are at the core of the suffering of the Brazilian people, of whom Lula is the primary representative. Indeed, in a letter released on April 7, 2019, President Lula makes this clear, writing, "They are getting richer, but their fortunes, which they obtained at the expense of the suffering of millions of Brazilians, do not bring them happiness ... their fear is not of Lula. They are afraid of the *millions of Lulas* because they know what we are capable of when we unite to transform this country" (Lula em carta, 2019, emphasis mine).

Highlighting the interconnectedness of the media, politics, and the nation, I began this book with similar examples from the respective presidencies of Collor, Rousseff, and Bolsonaro. Such an observation is not an original one. Indeed, Hamburger (2000) and Porto (2011 and 2012), among others, have published important studies regarding the role of the TV Globo *telenovela* as a public forum for debating, playing out, and understanding Brazilian politics and, by extension, *Brazilianness* itself. What is fascinating about the centrality of *The Mechanism* in discussions surrounding the contemporary political milieu in Brazil is that it is neither a TV Globo production nor a *telenovela*. What is more, considering that Netflix has far fewer subscribers than the tens of millions of viewers that make up TV Globo's audiences, the fact that the series has drawn so much attention highlights the Internet's role in creating the conditions for myriad fragmented conversations, representations, and social commentaries that together are capable of structuring the public debate in ways the TV Globo *telenovela* historically has. Thus, *The Mechanism*, the discussions surrounding it, and the varied responses to it, such as "The

System," exemplifies the extent to which the new Brazilian mediascape is defined by local and global players entrenched in a competition for viewers that increasingly plays out through the distribution and consumption of nonlinear content.

Throughout the introduction and the six chapters that followed, I have argued that legislative, technological, economic, and creative developments during the period 2011 to 2018 have combined to shift the deeply entrenched, TV Globo, *telenovela*-centric Network Era into the emergent post-2011 mediascape. Unlike the one that preceded it, the new Brazilian mediascape is not marked by a lone media behemoth and a single medium-defining genre but instead by more diversity in producers, production, and distribution. Despite this broad shift, the post-2011 mediascape must be understood as a transitional moment. Some of the advances during the last seven years—particularly those related to the pay-television sector, which has shown signs of weakening—have already begun to lose steam. Overall, the production of a genre like the series is up under the auspices of the Pay-TV Law. Additionally, the Law establishes the conditions for the funding and distribution of those productions. Nonetheless, as Sousa notes, the mere existence of domestically produced works for pay-television does not guarantee that audiences will see them (2018). If, as has been the case over the last two years, households continue to cancel their pay-television subscriptions, the quotas established by Law 12.485/11 to spur a virtuous cycle of production and subscription will eventually lose their impact.

What is more, depending on the aims of a particular administration, the dependence of domestic production for the pay-television sector on the State places it in a potentially precarious position. Those familiar with ongoing scholarly debates surrounding Brazilian cinema's production, audiences, and government-financing mechanisms will readily recognize the validity of this point. Indeed, the fragility of State dependence became apparent recently when an audit by the *Tribunal de Contas* (Accountability Office, TCU) of films and television programs funded by ANCINE over the last fifteen-plus years unearthed questionable accounting practices. In response, the TCU suspended the release of FSA funds for at least sixty days, effectively bringing industry-wide production to a halt. Consequently, the entity's decision has thrown the audiovisual sector into a burgeoning crisis, leaving some to wonder if it might not once again crumble as it did under President Collor's administration.

Importantly, the new Brazilian mediascape is dramatically different from the one that characterized the early 1990s. At that time, pay-television and the Internet were virtually nonexistent, television fiction was largely synonymous with TV Globo *telenovelas*, and the independent production sector produced virtually no series and fewer than thirty films per year. By the end of 2018, over seventeen million households subscribed to pay-television, another ten million plus to Netflix and Globo Play, and more than 50 percent of the population had regular access to the Internet. Moreover, the local independent production sector produced roughly ninety series and 150 films per year, employed more than three hundred thousand people, and secured yearly revenues of approximately R$25 billion (slightly more than $7 billion US). The growth of the sector combined with increased access to the Internet lends support to the argument that even in the face of a potential crisis and cord-cutting consumers slowly leaving behind their pay-television services, the competitiveness and diversity that has characterized the shift away from the Network Era since 2011 will persist through the further amplification of broadband and mobile technologies and the solidification of national and international portals distributing content over the Internet.

With regard to the latter, one is left to ponder—as do Massarolo and Mesquita (2016: 16–17)—whether Brazilian legislators will propose new regulations that, similar to Law 12.485/11, establish quotas for subscription video-on-demand (SVOD) catalogues. Considering that the local independent production sector was a major force behind getting the Pay-TV Law passed in the first place, and accounting for the fact that the sector has expanded greatly during the post-2011 era, it seems unlikely that it would not throw its economic and political capital behind legislation that would ensure its members a meaningful place in Brazil's future mediascape. What is more, interested parties need not look far for a viable model. Toward the end of 2018, the European Union determined that the catalogues of global streaming services like Netflix and Amazon must include at least 30 percent European content. Whether Brazil does the same—and I believe that history suggests it will—as I have outlined in chapter 6, foreign streaming services, even if not mandated by law to do so, will almost certainly continue to include and likely even increase the number of domestically produced works in their respective catalogues as they seek to draw viewers away from TV Globo, Globo Play, and other local sources of content. In response, as has been the case in recent years, one can expect companies like Globo to provide Brazilians with the genre consistently found in the catalogues of the foreign streaming services: the series.

Indeed, one of the key takeaways from the study of the new Brazilian mediascape is the rise in the production of series, a genre that has only recently taken hold in Brazil. As I have argued, why this is the case has much to do with economic factors. Over the decades leading up to 2011, TV Globo had mastered the *telenovela* genre, which was, and to a lesser degree still is, enormously popular. Importantly, as Brazil's largest creator of content, not unlike the Hollywood Studio System of the 1940s, Globo produced all their *telenovelas* in-house. At the same time, other national networks also produced (generally in-house) *telenovelas*—which were nearly always, in qualitative terms, inferior to those produced by Globo—or they aired relatively inexpensive content imported from the United States or other foreign markets. Excluding the rare example from HBO, during their first two decades of existence in Brazil, pay-television channels similarly presented subscribers with mostly imported content. The combination and interrelatedness of these different modes of production and economic strategies employed by both over-the-air networks and pay-television channels made it impossible for the Brazilian independent production sector—with the exception of a few large companies—to establish itself within the field of television production. Indeed, it was precisely for this reason that independent production companies united to support the development of Law 12.485/11.

As demonstrated at various points throughout this book, the longstanding popularity and cost-effectiveness of the *telenovela* genre provided TV Globo with little incentive to invest its time and money in a genre like the series. What is more, restricted access to pay-television and the Internet leading up to 2011 limited the contact with the series genre of the vast majority of Brazilians. However, the growth of production for pay-television and the increased access to the Internet, spurred by Law 12.485/11, combined with the expansion of Netflix and Globo Play in Brazil, exposed millions of Brazilians to the genre that had been capturing the imagination of audiences in the United States since the end of the twentieth century. As a result of these shifts, Brazilian television audiences have become increasingly fragmented. Though not gone entirely, the *telenovela*-informed public sphere is quickly becoming a relic of Brazil's fading Network Era. While some might long for those days, one must not forget that, despite their many positive qualities, in their drive to attract the largest possible audiences, TV Globo's *telenovelas* have long erred on the side of caution, while also imagining an ideal spectator who was, more often than not, a white, middle-class Brazilian. Along these lines, Lotz makes an excellent point regarding the contemporary television landscape in the United States: "We must be wary," she cautions, "of viewing past cultural constitution with nostalgia and carefully weigh perceptions of lost common culture against the reality of how narrow a view of the world advertiser-supported, broadcast-and-cable-distributed television permitted. It is easy for those whose culture was prevalent to see a shift from this forced, shared culture as a loss, but that shared culture was alienating and foreign to many that now see themselves or their lives represented" (2017: 58). In Brazil, the post-2011 mediascape has *reframed* the social imaginary, creating the conditions for more Brazilians than ever before to imagine lives that extend far beyond the possibilities previously on display in TV Globo's *telenovelas*.

Notes

Introduction: Brazil Reframed

1. Though a presidential election was held in 1985, the vote to determine the winner occurred indirectly—that is, only members of the Electoral College were allowed to participate.

2. Throughout this book, I will use TV Globo to refer to the over-the-air broadcast network. When I use the term Globo, I am referring to the media conglomerate that controls TV Globo. As is the case with the broadcast network, the Marinho family fully owns and controls the media conglomerate.

3. About the debate, Memória Globo—a Globo-run website dedicated to recording the company's history and archiving its institutional memory—admits to the network's questionable role in the proceedings. Although the site's version of the events surrounding the debate hedges, so as to not declare the network fully responsible, it does point out that the media conglomerate has since made it a policy to not edit presidential debates (Debate Collor X Lula).

4. As used throughout the book, mediascape will refer to the current state of Brazilian television in its varied forms. I borrow the term from Arjun Appadurai (1996: 32–33), who employs it as a central aspect of the theoretical framework he develops to contemplate global flows and the "disjunctures between economy, culture, and politics" that inform them. Building on Benedict Anderson's seminal work on the imagined community, Appadurai proposes five landscapes as the building blocks of what he refers to as *imagined worlds*—"that is, the multiple worlds that are constituted by the historically situated imaginations of persons and groups spread around the world" (1996: 37). In addition to mediascapes, the four other scapes introduced by Appadurai are ethnoscapes, technoscapes, financescapes, and ideoscapes. He argues that "the global relationship among ethnoscapes, technoscapes, and financescapes is deeply disjunctive and profoundly unpredictable because each of these landscapes is subject to its own constraints and incentives (some political, some informational, and some technoenvironmental), at the same time as each acts as a constraint and a parameter

for movements in the others" (37). Regarding mediascapes, Appadurai argues that it is emergent forms of media that "transform the field of mass mediation because they offer new resources and new disciplines for the construction of imagined selves and imagined worlds" (3). It is in this sense that I refer to the Brazilian mediascape post-2011.

5. When provided, I use the English translations for films, interviews, newspaper articles, scholarly works, *telenovelas,* and television and web series. In the case that they are unavailable, the English translations are my own. For certain translations—namely, those I deem to be of particular importance—I include the original Portuguese in a note.

6. Media outlets, both in Brazil and abroad, frequently refer to Bolsonaro as the "Trump of the Tropics" (Trump dos trópicos).

7. Rede Record was founded in 1953 by attorney and businessman Paulo Machado de Carvalho. Experiencing significant financial and audience struggles toward the end of the 1980s, the small network was acquired by Edir Macedo, the founder of the Neo-Pentecostal Christian denomination, the Igreja Universal do Reino de Deus (Universal Church of the Kingdom of God). Since 2007, Bishop Macedo's acquisition has morphed into a successful national network, ranking only behind TV Globo—albeit by a very wide margin—in terms of audience share (Porto, 2011: 72). The network has become (in)famous, particularly in recent years, for its production of religious-themed *telenovelas* such as *Os dez mandamentos* (*The Ten Commandments*, 2015–16), which broke the network's audience-share records and proved to be a potential threat to TV Globo's audience hegemony.

8. I use conjuncture here as employed in Cultural Studies. More precisely, I draw on the concept as defined by Lawrence Grossberg (2006 and 2010), who follows Stuart Hall's definition. According to Hall, the concept of a conjuncture describes "the complex historically specific terrain of a crisis which affects / but in uneven ways / a specific national-social formation as a whole" (qtd. in Grossberg, 2010: 4–5). "It is not a slice of time or a period but a moment defined by an accumulation/condensation of contradictions, a fusion of different currents or circumstances. A conjuncture is always a social formation understood as more than a mere context / but as an articulation, accumulation, or condensation of contradictions" (2006: 5). For Grossberg, a conjuncture is "a description of a social formation as fractured and conflictual, along multiple axes, planes and scales, constantly in search of temporary balances or structural stabilities through a variety of practices and processes of struggle and negotiation" (2010: 4–5).

9. Although it was neither the first nor the only broadcast network in Brazil, for decades TV Globo was so far ahead of competitors such as TV Tupi, Manchete, SBT, and Rede Record that it often seemed to be peerless.

10. While the Rio de Janeiro–based network did not begin to operate until 1965, TV Globo and Time-Life officialized their partnership in 1962. As Sérgio Caparelli notes, the contract was in direct violation of Article 160 of the Brazilian Constitution, which prohibited foreign companies from participating in the intellectual and administrative orientation of national television concessions (Caparelli, 1982: 25–29, 60–61). However, according to Caparelli, in line with its plan for national integration and security, the recently installed military dictatorship longed for access to the country's vehicles of mass communication, of which television was understood to be the most important. As a result, the illegitimate government did nothing to annul the agreement between TV Globo and Time-Life until the late 1960s. By the time President Castelo Branco gave TV Globo a ninety-day period to legitimize its existence in line with the law, the network had already received both financial and technical support from Time-Life, as the latter, among other things, gave the former approximately $5 million, trained TV Globo professionals in New York City, and advised on business dealings (Mattos, 2002: 95).

11. In 2011, the 8 PM *telenovela* (*novela das oito*) moved to the 9 PM slot. Similarly, in 2011, the 10 PM (*novela das dez*) became Super Series (*Superséries*). With an average of sixty-seven chapters, Super Series are essentially longer miniseries (which average roughly forty chapters) that air in the 11 PM slot.

12. According to Adorno, "The culture industry fuses the old and familiar into a new quality. In all its branches, products which are tailored for consumption by masses, and which to a great extent determine the nature of that consumption, are manufactured more or less according to plan. The individual branches are similar in structure or at least fit into each other, ordering themselves into a system almost without a gap. This is made possible by contemporary technical capabilities as well as by economic and administrative concentration. The culture industry intentionally integrates its consumers from above" (2001: 98). Adorno notes that "the expression 'industry'" should not be taken literally. Instead, he argues, "'industry' refers to the standardization of the thing itself and to the rationalization of distribution techniques, but not strictly to the production process" (100–101). Film (and by extension television), however, which is the culture industry's central area of production, is closer to actual industry: "the production process resembles technical modes of operation in the extensive division of labor, the employment of machines and the separation of the laborers from the means of production—expressed in the perennial conflict between artists active in the culture industry and those who control it—individual forms of production are nevertheless maintained" (100–101).

13. While his focus is on Latin American cinema, Paul A. Schroeder Rodríguez's (2016) use of *melorealism* is apt for discussing Brazilian telenovelas, which, among Latin American iterations of the genre, are known for their realist

aesthetic and treatment of contemporary social issues (López, 1995; Straubhaar, 2012). According to Rodríguez, *melorealism* applies to "narratives that center on affect and emotion, yet without the excess emotion associated with much of classical melodrama . . . [it] also points to the prevalence of a realist visual style constructed through the use of natural acting, continuity editing, on-location shooting, and the restrained use of nondiegetic sound" (2016: 250).

14. Similarly, Straubhaar notes that "radio and television are for the 20th century what the print media of newspapers and books were to the 19th century: the primary means of building and reinforcing national identity. Television becomes a crucial medium to unify geographically and ethnically dispersed and diverse peoples into a sense of nationhood" (2007: 61).

15. Over-the-top (OTT) refers to standalone subscription services that allow for the streaming of select content over the Internet. Examples include HBO Go and the more recent DAZN.

Chapter 1. The Pay-TV Law and the New Brazilian Mediascape

1. According to Lotz, in the United States, among other factors, the Network Era was characterized by the following: television as the main technology, deficit financing for production, exclusivity and limited windows for distribution, and 30-second advertisements at the core of the business model (2014: 9). By comparison, the Post-Network Era, again as defined by Lotz, is characterized by the following: the simultaneous presence of multiple technologies such as DVRs, Video-on-Demand, portable devices, tablets, and digital cable, varied financing norms, opportunities for amateur production, nonlinear distribution, widespread, often nonexclusive access, and the coexistence of thirty-second advertisements, branded and sponsored content with multiple-user supported models like the purchasing of specific films or television programs and subscription packages (2014: 9).

2. An exchange rate of 3.20 Brazilian Reais to 1 US dollar was used to calculate all the approximate US dollar values here and throughout the book.

3. The original Portuguese reads as follows: "De fato, a ANCINAV representou a primeira tentativa sistêmica do governo de regulação do conteúdo e promoção da diversidade cultural nas comunicações" (107).

4. Ikeda notes that the preliminary draft resulted in an uneven increase in the CONDECINE surcharge and impacted all sectors of the industry (2015: 107). As it pertained to movie theaters, for example, the surcharge would depend on the total number of commercial copies. According to the norms already in place, the release of a foreign feature-length film in local theaters resulted in the collection of R$3,000. However, in line with the new values proposed by the ANCINAV draft, if this same feature was released with more than two hundred copies,

the amount to be collected would rise to R$600,000. Additionally, movie-goers would pay a 10 percent tax on the price of admission.

5. In December of 1991, after purchasing Canal+ from Matias Machline, the entrepreneur who introduced the channel to Brazil, the Abril Group prepared a five-channel pay-television package for potential São Paulo subscribers. Channels in the package included TVA Clássicos (films), TVA Esportes (ESPN), TVA Filmes (later Showtime), and TVA Notícias (CNN) (Possebon, 2009: 43).

6. With the objective of countering TVA's early moves, the Globo Group founded Globosat in 1991. The programmer focused on reaching Brazil's wealthiest socioeconomic groups. To this end, Globosat developed four channels: GNT (news), Multishow (entertainment), Telecine (films), and Top Sports (later SporTV).

7. The origins of Net Brasil lie in 1993, when the Marinho family purchased 30 percent of Multicanal, then owned by Antônio Dias Leite. By 1996, Multicanal had become the largest cable operator in Brazil, prompting the company to go public on the New York Stock Exchange in 1997. During that same year, perhaps due to a lingering discontent with Multicanal's interest in programming, Globo's bread and butter, the Marinho family purchased all of Leite's and Garantia's shares in Multicanal for $180 million each, making Globo the owner of 60 percent of the pay-television market share. In 2004, the Carlos Slim–owned Telemex purchased 49 percent of Net Serviços, the maximum permitted by the Cable TV Law for a foreign investor (Possebon, 2009: 60, 77, 121, 133–34). Following the passing of the Pay-TV Law, which allows for up to 100 percent of foreign investment in Pay-TV operators and also restricts operators from being programmers and vice versa, Globo sold nearly all of its shares in Net Serviços to Embratel, Net's parent company, which is owned by Carlos Slim.

8. Not unlike the deal between Globo and Telemex, in 2006, the Civitas sold 49 percent of their shares in TVA to the Spanish telecommunications giant, Telefónica. Under the name of Vivo in Brazil, Telefónica purchased the rest of TVA shares in 2012 (Possebon, 2009: 225).

9. For an expansive list of the many players involved in the early development of the Brazilian pay-television industry, see Possebon (2009), particularly chapters 3 and 6.

10. Recent reports have shown that because of the economic downturn in Brazil, the pay-television sector has lost slightly more than 260,000 subscribers over the twelve-month period between May of 2016 and May of 2017 (TV paga registra, 2017).

11. According to paragraphs XVIII and XIX of Article 2, a Brazilian production company must (a) be incorporated under Brazilian law; (b) have its headquarters and administration located in Brazil; (c) have 70 percent of its total capital and

voting rights under the ownership, either directly or indirectly, of native Brazilians or those individuals that have been naturalized for more than ten years; and (d) place the administration of the company and editorial responsibility over the content under the control of native Brazilians or those individuals that have been naturalized for more than ten years. In addition to each of the aforementioned, a Brazilian *independent* production company must not in any way control, be controlled by, or be affiliated with programmers, packers, distributors, or dealers of sound and image broadcasting services (Lei da TV, 2011).

12. Sousa shows that the total number of pay-television channels in Brazil rose from 177 in 2012 to 246 in 2016 (2018: 200). During that same period, the number of Brazilian channels increased from thirteen in 2012 to twenty-seven in 2016.

13. Of course, one might easily imagine the potential problems of such a setup. The centrality of the state in the decision-making process could, particularly under the watch of an ideologically charged administration, lead to arbitrary conclusions regarding what does and does not get funded. Indeed, at the time of this writing, President Bolsonaro has invoked the State's power in this process, threatening to take a more active role in ensuring that nonconservative conforming content does not get made (Bolsonaro volta, 2019).

14. Specifically, those attempts were in the form of Article 39 of Provisional Measure 2.228-1/01 and Article 3 A of the aforementioned Audiovisual Law. The former aims to benefit pay-television programmers, offering them the opportunity to invest a portion of taxes owed in independent productions. The latter offers the same investment opportunity to broadcast networks.

15. Sousa correctly notes that during the early, first phase of Law 12.485/11, those production companies that benefited from of the established quotas were primarily medium- or large-sized production companies located in Rio de Janeiro and São Paulo (2014: 10). Not surprisingly, Sousa points out that when one considers the country as a whole, the diversity in production and participants the Law sought to establish was, during the first few years of its rollout, still far from a reality.

16. Though writing in the late 1980s, Mattelart and Mattelart's description of Globo's vertical integration and the lack of production outside its structure describes well the field leading up to 2011. They say: "Unlike the United States networks, which have been forced by the federal legislation to separate the functions of production and distribution, Globo has combined them from the beginning. As one Brazilian independent producer remarked: 'For a long time, the idea of the U.S. government was to protect film studios that were crippled when commercial television appeared. Up until now, the film studios have fed the television channels. If we were to pass legislation of this type in Brazil, television channels would have to cease activity. For independent producers would

have neither the know-how nor the equipment to maintain quality production in sufficient quantity. . . . In the Brazilian case, one remarks, this is the opinion of independent producers—a clear lack of competence in the channels competing with Globo as soon as it is a question of doing anything different. They limit themselves to imitating Globo in what is inimitable, namely the production of *telenovelas*'" (Mattelart and Mattelart, 1990: 25).

Chapter 2. Pay-Television Welcomes Brazil

1. I am using the term "series" in the broadest sense to include situational comedies, serial comedies, and serial dramas. Importantly, unlike the open-ended and narratively dynamic *telenovelas*, series are constructed around seasons and are shot in their entirety prior to going to air. For the purposes of providing the necessary certifications to meet content quotas, ANCINE defines series as works produced in chapters or episodes and organized into a single season or multiple seasons.

2. With an updated cast, the sitcom returned to Globo for a fourteen-season run between 2001 and 2014.

3. As with *Grande família*, *Carga pesada* received a reboot in 2003. The series, which starred original cast members Antônio Fagundes and Stênio Garcia, produced another sixty-four episodes over five seasons, before finally ending in 2007.

4. Part of the *Fome Zero* (Zero Hunger) social welfare program, *Bolsa Família* is a cash transfer initiative designed to reduce short- and long-term poverty among Brazil's D and E Classes.

5. Regarding socioeconomic groups, Brazil employs a classification tool that places individuals into one of five classes: A, B, C, D, and E. With monthly incomes at or above R$8,641, the A and B Classes are made up of the country's highest earners. At the other end of the spectrum are the D and E Classes, which have monthly household incomes between R$0 and R$2,004. C Class households earn a monthly income between R$2,005 and R$8,640 (Qual a faixa de renda, 2014). As already mentioned, Escosteguy and Coutinho (2017) point out that nineteen million Brazilians moved from the highly impoverished D and E Classes to the working middle-class, also known as the C Class. Indeed, recent demographic research from the Brazilian Institute of Geography and Statistics (Instituto Brasileiro de Geografia e Estatística) estimates that the C Class makes up 52 percent of Brazil's population, approximately 105 million people. By comparison, the A and B Classes comprise approximately 28 percent of Brazil's total population, while the D and E Classes total 20 percent of the population.

Escosteguy and Coutinho argue that the growth of the C Class from 2003 to 2011 was "accompanied by a rise in the visibility of disadvantaged economic classes within the country's mediascape" (2017: 38). According to Escosteguy and Coutinho, TV Globo's portrayals of such classes in *telenovelas* and series was especially frequent during the first decade of the twenty first century. Series like *Cidade dos homens* (2002–2005), *Antonia* (2006–2007), *Ó pai ó* (2008–2009), and *Subúrbia* (2012) and *telenovelas* like *Duas caras* (2007–2008), *Fina estampa* (2011–2012), and *Avenida Brasil* (2012) all included characters from and plotlines related to the C Class. However, the authors (2017: 48, 49) make it clear that, in general terms, TV Globo's heterogeneous representations of this socioeconomic group, which largely flamed out after 2012, favored certain meanings, beliefs, and behaviors, enacting what Stuart Hall (1997) refers to as a process of regulation by culture and thereby masking social inequality.

6. The specific breakdown of the channels is as follows: eighty-two qualified space channels (CEQ); fifteen Brazilian qualified space channels (CABEQ); and four super Brazilian qualified space channels (CABEQ SB).

7. According to multiple media reports from 2018, the series has been picked up for a fourth season.

8. Information was not available for season one.

9. In 2001, Silveira directed the television documentary, *Mar sem fim* (*Endless Sea*). It was *2 filhos de Francisco*, however, that provided him national and international recognition. The film is based on the childhood and rise to fame of Brazilian singer Zezé Di Camargo who, following the death of his brother and bandmate, Emival, turns to his younger brother, Luciano, to form the immensely popular country duo Zezé Di Camargo and Luciano.

10. The films Silveira directed were *Era uma vez* (*Once Upon a Time*, 2008), *Gonzaga—de pai pra filho* (*Gonzaga—From Father to Son*, 2010), *À beira do caminho* (*On the Edge of the Road*, 2012), and *Entre irmãs* (*Between Sisters*, 2017).

11. Helder Aragão is also listed as a co-director and composer. Aragão, who is best known by his professional name, DJ Donovan, was an influential member of the *manguebeat* movement. He also did the soundtrack for *Lama dos dias*, producing all of Psicopasso's original songs.

12. Chico Science composed the music for *Baile perfumado*.

13. França, who plays Luli, is Chico Science's daughter.

14. For both of these reasons, Lacerda's series is similar to another singular work of Brazilian television: Luiz Fernando Carvalho's excellent TV Globo microseries, *A pedra do reino* (*The Stone Kingdom*, 2007).

15. I have argued elsewhere that some of Luiz Fernando Carvalho's work in television, namely *Hoje é dia de Maria* (*Today is Maria's Day*, 2005) and *Capitu* (2008), similarly reappropriates discarded objects and draws from and reinterprets a number of Brazilian and non-Brazilian artistic forms, mediums, and schools (Carter, 2018).

Chapter 3. The New Frontier: Internet Fiction

1. In July of 2018, numerous media outlets reported that Globo's pay-television channel Multishow ordered twenty episodes of the sitcom *Família nordestina* (*Northeastern Family*), which is set to star Nunes, GKAY (Paraíba), Tirulipa (Ceará), and Carlinhos Maia (Alagoas), all famous social media personalities from Northeastern Brazil.

In 2011, having already acquired Internet fame, Neto was hired by Globo's daily sports program *Esporte espetacular* to create and star in "Sem noção" (Without a Clue), a segment of brief sketches poking fun at the world of sports. Roughly a year later, Globo canceled the segment and did not renew Neto's contract. Around the time he signed on to do "Sem Noção," Neto made his debut as the host of *Até que faz sentido* (*Until it Makes Sense*), a thirty-minute program on Multishow that centered on Neto exploring things he did not understand through interviews with guests and encounters with random individuals on the streets of Rio de Janeiro. The pay-television channel canceled the program in 2012 after the airing of the thirteenth episode.

2. Neto's eponymous channel, which ranks third in Brazil in terms of total subscribers, currently has over thirty-three million along with nearly 7.5 billion views (Top 50, 2019).

3. The original Portuguese reads: Sou Nátaly Neri, mulher negra, feminista, apaixonada por brechó, costura, moda e faça você mesmo

4. The original Portuguese reads: "O ALEXANDRISMOS é um canal criado pela jornalista Alexandra Gurgel, que viveu por anos com complexos em relação ao seu corpo. Depois de uma busca incessante por autoconhecimento, a carioca deu play no YouTube com vídeos sobre body positive, amor-próprio, autoestima, cabelo, saúde mental e relacionamentos. Em todos os vídeos, Alexandra traz, com bom-humor e sem papas na língua, uma mensagem positiva em relação a ser quem você é, independentemente do seu formato de corpo, cor da pele, crença ou gênero. Afinal de contas, se amar, se aceitar e gostar de quem você é, é uma prerrogativa para viver em sociedade!"

5. According to data from 2017, Brazil has the fourth most Internet users at approximately 121 million. China is first with over 700 million and is followed by India (over 400 million) and the United States (over 300 million). With around 85 million Internet users, Mexico is second to Brazil in Latin America (Statista, 2017).

A 2018 study from Hootsuite found the average Brazilian, independent of connecting device, uses the Internet slightly over nine hours per day. According to the study, such usage places Brazil behind only Thailand and the Philippines (Estudo comprova, 2018).

6. For a breakdown of the classes, see chapter 2, note 5.

7. The original Portuguese reads: "Sabemos que no Brasil existe um grande público LGBTQ+ que deseja se ver representado fielmente. A cada episódio, as personagens costuram uma história que emociona, sem ser piegas, e trata o relacionamento entre duas mulheres de forma realista e natural. Também queremos que SEPTO possa contribuir de alguma forma com o avanço da discussão sobre visibilidade LGBTQ+, já que o Rio Grande do Norte figura como o terceiro estado mais perigoso do Brasil para homossexuais" (Dantas, 2016).

8. Based in Olinda, Pernambuco, Brasileiríssimos, which describes itself as the "o maior projeto de valorização da cultura brasileira" (the largest valorization project of Brazilian culture), was founded in December of 2012. Though it states it focuses on music, culture, cinema, and history, the project's website is heavily weighted to the dissemination of music from independent Brazilian musicians. Brasileiríssimos created its YouTube channel in August of 2014 and currently has 19,000 subscribers. In addition to *Septo*, the Brasileiríssimos YouTube channel, which has posted a total of fifty-one videos, has a series of interviews with Brazilian musicians and a number of music videos. Of all the channel's videos, *Septo*'s "Obrigação" has received the most views.

9. Those lyrics that can be heard in the scene are as follows: "Quando abre teus olhos, sou o sol. Quando abre esta boca, o universo . . ." (When you open your eyes, I am the sun. When you open your mouth, the universe).

10. In 2003, Alinne Moraes and Paula Picarelli's characters pecked on the lips in Manoel Carlos's telenovela *Mulheres apaixonadas*. However, because the kiss—not to mention the largely asexual nature of the couple's relationship on the whole—was not like that most common among heterosexual couples in *telenovelas*, it is not widely considered to be the first lesbian kiss on Brazilian television, even though it occurred nearly eight years before *Amor e revolução*.

11. As of this writing, the original videos posted by *serie3porcento* have accumulated 1,374,298 YouTube views.

12. The objective of the first and only edition of the FICTV (Fictional Television) competition was to foment the production of innovative independent television fiction directed at audiences comprised of young people from the least economically privileged socioeconomic classes. Among the 225 proposed projects, eight were awarded with approximately R$250,000 (roughly $78,000 US) to produce a twenty-six-minute pilot. At 6:30 PM, on April 6–16, 2011, TV Brasil aired each of the eight pilots. The channel encouraged audiences to vote for the three best pilots, which were to be turned into thirteen-episode series (FICTV).

13. Uploaded to YouTube by creator Felipe Reis in April of 2007, *Conversas de elevador* is considered to be the first Brazilian web series. By contrast, Scott Zakarin created what is widely considered to be the first U.S. web series, *The Spot* in 1995.

14. The majority of the actors listed here have appeared in TV Globo

productions in the past. Importantly, however, this does not prove that TV Globo's works are diverse. One must not forget that numerous studies, many of which are cited in this book, have shown that the network has historically over-emphasized upper-middle-class whiteness to the detriment of other races and socioeconomic groups. In the pre-2011 mediascape, then, employment options were largely restricted to the country's largest producer—TV Globo. Considering that there was documented underrepresentation in the network's *telenovelas*, the roles for people of color were limited. Thus, in an era of limited competition, it follows that actors of color competed for the relatively few roles available to them at TV Globo. Those who did not get the roles had few other options. The increased competition in the post-2011 mediascape expands the possibilities for more employment for more actors of color.

Chapter 4. Entering Television through the *Porta dos Fundos*

1. The two *telenovelas*, both directed by television auteur Luiz Fernando Carvalho, achieved average penetration rates of 60 percent and 51.1 percent, respectively (Sabbatino, 2013; *O Rei do Gado*, 1997).

2. The Sistema Brasileiro de Televisão (SBT) began operating in 1981, shortly after the Military Dictatorship suspended TV Tupi license (Mira, 1995). SBT is the primary asset of the Silvio Santos Group (Grupo Silvio Santos), which, as the group's name suggests, is controlled by Silvio Santos, the famous television presenter. With a programming grid heavy on imported content and variety shows, SBT frequently figures among Brazil's largest television networks, well behind TV Globo but in direct competition with Rede Record.

3. See note 7 from the Introduction.

4. Alongside the nightly national news, the jewel of TV Globo's programming grid is the *novela das nove* (nine o'clock *telenovela*). Though it was previously known as the *novela das oito* for having aired in the eight o'clock timeslot, I will use the *novela das nove* to refer to both the present and the pre-2011 period when it carried the former moniker. In general terms, the *novela das nove* features Brazil's most famous writers and stars in a relatively high-budget production that explores pressing social issues through a *melorealist* mode.

5. When discussing *telenovelas*, in Brazil it is common to refer to the individual airings of the genre as *capítulos* (chapters) and not episodes.

6. In Brazil, the agency that measures audience share is the Instituto Brasileiro de Opinião Pública e Estatística (IBOPE, Brazilian Institute of Public Opinion and Statistics). In 2014, following a sale to the Kantar Group, the company's name changed to Kantar IBOPE Media. According to the company's current metrics, one IBOPE point (*ponto*) is the equivalent to 71,855 households in the city of São Paulo. In terms of viewers in that same city, one point translates to an approximate total of 201,000 (assuming a conservative average of three

viewers per household). In Rio de Janeiro, Brazil's other major city, one point is the equivalent of 45,253 households, or roughly 118,000 viewers (Forato, 2017). The average numbers cited for *Renascer, O Rei do Gado, Laços de família,* and for each of those that follow are based on Brazil's two largest markets (São Paulo and Rio de Janeiro). While these two urban metropolises comprise a significant share of the overall television audience, and while media outlets often employ their respective shares as representing broader audience trends, they cannot be generalized to the country as whole.

7. The individual average audience share numbers for the thirty total *telenovelas* for the periods between 2000 and 2010 (15) and 2010 and 2019 (15) were collected from a diverse selection of Brazilian newspapers (e.g., *Folha de São Paulo, O Globo,* etc.) and websites dedicated to covering television (e.g., *TV foco, Tela viva, Na telinhana,* etc.). The consistency of the numbers across the publications suggests accuracy. However, because in most cases they do not come directly from IBOPE, I employ them not as exact or authoritative but as representative of broader, ongoing trends regarding declines in audience share.

Along with the years they aired, the fifteen *telenovelas* and their overall average audience shares for the period 2000–2010 are as follows: *Laços de família* (2000–2001, 45), *Porto dos Milagres* (2001, 45), *O clone* (2001–2002, 47), *Esperança* (2002–2003, 38), *Mulheres apaixonadas* (2003, 45), *Celebridade* (2003–2004, 46), *Senhora do destino* (2004–2005, 50), *América* (2005, 49), *Belíssima* (2005–2006, 48), *Páginas da vida* (2006–2007, 47), *Paraíso tropical* (2007, 43), *Duas caras* (2007–2008, 41), *A favorita* (2008–2009, 39), *Caminho das Índias* (2009, 39), and *Viver a vida* (2009–2010, 36).

8. Along with the years they aired, the fifteen *telenovelas* and their overall average audience shares for the period 2010–2019 are as follows: *Insensato coração* (2011, 36), *Fina estampa* (2011–2012, 38), *Avenida Brasil* (2012, 39), *Salve Jorge* (2012–2013, 34), *Amor à vida* (2013–2014, 35), *Em família* (2014, 30), *Império* (2014–2015, 33), *Babilônia* (2015, 25), *A regra do jogo* (2015–2016, 28), *Velho Chico* (2016, 29), *A lei do amor* (2016–2017, 27), *A força do querer* (2017, 36), *O outro lado do paraíso* (2017–2018, 39), *Segundo sol* (2018, 33), and *O sétimo guardião* (2018–2019, 29).

9. Though Netflix has famously described itself as a global television network and though it is indeed present in over 130 countries worldwide, Ramon Lobato (2019: 184) makes a convincing case that due to increased and varied regulatory pressures in different countries throughout the world, "in some senses it may now be more appropriate to see Netflix as a collection of *national media services* tied together in one platform rather than as a uniform global service" (emphasis in original).

10. The founding members of Porta dos Fundos were screenwriter and actor Antônio Tabet; director and producer Ian SBF; stand-up comedian, screenwriter,

actor, and television host Fábio Porchat; screenwriter and actor Gregório Duvivier; and publicist and actor João Vicente de Castro.

11. In addition to Endemol Brasil's percentage, Joá Investimentos controlled as much as 16 percent of Porta dos Fundos in 2017 (Jardim, 2017). Joá Investimentos is a Rio de Janeiro–based investment company that belongs to Luciano Huck, the host of *Caldeirão do Huck*.

12. Letícia Lima, who was married to Ian SBF, was one of Porta dos Fundos' main protagonists until 2015, when she signed a contract with TV Globo to appear in the João Emanuel Carneiro–penned *telenovela*, *A regra do jogo* (2015–2016).

13. The web series' first episode is the most watched video on the Fondo Filmes' channel with approximately 1.4 million views to date.

14. The original Portuguese reads: "Amanda, o meu marido me senta porrada toda vez que ele chega em casa bêbedo. O que você queria que eu fizesse; que viesse pro trabalho que nem a Cheetara das *Thundercats*, toda cheia de mancha pelo corpo?"

The question of the day, which appears in a speech balloon, reads: "Como faço pra evitar os roxos, os hematomas amarelos e as bolhas com sangue?" ("Amanda episódio 1").

15. As of this writing, the web series has accumulated nearly 3.7 million views.

16. *Viral* was the company's first foray into a full-fledged serial format. However, unlike *Refém*, *O Grande Gonzalez*, and *Borges*, all of which have been or currently are available on both the Internet and television, *Viral* is, at least to this point, exclusively available on YouTube. Starting on April 5, 2014, thirteen-minute episodes were released onto YouTube at 7 PM over four consecutive Saturdays. The web series revolves around Porta dos Fundos' cast members Fábio Porchat (Rafael) and Gregório Duvivier (Beto), who has recently learned that he is carrying the AIDS virus. Beto decides that it is his obligation to inform his past partners of this news. The web series, then, follows Beto and his best friend Rafael as they move through Rio de Janeiro with the objective of confronting Beto's past partners and asking them to take a test. At the time of writing, each of *Viral*'s four episodes on average had approximately 3.7 million views.

17. *Porta afora* is hosted by Fábio Porchat and Rosana Hermann, author, screenwriter, and television personality. In addition to its weekly YouTube releases every Tuesday at 7 PM, the informal travel show airs every Saturday at 9:50 PM on Multishow, one of the Globo Group's channels from its pay-television programming division, Globosat.

18. In 2011, Fondo Filmes released the SBF-directed *Teste de elenco* (*Casting Call*). The film stars Porchat as a director who is conducting a casting call for the female lead in his upcoming film. Released exclusively on the Anões em chamas

website, the Fondo Filmes production was the first feature-length Brazilian film made specifically for Internet distribution. Following the 2015 release of the dramatic feature, *Entre abelhas* (*Between Bees*), which was directed by SBF and starred Porchat, both of whom also wrote the screenplay, Porta dos Fundos premiered its first feature-length film, *Porta dos Fundos: Contrato vitalício*. Also directed by SBF and written by Porchat, the film centers on the disastrous relationship between Rodrigo, a budding actor played by Porchat, and Miguel, an upstart filmmaker played by Duvivier. After the two win the main prize at an esteemed international film festival, an inebriated Rodrigo signs a contract to be in Miguel's next film. Miguel then disappears for ten years, only to return to enact their contract when Rodrigo is at the height of his fame. Rodrigo, aware that appearing in Miguel's incomprehensible film may lead to the end of his career, believes he has no choice but to honor what has now seemingly become a "lifetime contract." The film was released to mixed reviews. In box-office terms, it did not fare much better, selling slightly less than 450 thousand tickets during its three-week run.

19. Performed by Gregorio Duvivier, João Vicente de Castro, Luis Lobianco, Gustavo Miranda, and in later iterations, Andres Giraldo, *Portátil* is a long-form take on improv comedy, popular in the United States. Based on an interview with an audience member, who answers a series of questions about his or her family, work, and dreams, the actors construct an immediate reconstitution of the interviewee's life. The play is directed by Barbara Duvivier, Gregório Duvivier's sister.

20. At the time of writing, the web series has accumulated an approximate average of 2.7 million YouTube views per episode.

21. Those individuals born in Rio de Janeiro.

22. To date, the video has accumulated more than seven million views. At the time of this writing, the case had not yet been decided.

Chapter 5. Blackness in the Post-2011 Mediascape

1. According to data from Brazil's most recent census from 2010, approximately ninety million of the country's total population of about 177 million self-declared as being black or brown. In his analysis of the consistency rates of racial self-reporting by Brazilians, Edward Telles argues that respondents and interviewers are "more able to agree on who is white than who is brown or black, which demonstrates that the white-non-white distinction is the most conceptually clear racial divide in the minds of Brazilians" (2004: 90). This lends support for collapsing "the brown and black categories into a single category," that of color, represented here as 50.8 percent of the total population.

2. When it first aired in 2005, "Somewhere in the Future" was supposed to be the series' finale. In 2017, however, the *Cidade dos homens* returned to TV

Globo for a four-episode run. Though the series was picked up for another four episodes in 2018, in 2019, TV Globo did not renew it for another season.

3. The first *telenovela* to feature a middle-class Afro-Brazilian (a secretary played by Léa Garcia) was the TV Globo–produced and Janete Clair–penned *Selva de pedra* (1973) (Araújo, 2000: 118).

4. Overall, the *Cidade dos homens* series had an approximate average viewership of 1.7 million households in the greater São Paulo area, which, for that time, was fair to middling (Bartolomei, 2005).

5. *Mister Brau* replaced the TV Globo sitcom *Tapas e beijos* (2011–2015). According to the *Folha de São Paulo* (2016), *Mister Brau*'s first season achieved an average audience share of 1.3 million homes in the greater São Paulo metropolitan area—the same audience share, according to the Brazilian Institute of Public Opinion and Statistics (IBOPE), as its predecessor.

6. *Mister Brau* received international attention for featuring an Afro-Brazilian couple. For example, writing for the "Shadow and Act: On Cinema of the African Diaspora," a subsection of the US website *Indie Wire*, Kiratiana Freelon (2015) published an article titled "Groundbreaking New Series—'Mister Brau'—Gives Afro-Brazilians Representations to Cheer Despite Flaws." Additionally, reporting from Rio de Janeiro, Bruce Douglas (2015) of the *Guardian* wrote an article titled, "Brazilian Television Slowly Confronts Country's Deeply Entrenched Race Issues." In addition to their own write-ups on the serial comedy, Brazilian media outlets such as *Globo*, *IG*, *Veja*, *Folha de São Paulo*, and the blog *Black Women of Brazil* reported on the attention the show received from the British publication.

7. Caldeira contends that the perpetuation of stories of crime and violence "serves to reinforce people's feelings of danger, insecurity, and turmoil" (2000: 19). Consequently, "the talk of crime," as she refers to it, "feeds a circle in which fear is both dealt with and reproduced, and violence is both counteracted and magnified."

8. In addition to showing how the scholarly work on race in Brazil transitioned from the idea of Brazil as a racial democracy to Brazil as racist, Telles argues that recent data suggest "young persons are socialized to identify increasingly in black and white categories" (2004: 33–46, 101). Thus, whereas an ideology of racial democracy "uses ambiguity and middle categories to avoid the placement of others in particularly stigmatized categories," the emergence of the black movement in Brazil has given rise to support for a system "that excludes the middle categories increase, forcing the vast majority of Brazilians (Asians and Indians excepted) to identify as either black or white" (105). While, as Telles correctly documents, by the 1950s Brazilian academia, in large part, had moved beyond the idea of a racial democracy, Smith notes that the broader Brazilian "society continues to hold on religiously to the ideology of racial democracy" (2016: 6).

9. On YouTube the three videos and series have accumulated more than thirty million views. During its Fox Brasil-run, *O Grande Gonzalez* achieved an audience share similar to that of *Mister Brau*.

10. While some will argue that *preto* does not carry the same negative connotation in the Brazilian context as the word *nigger* does in the US context, there can be no argument that when the word is used to refer to one's skin color it becomes a pejorative term. As such, like the term "nigger," *preto* is to be avoided when referring to people of color.

11. The original Portuguese reads: "Todos sabemos que o Brasil é uma democracia racial. É só olhar pelas suas câmeras de vigilância, do alto dos seus muros ou pelas grades do condomínio que veremos que todas as pessoas se dão bem e são felizes. Como é que pode haver racismo se a favela é tão perto do asfalto? O negro no Brasil tem tantos direitos quanto outra pessoa qualquer. Contanto que ele se coloque no lugar que os outros destinaram pra ele. Sair disso é só querer tumultuar o que já vem dando certo . . ." (SBF, 2015b).

12. The original Portuguese reads: "A pessoa merece solidariedade e um tratamento diferencial. O indivíduo, ao contrário, é o sujeito da lei, foco abstrato para quem as regras e a repressão foram feitas . . . Em termos da dialética do indivíduo e da pessoa, temos um universo formado de um pequeno numero de pessoas, hierarquizado, comandando a vida e o destino de uma multidão de indivíduos, esses que devem obedecer à lei (218, 231).

Chapter 6. Globo *Plays* Series

1. By the end of 2018, Netflix Brasil had a total of five original series: *3%, O mecanismo, Samantha!, Super Drags,* and *Vai Anitta*. Before 2019 even began, Netflix Brasil had already announced plans to release seven more Brazilian original series: *A facção (The Faction), Cidades invisíveis (Invisible Cities), Coisa mais linda (The Most Beautiful Thing), Ninguém está olhando (Nobody's Looking), O escolhido (The Chosen One), Sintonia,* and *Spectros*.

2. The year with most subscribers was in 2014 when the sector reached 19.6 million households.

3. *The Good Doctor* is an ABC medical drama about surgery resident Dr. Shaun Murphy and the ways in which he uniquely uses his autism and savant syndrome to save the lives of his patients. The series is based on a homonymous South Korean series from 2013. Over its two seasons, *The Good Doctor* has been a ratings success in the United States.

4. For example, at the time of this writing, Cynthia Littleton of *Variety* reported that Disney planned to invest over $16 billion in 2019 in content for its forthcoming streaming service, outpacing Warner and Netflix, both with targets of slightly over $14 billion (2019).

5. In addition to *Supermax* and *Assédio* and a number of other series, Globo

has produced such Globo Play originals as *Além da Ilha* (*Beyond the Island*, 2018–) and *Ilha de Ferro* (*Iron Island*, 2018–).

6. Though frequently employed when discussing series from the United States, as far as I am aware, *Supermax* represents the first time the Brazilian media refers to the creators of a domestic series as "showrunners."

7. Draccon, whose real name is Raphael Albuquerque Pereira, has sold over 250,000 copies of his trilogy, *Dragões de éter* (*Dragons of Ether*, 2007–2010). Though not nearly as successful, Montes's police novels, *Suicidas* (*Suicides*, 2012), *Dias perfeitos* (*Perfect Days*, 2014), and *Jantar secreto* (*Secret Dinner*, 2016), have done quite well in commercial terms, reaching over fifty thousand sales in Brazil alone.

8. Kotscho and Mantovani, who are married to each other, have also worked in television, albeit to a lesser extent. In the early 2000s, after the release of *Cidade de Deus*, Mantovani wrote some of the episodes for the O2 Filmes/Globo co-production, *Cidade dos homens*. Some years later, Kotscho and Mantovani teamed up to write ten episodes for *A teia* (*The Web*, 2014*)*, a TV Globo–produced crime drama starring José Miguel.

9. Marins is the pioneer of the horror genre in Brazil. In the 1960s, he directed, wrote, and starred in *À meia-noite levarei sua alma* (*At Midnight I Will Take Your Soul*, 1963) and *Esta noite encarnarei no teu cadáver* (*This Night I Will Possess Your Corpse*, 1967). Over forty years later, *Encarnação do demônio* became the final installment of Marins's horror trilogy. Famously, each of the three films feature the cult figure Zé do Caixão, played by Marins.

10. In addition to a number of shorts, Rojas and Dutra have collaborated on the following feature-length films: *As boas maneiras* (2017), *Sinfonia da necrópole* (2014), *O duplo* (2012), and *Trabalhar cansa* (2011).

11. Debuting in 2002, *Big Brother Brasil* is currently in its nineteenth edition.

12. A Globo reporter, Bial became especially known for hosting *Big Brother Brasil* from 2002 to 2016.

13. More recent reports indicate that, due to a lack of adequate or desired programming for the 11 PM time slot, *Assédio* could air on Globo sometime in 2019 (Castro, 2018).

14. In Brazil, *Assédio* was largely hailed by critics. The series also received recognition abroad. At the 2019 National Association of Television Program Executives (NATPE) in Miami, Globo sold the series to Mega, Chile's most successful broadcast network in terms of audience share. Moreover, the lone long-form serial from Latin America to be selected, *Assédio* was tabbed by the Berlin Festival to participate in its distinguished Drama Series Days.

15. In 2018, the Associação Paulista de Críticos de Arte (The São Paulo Art Critics Association, APCA) recognized Mautner's work on *Assédio* with the award for best director of a drama.

16. It is worth noting that the TV Globo *telenovela Mulheres apaixonadas* (*Women in Love*, 2003) also explicitly dealt with domestic abuse by featuring real Brazilian women sharing their own experiences of domestic violence. The major difference between the *telenovela* and *Assédio* is qualitative. Whereas *Mulheres apaixonadas*, like virtually every other *telenovela*, overly emphasizes expository dialogue to the detriment of the audiovisual construction, *Assédio* inverts that practice. Additionally, whereas the *telenovela* lacks contextualization and more precise critique of the hegemonic structures that permit such behavior, *Assédio* goes after those very structures, making it clear that Dr. Sadala's crimes are not reducible to a deranged individual.

17. The *Central de atendimento à mulher em situação de violência* began operating in late 2006 when the Lei da Maria da Penha was passed, making domestic violence against women a crime in Brazil.

References

1 contra todos (2016–). TV series. Dir. Breno Silveira. Fox Brasil.

3% (2016–). Web series. Writ. Pedro Aguileira. Netflix.

Adorno, T.W. (2001). *The Culture Industry: Selected Essays on Mass Culture*. New York: Routledge.

Aguilera, P. (2011). Série *3 por cento* piloto ep. 1. YouTube. www.youtube.com/watch?v=R_rvS7nX7pM&index=20&list=PLbqhalCwkiNWbeAQCRrbBvNo0ATKNl-Nn

Alves da Silva, L.M.R., et al. (2018). *Informe de mercado: TV paga 2017* (01 de janeiro a 31 de dezembro). www.oca.ancine.gov.br/sites/default/files/repositorio/pdf/informe_tv_paga_2017.pdf

Anderson, B. (2006). *Imagined Communities: Reflections on the Origin and Spread of Nationalism*. New York: Verso Books.

Aposta da Globo dá certo: Tela Quente tem maior ibope em 6 anos com série (2018). *Notícias da TV* www.noticiasdatv.uol.com.br/noticia/audiencias/aposta-da-globo-da-certo-tela-quente-tem-maior-ibope-em-6-anos-com-the-good-doctor-22063?cpid=txt

Appadurai, A. (1996). *Modernity at Large: Cultural Dimensions of Globalization*. Minneapolis: University of Minnesota Press.

Araújo, J.Z. (2000). *A negação do Brasil: o negro na telenovela brasileira*. São Paulo: Senac.

Araújo, J.Z. (2008). O negro na dramaturgia, um caso exemplar da decadência do mito da democracia racial brasileira. *Estudos Feministas* 16(3): 979–85.

Assédio (2018). Series. Dir. Amora Mautner. Globo Play.

Autran, A., and Fernandes, M.R. (2017). A ANCINAV e os conflitos no meio cinematográfico. *Cotracampo* 36(2): n.p.

Bahia, L. (2008). Cinema e identidade cultural: O debate contemporâneo sobre as políticas publicas do audiovisual no Brasil. In E. Hamburger et al. (eds.), *Estudos de Cinema—Socine, IX*, 367–76. São Paulo: Annablume; Fapesp; Socine.

Bakhtin, M., and Medvedev, P.N. (1991). *The Formal Method in Literary Scholarship: A Critical Introduction to Sociological Poetics*. Baltimore: Johns Hopkins University Press.

Bartolomei, M. (2005). Cidade de Deus deixa herança desigual. *Folha de São Paulo*. www1.folha.uol.com.br/fsp/ilustrad/fq0805200511.htm

Base de usuários da Netflix no Brasil dobra em um ano: empresa planeja ex pansão (2017). *Canal Tech*. www.canaltech.com.br/entretenimento/base-de-usuarios-da-netflix-no-brasil-dobra-em-um-ano-empresa-planeja-ex pansao-89080

Bauman, Z. (2004). *Wasted Lives: Modernity and Its Outcasts*. Cambridge: Polity.

Bentes, I. (2005). The Aesthetics of Violence in Brazilian Film. In E.R.P. Vieira (ed.), *City of God in Several Voices: Brazilian Social Cinema as Action*, 82–92. Nottingham: Critical, Cultural and Communications Press.

Bentes, I. (2007). Sertões e favelas no cinema brasileiro contemporâneo. In I. Bentes (ed.), *Ecos do cinema—de Lumière ao digital*, 191–224. Rio de Janeiro: Editora da UFRJ.

Bernardet, J.C. (2008). *Historiografia clássica do cinema brasileiro*. 2a edição. São Paulo: Annablume.

Billig, M. (2005). *Laughter and Ridicule: Towards a Social Critique of Humour*. London: Sage Publications.

Bolaño, C., and Brittos V.C. (2005). *Rede Globo: 40 anos de poder e hegemonia*. São Paulo: Paulus.

Bolsonaro volta a atacar Ancine: 'Poder público não faz filme' (2019). *Veja*. www.veja.abril.com.br/entretenimento/bolsonaro-vou-buscar-extinguir-a-ancine-poder-publico-nao-faz-filme

Borelli, S.H.S., and Priolli, G. (2000). *A deusa ferida: Por que a Rede Globo não é mais a campeã absoluta de audiência*. São Paulo: Summus Editorial.

Bourdieu, P. (1993). *The Field of Cultural Production*. Edited by R. Johnson. New York: Columbia University Press.

Branco, F.C. (2003). Conheça os sucessos e fracassos das telenovelas da Globo. *Terra*. www.terra.com.br/exclusivo/noticias/2003/04/16/002.htm

Brasil 247 (2017). Dilma: Globo tem sido arma contra nossa democracia. www.brasil247.com/pt/247/brasil/291041/Dilma-Globo-tem-sido-arma-contra-nossa-democracia.htm

Brazil, Observatório Brasileiro do Cinema e do Audiovisual—Agência Nacional do Cinema (2016). Bilheterias—2002 a 2015. www.oca.ancine.gov.br/sites/default/files/cinema/pdf/2101.pdf

Brazil, Agência Nacional do Cinema, Observatório Brasileiro do Cinema e do Audiovisual (2016). CONDECINE—Valores arrecadados—2006–2015.

www.oca.ancine.gov.br/sites/default/files/recursos_publicos/pdf/2901_1.pdf

Brazil, Agência Nacional do Cinema (n.d.). Mecanismos de fomento. www.cartadeservicos.ancine.gov.br/?pg=fomento

Brazil, Agência Nacional do Cinema (2016). Valores investidos em cada linha de ação. www.fsa.ancine.gov.br/?q=resultados/investimentos/valores-investidos

Breno Silveira estreia na TV pela FOX, com a série 'Um Contra Todos' (2016). *Isto É*. www.istoe.com.br/breno-silveira-estreia-na-tv-pela-fox-com-a-serie-um-contra-todos

Brittos, V.C., and Simões, D.G. (2010). A reconfiguração do mercado de televisão pré-digitilização. In A.P.G. Ribeiro, I. Sacramento, and M. Roxo (eds.), *História da televisão no Brasil: Do início aos dias de hoje*, 219–38. São Paulo: Contexto.

Burgoyne, R. (2010). *Film Nation: Hollywood Looks at U.S. History*. Minneapolis: University of Minnesota Press.

Butcher, P. (2006). *A dona da história: origens da Globo Filmes e seu impacto no audiovisual brasileiro*. Unpublished doctoral dissertation, Universidade Federal do Rio de Janeiro, Rio de Janeiro.

Cajueiro, M. (2017). Viacom International Media Networks Buys Majority Stake in Brazil's Porta dos Fundo [sic]. *Variety*. www.variety.com/2017/tv/festivals/viacom-buys-majority-stake-porta-dos-fundos-1202390624

Caldeira, T.P.R. (2000). *City of Walls: Crime, Segregation, and Citizenship in São Paulo*. Berkeley: University of California Press.

Campos, L.A., Candido, M.R., and Feres, J. Jr. (2014). A raça e o gênero nas novelas dos últimos 20 anos. *Grupo de Estudos Multidisciplinares da Ação Afirmativa*. www.gemaa.iesp.uerj.br/publicacoes/infografico/infografico3.html

Candido, A. (1970). Dialética da malandragem. *Revista do Instituto de Estudos Brasileiros* 8: 67–89.

Cannito, N.G. (2010). *A televisão na era digital: Interatividade, convergência e novos modelos de negócio*. São Paulo: Summus.

Caparelli, S. (1982). *Televisão e capitalismo no Brasil: Com dados da pesquisa da ABEPEC*. Porto Alegre: L&PM Editores.

Capoano, E. (2016). Globo Play: comodidade e mobilidade como novos conceitos de valor para maior TV do Brasil. *ComuniCon: Congresso Internacional de Comunicação e Consumo* October 14–15, 1–13.

Carpanez, J. (2006). Kibe Loco vira TV, apimenta *Caldeirão* e engorda ibope. *Folha de São Paulo*. www1.folha.uol.com.br/folha/ilustrada/ult90u59533.shtml

Carter, E. (2018). *Reimagining Brazilian Television: Luiz Fernando Carvalho's Contemporary Vision*. Pittsburgh, PA: University of Pittsburgh Press.

Carvalho, B. (2015). Crítica: O grandioso acerto de *O Grande Gonzalez*. *Ligado em Série*, www.ligadoemserie. com.br/2015/10/critica-o-grandioso-acerto-de-o-grande-gonzalez

Carvalho, J.M.D. (2000). The Edenic Motif in the Brazilian Social Imaginary. *Revista Brasileira de Ciências Sociais* (SPE1), 111–28.

Carvalho, M.S.R.M. (2006). A trajetória da Internet no Brasil: do surgimento das redes de computadores à instituição dos mecanismos de governança. Unpublished doctoral dissertation, Universidade Federal do Rio de Janeiro, Rio de Janeiro.

Castro, D. (2018). Globo cancela novela das onze e exibe série sobre médico estuprador. *Notícias da TV.* www.noticiasdatv.uol.com.br/noticia/novelas/globo-cancela-novela-das-onze-exibe-serie-sobre-medico-estuprador-23641

Castro, Rocha J. (2005). The "Dialectic of Marginality": Preliminary Notes on Brazilian Contemporary Culture. *Centre for Brazilian Studies, University of Oxford, Working Paper.* 62: 1–39.

Cesnik, F., and Juca, R. (2014). Brasil. In S. Solot (ed.), *Current Mechanisms for Financing Audiovisual Content in Latin America 2*, 39–48. Rio de Janeiro: Latin American Training Center.

Christian, A.J. (2012). The Web as Television Reimagined? Online Networks and the Pursuit of Legacy Media. *Journal of Communication Inquiry* 36(4): 340–56.

Christian, A.J. (2018). *Open TV: Innovation beyond Hollywood and the Rise of Web Television*. New York: NYU Press.

Com paródia de série da Netflix, vídeo define o 'Sistema' que aprisiona Lula (2019). *Rede Brasil Atual*. www.redebrasilatual.com.br/politica/2019/04/com-parodia-de-serie-da-netflix-video-define-o-sistema-que-aprisiona-lula

Crook, L., and Johnson, R. (1999). Introduction. In L. Crook and R. Johnson, *Black Brazil: Culture, Identity, and Social Mobilization*, 1–13. Los Angeles: UCLA Latin American Center Publications.

Dados do Setor (2018). Associação Brasileira de Televisão por Assinatura. www.abta.org.br/dados_do_setor.asp

DaMatta, R. (1979). *Carnavais, malandros e heróis: para uma sociologia do dilema brasileiro*. Rio de Janeiro: Rocco.

Dantas, R. (2018). Televisão perdeu relevância na campanha eleitoral, constatam marqueteiros. *Uol.* www.noticiasdatv.uol.com.br/noticia/televisao/televisao-perdeu-relevancia-na-campanha-eleitoral-dizem-marqueteiros—22635

Dantas, J.B.D., and Rodrigues, G. (2016). A configuração contemporânea da economia criativa do audiovisual no contexto brasileiro. *Chasqui. Revista Latinoamericana de Comunicación* 132: 183–203.

Dantas, P. (2016). Septo. *Catarse*. www.catarse.me/septowbs#about

Debate Collor X Lula (n.d.). Memória Globo. www.memoriaglobo.globo.com/erros/debate-collor-x-lula.htm

Deodoro, J., and Padiglione, C. (2012). Com maior audiência da TV no ano, final de 'Avenida Brasil' para a cidade. *Estadão*. www.brasil.estadao.com.br/noticias/geral,com-maior-audiencia-da-tv-no-ano-final-de-avenida-brasil-para-a-cidade,948144

Denninson, S., and Shaw, L. (2007). *Brazilian National Cinema*. London and New York: Routledge.

Douglas, B. (2015). Brazilian Television Slowly Confronts Country's Deeply Entrenched Race Issues. *The Guardian*. www.theguardian.com/world/2015/oct/07/brazil-television-mister-brau-black-couple-race-issues

Eakin, M.C. (2017). *Becoming Brazilians: Race and National Identity in Twentieth-century Brazil*. Cambridge: Cambridge University Press.

Em algum lugar do futuro (2006). *City of Men: The Complete Series*. DVD. Writ. G. Arraes, J. Furtado, F. Meirelles, and G. Moura. Dir. F. Meirelles. Palm Pictures, O2 Filmes, and Globo Video.

Entrevista com Daina Giannecchini, uma das diretoras da série de ficção brasileira *3%* (2011). *Nerd Maldito*. www.nerdmaldito.com/2011/06/entrevista-com-daina-giannecchini-uma.html

Entrevista com a diretora da série 3% (Interview with the director of 3%). (2016). *Esquerda Diário*. www.esquerdadiario.com.br/Entrevista-com-a-diretora-da-serie-3

Escosteguy, A.C., and Coutinho, L.L. (2017). The Rise of the Working Poor within the Brazlian Mediascape: The Mythology of Social Inequality. *Studies in Media and Communications* 13: 37–51.

Estreia de *O Grande Gonzalez* deixa a FOX em segundo lugar na TV Paga (2015). *Revista da TV*. www.revistadatv.com/2015/11/10/estreia-de-o-grande-gonzalez-deixa-a-fox-em-segundo-lugar-na-tv-paga

Estudo comprova que Brasil é o terceiro país que passa mais tempo na internet (2018). *Tudocelular*. www.tudocelular.com/mercado/noticias/n119125/brasil-internet.html

Evolução do número de acessos no tempo (2018). *ANATEL*. www.anatel.gov.br/dados/acessos-telefonia-movel

Ex-presidente Lula afirma que processará a Netflix (2018). *Correiro Braziliense*. www.correiobraziliense.com.br/app/noticia/diversao-e arte/2018/03/30/interna_diversao_arte,669773/lula-netflix.shtml

Falcheti, F. (2018). Exibição especial de 'Assédio' tem mais audiência que séries da faixa *Natelinha*. www.natelinha.uol.com.br/televisao/2018/10/16/exibicao-especial-de-assedio-tem-mais-audiencia-que-series-da-faixa-i-120901.php

Fechine, Y. (2007). O Núcleo Guel Arraes e sua 'pedagogia dos meios.' *E-Compós, São Paulo* 8: 1–22.

Feltrin, R. (2018). No Brasil, Netflix fatura R$ 1.4 bi, tem 50 funcionários e nenhum chefe. *Uol*. www.tvefamosos.uol.com.br/noticias/ooops/2018/12/26/no-brasil-netflix-fatura-r-14-bi-tem-50-funcionarios-e-nenhum-chefe.htm

Fernando, J. (2013). Diretor de *Amores Roubados* fala sobre sertão reformulado: Produção quer brigar com grandes produções da TV paga. *Estadão de São Paulo*. www.cultura.estadao.com.br/noticias/televisao,diretor-de-amores-roubados-fala-sobre-sertao-reformulado,1101896

FICTV (2017). *Ministério da Cultura*. www.cultura.gov.br/programas8/-/asset_publisher/QTN9rjJEc1bg/content/fictv-307785/10889

Flaksman, A. et al. (2012). *Informe de acompanhamento do mercado: TV paga monitoramento da programação 2011.* www.oca.ancine.gov.br/sites/default/files/repositorio/pdf/Informe_TVPaga_2011.pdf

Forato, T. (2017). Kantar Ibope atualiza representatividade de 1 ponto de audiência. *Natelinha*. www.natelinha.uol.com.br/noticias/2017/12/31/kantar-ibope-atualiza-representatividade-de-1-ponto-de-audiencia-113176.php

Freelon, K. (2015). Groundbreaking New Series—"Mister Brau"—Gives Afro-Brazilians Representations to Cheer Despite Flaws. *Indie Wire*. www.blogs.indiewire.com/shadowandact/groundbreaking-new-series-mister-brau-gives-afro-brazilians-representation-to-cheer-despite-flaws-20151007

Freyre, G. (1946). *The Masters and the Slaves: A Study in the Development of Brazilian Civilization*. New York: Knopf.

Furtado, R. (2018). Rio2C 2018: Produtor de *1 contra todos* confirma quarta temporada e adaptação mexicana (Entrevista Exclusiva). *Adoro Cinema*. www.adorocinema.com/noticias/series/noticia-139192

Geraldes, E.C., and Caribé, P.A. (2016). A seletividade do audiovisual brasileiro e, ou, independente na Lei da TV paga. *Revista Comunicação Midiática* 10(2): 109–25.

Globo quer emplacar série 'Assédio' na TV e exibe primeiro episódio sem cortes na segunda (2018). *Folha de São Paulo*. www.f5.folha.uol.com.br/televisao/2018/10/globo-exibira-primeiro-capitulo-da-serie-assedio-na-segunda.shtml

Globo inova, compartilha ideias e conteúdo no NATPE 2019 (2019). *Rede Globo* January 23. www.redeglobo.globo.com/novidades/noticia/globo-inova-compartilha-ideias-e-conteudo-no-natpe-2019.ghtml

Goes, T. (2018). Sem muito alarde, a Globoplay se prepara para enfrentar a Netflix. *Folha de São Paulo*. www.f5.folha.uol.com.br/colunistas/tony-goes/2018/08/sem-muito-alarde-a-globoplay-se-prepara-para-enfrentar-a-netflix.shtml

Gray, H. (1995). *Watching Race: Television and the Struggle for "Blackness."* Minneapolis: University of Minnesota Press.

Grijó, W.P., and Sousa, A.H.F. (2012). O negro na telenovela brasileira: A atualidade das representações. *Estudos em Comunicação* 11: 185–204.

Grossberg, L. (2006). Does Cultural Studies Have Futures? Should it? (Or What's the Matter with New York?) *Cultural Studies*, 20(1): 1–32.

Grossberg, L. (2010). *Cultural Studies in the Future Tense*. Durham, NC: Duke University Press.

Guaraldo, L. (2018). Globoplay terá 100 séries internacionais em seu catálogo até o fim de 2019. *Notícias da TV*. www.noticiasdatv.uol.com.br/noticia/mercado/globoplay-tera-100-series-internacionais-em-seu-catalogo-ate-o-fim-de-2019—23637

Hall, S. (1993). What is this "black" in black popular culture? *Social Justice* 20.1/2(51–52): 104–14.

Hamburger, E. (2000). Politics and Intimacy: The Agrarian Reform in a Brazilian Telenovela. *Television & New Media* 1(2): 159–78.

Hamburger, E. (2005). *O Brasil antenado: A sociedade da novela*. Rio de Janeiro: Jorge Zahar Editor.

Heise, T.S. (2012). *Remaking Brazil: Contested National Identities in Contemporary Brazilian Cinema*. Cardiff: University of Wales Press.

Hopewell, J. (2016). Brazilian Giant Globo Reveals First Results, Strategies of New VOD Service Globo Play. *Variety*. www.variety.com/2016/tv/global/globo-vod-globo-play-1201712749

Hunt, D.M. (2005). *Channeling Blackness: Studies on Television and Race in America*. New York: Oxford University Press.

Ikeda, M. (2015). *Cinema brasileiro a partir da retomada*. São Paulo: Summus.

Jardim, L. (2017). Venda do Porta dos Fundos rende R$ 8 milhões a cada um dos sócios. *O Globo*. www.blogs.oglobo.globo.com/lauro-jardim/post/venda-do-porta-dos-fundos-rende-r-8-milhoes-cada-um-dos-socios.html

Johnson, R. (1987). *The Film Industry in Brazil*. Pittsburgh, PA: University of Pittsburgh Press.

Johnson, R. (2005). TV Globo, the MPA, and Contemporary Brazilian Cinema. In L. Shaw and S. Dennison (eds.), *Latin American Cinema: Essays on Modernity, Gender and National Identity*, 11–38. Jefferson, NC: McFarland.

Johnson, R. (2007). The Brazilian Retomada and Global Hollywood. In G. Lillo and W. Moser (eds.). *History and Society: Argentinian and Brazilian Cinema Since the 1980s*, 87–100. Ottawa: Legas Publishing.

Johnson, R. (2017). Television and the Transformation of the Star System in Brazil. In M. Delgado, R. Johnson, and S. Hart (eds.), *A Companion to Latin American Cinema*, 21–35. Malden, MA: John Wiley & Sons.

Joyce, N.S. (2012). *Brazilian Telenovelas and the Myth of Racial Democracy*. Lanham, MD: Lexington Books.

Kehl, M.R. et al. (1986). *Um país no ar: história da TV brasileira em 3 canais*. São Paulo: Brasiliense/FUNARTE.

Kibe Loco desconstrói talk show no canal TBS (2015). *Estadão Conteúdo São Paulo*. www.portal.tododia.uol.com.br/_conteudo/2015/04/cultura_e_entretenimento/71268-kibe-loco-desconstroi-talk-show-no-canal-tbs.php

La Pastina, A.C., Straubhaar, J.D., and Sifuentes, L. (2014). Why Do I Feel I Don't Belong to the Brazil on TV? *Popular Communication* 12(2): 104–16.

Lama dos dias (2018). TV series. Dir. Hilton Lacerda. Canal Brasil.

Laporta, T. (2016). Mercado audiovisual cresce com Lei da TV Paga e recursos públicos. *G1*. www.g1.globo.com/economia/midia-e-marketing/noticia/2016/11/mercado-audiovisual-cresce-com-lei-da-tv-paga-e-recursos-publicos.html

Leichtman Research Group (2018). About 580,000 Added Broadband in 3Q 2018. www.leichtmanresearch.com/about-580000-added-broadband-in-3q-2018

Lei do Audiovisual, 8.685, Presidência da República Casa Civil, 1993.

Lei do Cabo 8.997, Presidência da República Casa Civil, 1995.

Lei da TV Paga, 12.485, Presidência da República Casa Civil, 2011.

Levin, T. (2012). Spoleto tira proveito de viral irônico. *Meio e Mensagem*. www.meioemensagem.com.br/home/marketing/2012/08/30/spoleto-tira-proveito-de-viral-ironico.html

Lima, H.S. (2015). *A lei da TV paga: impactos no mercado audiovisual*. Unpublished master's thesis, Universidade de São Paulo, São Paulo.

Lista de CPBs 2012–2017 (2018). Agência Nacional do Cinema, Demanda E-SIC.

Littleton, C. (2019). Inside Disney's Daring Dive into the Streaming World. *Variety*. www.variety.com/2019/biz/features/disney-plus-streaming-plans-bob-iger-1203120734

Lobato, R. (2019). *Netflix Nations: The Geography of Digital Distribution*. New York: NYU Press.

Lopez, A.M. (1995). Our Welcomed Guests: Telenovelas in Latin America. In R.C. Allen (ed.), *To Be Continued: Soap Operas around the World*, 256–75. UK: Psychology Press.

Lotz, A.D. (2014). *The Television Will Be Revolutionized*. New York: NYU Press.

Lotz, A.D. (2017). *Portals: A Treatise on Internet-Distributed Television*. Ann Arbor: Michigan Publishing.

Lotz, A.D. (2018). *We Now Disrupt This Broadcast: How Cable Transformed Television and the Internet Revolutionized It All*. Cambridge, MA: MIT Press.

Lula em carta ao povo brasileiro: 'O medo deles não é do Lula. Eles têm medo é dos milhões de Lulas' (2019). *Revista Forum*. www.revistaforum.com.br/lula-em-carta-ao-povo-brasileiro-o-medo-deles-nao-e-do-lula-eles-tem-medo-e-dos-milhoes-de-lulas

Marcos: Uma websérie quase original (2015–2016). 1quarto. YouTube. www.youtube.com/watch?v=y6x8XdMnvfI&list=PLxXfFdmIGOID52ishbGjC3 0JvRcwnJb2Q&index=2

Marinoni, B. (2015). Concentração dos meios de comunicação de massa e o desafio da democratização da mídia no Brasil. *Intervozes—Coletivo Brasil de Comunicação Social*. 13: 1–28.

Martín-Barbero, J. (1993). *Communication, Culture, and Hegemony: From the Media to Mediations*. Thousand Oaks, CA: Sage.

Martins, L. (2012). Netflix Brasil, ano um: Os altos e baixos de um serviço ainda em construção. *Gizmodo*. www.gizmodo.uol.com.br/netflix-brasil-um-ano-os-altos-e-baixos-de-um-servico-ainda-em-construcao

Massarolo, J.C., and Mesquita, D. (2016). "Vídeo sob demanda: uma nova plataforma televisiva." Available at: http://www.compos.org.br/biblioteca/compos2016videosobdemanda_3397.pdf.

Mattelart, A., and Mattelart, M. (1990). *The Carnival of Images: Brazilian Television Fiction*. Westport, CT: Greenwood Publishing Group.

Mattos, S. (1990). *Um pérfil da TV brasileira: 40 anos de história—1950–1990*. Salvador: A Tarde.

Mattos, S. (2002). *História da televisão brasileira: Uma visão econômica, social e política*. Petrópolis: Editora Vozes.

Maurício, P. (2015). Regulação do audiovisual no Brasil: Tudo outra vez de novo. *Eptic online: Revista eletrônica internacional de economia política da informação, da comunicação e da cultura* 17(2): 137–52.

Mbembe, A. (2017). *Critique of Black Reason*. Durham, NC: Duke University Press.

Mesquita, L. (2015). 'Os negros não são representados na dramaturgia,' diz Jorge Furtado. *Folha de São Paulo*, www.f5.folha.uol.com.br/televisao/2015/10/1692618-negros-nao-estao-representados-na-teledramaturgia-diz-jorge-furtado-autor-de-mister-brau.shtml

Mídia fatos (2018). *Dados*. www.midiafatos.com.br/dados

Mira, M.C. (1994). *Circo eletrônico: Silvio Santos e o SBT*. Edições Loyola.

Miranda, A. (2011). Aprovada após cinco anos de polêmica, lei da TV por assinatura cria cotas para o conteúdo nacional. *O Globo*. www.oglobo.globo.

com/cultura/aprovada-apos-cinco-anos-de-polemica-lei-da-tv-por-assinatura-cria-cotas-para-conteudo-nacional-2695231

Mister Brau (2015). TV series. Writ. Jorge Furtado. TV Globo. Channel 4. Rio de Janeiro.

Mitchell, J. (2013). *Popular Culture Imaginings of the Mulatta: Constructing Race, Gender, Sexuality, and Nation in the United States and Brazil.* Unpublished doctoral dissertation, University of Minnesota, Minneapolis, Minnesota.

Morais, de K.S. (2019). Cota de tela (Lei nº 12.485/2011) e a produção independente na TV paga. *Significação: Revista De Cultura Audiovisual*, 46(52): 270–92.

"Mr. Brau" iguala "Tapas & Beijos" na audiência em São Paulo (2016). *Folha de São Paulo*, www.f5.folha.uol.com.br/televisao/2016/01/1724864-mr-brau-iguala-tapas—beijos-na-audiencia-em-sao-paulo.shtml

Nagib, L. (2002). *O cinema da retomada*. São Paulo: Editora 34.

Netflix diz não temer restrições ao serviço de vídeo no Brasil (2017). *Folha de São Paulo*. www1.folha.uol.com.br/mercado/2017/02/1856535-netflix-diz-nao-temer-restricoes-ao-servico-de-video-no-brasil.shtml

Nogueira, I. (2018). 'Netflix não está sabendo onde se meteu,' diz Dilma sobre 'O Mecanismo.' *Folha de São Paulo*. www1.folha.uol.com.br/ilustrada/2018/03/dilma-diz-que-alertara-liderancas-estrangeiras-contra-netflix.shtml

Nudeliman, S., and Pfeiffer, D. (2010). Novas janelas. In A. Meleiro (ed.), *Cinema e Mercado: Indústria Cinematográfica e Audiovisual Brasileira Vol. III*, 103–18. São Paulo: Escrituras Editora.

O Rei do Gado: Audiência detalhada (1997). Gabriel Farac Blogspot. www.gabrielfarac.blogspot.com/1997/02/o-rei-do-gado-audiencia-detalhada.html

O Sistema (2019). *YouTube*. www.youtube.com/watch?v=97NE-LdIxXc

O site de Humor *Kibe Loco* estreia no R7 (2012). *R7*. www.entretenimento.r7.com/humor/noticias/kibe-loco-e-o-novo-parceiro-do-r7-20120302.html

Orozco, G., and Miller, T. (2018). Television beyond Itself in Latin America. *MATRIZes* 12(3): 59–75.

Ortiz, R. (1988). *A moderna tradição brasileira: Cultura brasileira e indústria cultural*. São Paulo: Editora Brasiliense.

Peccoli, V. (2017). Final de "A Força do Querer" bate recorde de audiência desde "Avenida Brasil"; confira os consolidados da sexta-feira (20/10/17). *TV Foco*. www.otvfoco.com.br/final-de-a-forca-do-querer-bate-recorde-de-audiencia-desde-avenida-brasil-confira-os-consolidados-da-sexta-feira-201017

Peccoli, V. (2018). O Outro Lado do Paraíso chega ao fim com maior ibope desde 2012: confira os consolidados de sexta-feira. TV Foco. www.otvfoco.com.br/o-outro-lado-do-paraiso-chega-ao-fim-com-maior-ibope-desde-2012-confira-os-consolidados-de-sexta-feira-11-05-18

Petró, G. (2012). 'Brasileiros ainda não entenderam o Netflix,' diz presidente da empresa. *G1*. www.g1.globo.com/tecnologia/noticia/2012/08/brasileiros-ainda-nao-entenderam-o-netflix-diz-presidente-da-empresa.html

Pinheiro, A. (2018). A importância dos cabais CABEQs. *Revista do Cinema*. www.revistadecinema.com.br/2018/04/a-importancia-dos-canais-cabeqs

Portela, K.G.B. (2017). *A TV na Internet: A transmidialidade em Porta dos Fundos*. Unpublished master's thesis, Universidade Federal de Mato Grosso do Sul, Campo Grande.

Porto, M. (2011). Telenovelas and Representations of National Identity in Brazil. *Media, Culture, & Society* 33(1): 53–69.

Porto, M. (2012). *Media Power and Democratization in Brazil: TV Globo and the Dilemmas of Political Accountability*. New York: Routledge.

Porta dos Fundos quer que entidade que o acusou pague custas de R$ 1 milhão (2018). *Paulopes*. www.paulopes.com.br/2018/02/porta-dos-fundos-pede-multa-entidade.html#.WxlWlDNKjGJ

Porta dos Fundos vai produzir seriado para a Fox em 2015 (2014). *Folha de São Paulo*. www.f5.folha.uol.com.br/televisao/2014/05/1453748-porta-dos-fundos-vai-produzir-seriado-para-a-fox-em-2015.shtml

Programa Brasil de Todas as Telas investe em novos projetos para TV (2016). *Agência Nacional do Cinema*. www.ancine.gov.br/pt-br/sala-imprensa/noticias/programa-brasil-de-todas-telas-investe-em-novos-projetos-para-tv

Qual a faixa de renda familiar das classes? (2014). Fundação Getúlio Vargas—Centro de Políticas Sociais. www.cps.fgv.br/qual-faixa-de-renda-familiar-das-classes

Ramos, F. et al. (1990). *História do cinema brasileiro*. São Paulo: Arte Editora.

Rêgo, C.M. (2005). Brazilian Cinema: Its Fall, Rise, and Renewal (1990–2003). *New Cinemas: Journal of Contemporary Film* 3: 85–100.

Rêgo, C. (2014). Centering the Margins: The Modern Favela in the Brazilian Telenovela. In N.P. Wood (ed.), *Brazil in Twenty-First Century Popular Media: Culture, Politics, and Nationalism on the World Stage*, 91–111. Lanham, MD: Lexington.

Rial, C.S. (1999). Japonês está para TV assim como mulato para cerveja: Imagens da publicidade no Brasil. In C. Eckert and P. Mont-Mór (eds.). *Imagem em Foco: Novas perspectivas em antropologia visual*, 231–55. Porto Alegre/Rio de Janeiro: UFRGS/UFRJ, pp. .

Rocha, P. (2018). Brasil tem número recorde de séries exclusivas para o streaming em 2018. *Estadão*. www.cultura.estadao.com.br/noticias/

televisao,brasil-tem-numero-recorde-de-series-exclusivas-para-o-streaming-em-2018,70002562261

Rodríguez, P.A.S. (2016). *Latin American Cinema: A Comparative History*. Oakland: University of California Press.

Roppa, B.F., Reis, M.M.S., and Leandro, T. (2016). *TV por assinatura no Brasil: Aspectos econômicos e estruturais*. Rio de Janeiro: Observatório Brasileiro do Cinema e do Audiovisual.

Rosas-Moreno, T.C. (2014). *News and Novela in Brazilian Media: Fact, Fiction, and National Identity*. Lanham, MD: Lexington.

Rousseff, D. (2018). José Padilha's Character Assassination Mechanism: Filmmaker Spreads "Fake News" in the TV Series Released by Netflix. Dilma Unmasks the Lies. *Dilma: Presidenta Eleita do Brasil*. www.dilma.com.br/jose-padilhas-character-assassination-mechanism

Russo, F. (2016). Supermax: "A gente foi livre para imaginar. Esta é a grande diferença que podemos propor neste momento à TV brasileira." *Adoro Cinema*. www.adorocinema.com/noticias/series/noticia-122702

Sá, N.D. (2018a). Globo lança Telecine e Premiere por internet, com assinatura avulsa. *Folha de São Paulo*. www1.folha.uol.com.br/mercado/2018/12/globo-lanca-telecine-play-e-pfc-por-internet-com-assinatura-avulsa-sem-cabo.shtml

Sá, N.D. (2018b). Netflix faz sete anos no Brasil e ganha concorrência no streaming. *Folha de São Paulo*. www1.folha.uol.com.br/ilustrada/2018/09/netflix-faz-sete-anos-no-brasil-e-ganha-concorrencia-no-streaming.shtml

Sá Pessoa, G. (2016). Globo segue tática da Netflix e estreia série 'Supermax' hoje on-line. *Folha de São Paulo*. www1.folha.uol.com.br/ilustrada/2016/09/1813812-globo-segue-tatica-da-netflix-e-estreia-serie-supermax-hoje-na-internet.shtml

Sabbatino, R. (2013). Audiência Detalhada: *Renascer*. TV Foco. www.otvfoco.com.br/audiencia-detalhada-renascer

Sacramento, I. (2008). *Depois da revolução, a televisão: Cineastas de esquerda no jornalismo televisivo dos anos 1970*. Unpublished doctoral dissertation, Universidade Federal do Rio de Janeiro.

Sanseverino, G., and Gruszynski, A. (2018). Ver TV sem TV: Mídias digitais, Internet e múltiplas telas. *Revista Memorare, Tubarão*, 5(3): 202–30.

Santos, S. (2009). The Central Role of Broadcast Television in Brazil's Film Industry: The Economic, Political, and Social Implications of Global Markets and National Concentration. *International Journal of Communication* 3: 695–712.

SBF I (2010). 'Amanda episódio 1.' YouTube. www.youtube.com/watch?v=zJZ2rX-Kyaw

SBF I (2011a). 'CSI: Nova Iguaçu episódio 2.' YouTube. www.youtube.com/

watch?v=xJUJ7F-cYDw&list=PL5imFqWD477zVw6xdQwh0On44rgXbZ RFU&index=6
SBF I (2011b). 'CSI: Nova Iguaçu episódio 5.' YouTube. www.youtube.com/watch?v=cwsTLJKwViA&list=PL5imFqWD477zVw6xdQwh0On44rgXbZRFU&index=3
SBF I (2012). 'Porta dos Fundos N°1.' YouTube. www.youtube.com/watch?v=eQmDdD5f-Ic
SBF I (2014). 'Negro.' YouTube. www.youtube.com/watch?v=Le8xjRufv-M
SBF I (2015a). 'Redução.' YouTube. www.youtube.com/watch?v=rc99KJh9nd8
SBF I (2015b). 'Amiguinho.' YouTube. www.youtube.com/watch?v=NxzUU-cZD1o
SBF I (2015c). *O Grande Gonzalez*. YouTube. www.youtube.com/watch?v=MHI9WQ9aVB0&list=PLT0Smhj8chMWxIF6Zctrn0PqVeq6AHQM
Schwarz, R. (2014). *As ideias fora do lugar: Ensaios selecionados*. Rio de Janeiro: Companhia das Letras.
Schwertner, S.F. (2007). Análise das condições de produção de *Cidade dos Homens*: Articulações entre educação e comunicação. *Educação e Pesquisa* 33(1): 47–61.
Septo (2015). Series. Writ. Aleixo F. et al. YouTube. www.*youtube.com/watch?v=1yQgim3bVuc&list=PL7N2DfMjTuxvUiOYxSn-UElvH_mv_CWOJ*
Sereza, H.C. (2009). Relação com a Globo 'ajudou bastante,' lembra Collor; senador diz ter pensado, na véspera, que perderia a eleição. *Uol* www.noticias.uol.com.br/especiais/eleicoes-1989/ultnot/2009/11/15/ult9005u10.jhtm
Série do Porta dos Fundos eleva em 43% a audiência da Fox (2015). *Veja.* www.veja.abril.com.br/entretenimento/serie-do-porta-dos-fundos-eleva-em-43-a-audiencia-da-fox
Silva, D.F. (1999). The Drama of Modernity: Color and Symbolic Exclusion in the Brazilian Telenovela. In L. Crook L. and R. Johnson R. (eds.), *Black Brazil: Culture, Identity, and Social Mobilization*, 339–61. Los Angeles: UCLA Latin American Center Publications.
Silva, G.R. (2013). Cinema e televisão: afastamentos e reaproximações na economia do audiovisual brasileiro contemporâneo. *Latitude* 6(2): 267–95.
Silva, G.R. (2015). *Cinema e televisão: Afastamentos e reaproximações na economia do audiovisual brasileiro contemporâneo*. Saarbrücken: Novas Edições Acadêmicas.
Silveira, B. (2018). Breno Silveira, da Conspiração, fala sobre o aquecimento do mercado de séries para TV no Brasil. *Acadêmia Internacional de Cinema*. www.aicinema.com.br/breno-silveira-da-conspiracao-fala-sobre-o-aquecimento-do-mercado-de-series-para-tv-no-brasil
Simpson, A. (1993). *Xuxa: The Mega-Marketing of Gender, Race, and Modernity*. Philadelphia, PA: Temple University Press.

Smith, C.A. (2016). *Afro-Paradise: Blackness, Violence, and Performance in Brazil*. Urbana: University of Illinois Press.

Smith, M.D., and Telang, R. (2016). *Streaming, Sharing, Stealing: Big Data and the Future of Entertainment*. Cambridge, MA: MIT Press.

Social Mission (2016). *Rede Globo*. www.redeglobo.globo.com/Portal/institucional/foldereletronico/ingles/g_rs_missao_social.html

Sodré, M. (2008). O jogo contra-hegemônico do diverso. In E.G. Coutinho (ed.), *Comunicação e contra-hegemonia*, 27–38. Rio de Janeiro: UFRJ.

Sodré, M. (2015). *Claros e escuros: Identidade, povo, mídia e costas no Brasil*. 3rd. edition. Petrópolis: Editora Vozes.

Sovik, L. (2004). We Are Family: Whiteness in the Brazilian Media. *Journal of Latin American Cultural Studies* 13(3): 315–25.

Sousa, A.P.D.S. (2014). Lei da TV Paga: Até que ponto a restrição a produtos estrangeiros estimula a produção local. Paper Presented at: *V Seminário Internacional—Políticas Culturais*, 7 a 9 de maio/2014. Setor de Políticas Culturais–Fundação Casa de Rui Barbosa, Rio de Janeiro.

Sousa, A.P.D.S. (2018). *Dos conflitos ao pacto: As lutas no campo cinematográfico brasileiro no século XXI*. Unpublished doctoral dissertation, Universidade de São Paulo, São Paulo.

Spigel, Lynn. *Make room for TV: Television and the family ideal in postwar America*. University of Chicago Press, 1992.

Stam R. (1997). From Hybridity to the Aesthetics of Garbage. *Social Identities* 3(2): 275–90.

Statista (2013). Household Adoption Rate of Internet in the United States from 1997 to 2011. www.statista.com/statistics/214662/household-adoption-rate-of-internet-access-in-the-us-since-1997

Statista (2017). Countries with the Highest Number of Internet Users as of December 2017. www.statista.com/statistics/262966/number-of-internet-users-in-selected-countries

Straubhaar, J.D. (1984). Brazilian Television: The Decline of American Influence. *Communication Research* 11(2): 221–40.

Straubhaar, J.D. (1991). Beyond Media Imperialism: Asymmetrical Interdependence and Cultural Proximity. *Critical Studies in Mass Communication* 8: 39–59.

Straubhaar, J.D. (2003). Choosing National TV: Cultural Capital, Language, and Cultural Proximity in Brazil. In M.G. Elasmar (ed.), *The Impact of International Television: A Paradigm Shift*, 75–106. Mahwah: Lawrence Erlbaum Associates.

Straubhaar, J.D. (2007). *World Television: From Global to Local*. Thousand Oaks, CA: Sage.

Straubhaar, J.D. (2012). Telenovelas in Brazil: From Travelling Scripts to a

Genre and Proto-format both National and Transnational. In T. Oren and S. Shahaf (eds.), *Global Television Formats: Understanding Television across Borders*, 148–77. New York: Routledge.

Straubhaar, J.D. (2013). The Dominant Markets—Brazil. In J. Sinclair and J.D. Straubhaar (eds.). *Latin American Television Industries*, 63–91. London: Palgrave.

Stycer, M. (2016). Pior audiência de série da Globo na história, Supermax atrai público jovem *UOl*. www.tvefamosos.uol.com.br/blog/mauriciostycer/2016/11/18/pior-audiencia-de-serie-da-globo-na-historia-supermax-atrai-publico-jovem

Subervi-Velez, F.A., and Omar, S.O. (1991). Negros (e outras etnias). em comerciais da televisão brasileira: Uma investigação exploratória. *Comunicação & Sociedade* 10(17): 79–101.

Supermax (2016). TV series. Writ. José Alvarenga Jr. et al. GloboPlay.

Tavares, T.S. (2015). O Brasil de todas as telas e seu financiamento pelo Fundo Setorial do Audiovisual. *Cambiassu: Estudos em Comunicação* 15(17): 230–44.

Telles, E.E. (2004). *Race in Another America: The Significance of Skin Color in Brazil*. Princeton, NJ: Princeton University Press.

TIC Domicílios (2005a). Proporção de domicílios com acesso à Internet, por tipo de conexão. www.data.cetic.br/cetic/explore

TIC Domicílios (2005b). Tipo de conexão para acesso à Internet no domicílio. www.data.cetic.br/cetic/explore?idPesquisa=TIC_DOM

TIC Domicílios (2005c). Tipo de equipamento para acesso à Internet no domicílio. www.data.cetic.br/cetic/explore

TIC Domicílios (2010). Proporção de domicílios com acesso à Internet, por tipo de conexão. www.data.cetic.br/cetic/explore

TIC Domicílios (2011). Tipo de conexão para acesso à Internet no domicílio. www.data.cetic.br/cetic/explore?idPesquisa=TIC_DOM

TIC Domicílios (2015). Proporção de domicílios com acesso à Internet, por tipo de conexão. www.data.cetic.br/cetic/explore

TIC Domicílios (2017a). Proporção de domicílios com acesso à Internet, por tipo de conexão. www.data.cetic.br/cetic/explore

TIC Domicílios (2017b). Proporção de domicílios que possuem TV Paga. www.data.cetic.br/cetic/explore?idPesquisa=TIC_DOM

TIC Domicílios (2017c). Tipo de conexão para acesso à Internet no domicílio. www.data.cetic.br/cetic/explore

TIC Domicílios (2017d). Tipo de equipamento para acesso à Internet no domicílio. www.data.cetic.br/cetic/explore

TIC Domicílios (2018). TIC Domicílios 2017 Pesquisa sobre o Uso das Tecnologias de Informação e Comunicação nos Domicílios Brasileiros. www.

cetic.br/publicacao/pesquisa-sobre-o-uso-das-tecnologias-de-informacao-e-comunicacao-nos-domicilios-brasileiros-tic-domicilios-2017

Top 50 Subscribed YouTube Channels (Sorted by Subscriber Count). (2019). *Socialblade.* www.socialblade.com/youtube/top/50/mostsubscribed

TV paga registra perda de 262 mil assinantes em 12 meses (2017). *Época Negócios.* www.epocanegocios.globo.com/Brasil/noticia/2017/07/tv-paga-registra-perda-de-262-mil-assinantes-em-12-meses.html

Um contra todos é série brasileira de maior audiência na TV paga (2016). *Folha de São Paulo.* www.f5.folha.uol.com.br/televisao/2016/08/um-contra-todos-e-serie-brasileira-de-maior-audiencia-na-tv-paga.shtml

Vieira, A.V., and Murta, C.M.G. (2017). Globo Play: A plataforma da Rede Globo. *Revista GEMInIS* 8(2): 31–47.

Zefr (2016). 2016 Influencers: A Year in Review. www.2016influencer.zefr.com/best-overall

Zeidan, R.M. et al. (2016). *Mapeamento e impacto econômico do setor audiovisual no Brasil.* São Paulo: Associação Brasileira da Produção de Obras Audiovisuais e Serviço Brasileiro de Apoio às Micro e Pequenas Empresas.

Index

Page numbers in *italics* refer to illustrations.

Abramson, Josh, 98
Abril Group, 22–25
ABTA (Brazilian Pay-Television Association), 27, 45
Academia de Filme, 44
Academia Internacional de Cinema, 51
Accountability office (TCU), 163
Adorno, Theodor, 8, 12
ad-supported model, 6–7, 29, 45, 147
Afro-Brazilians in Brazilian media: *City of Men,* 116–120; *Grande Gonzalez,* 130–134; *Mister Brau,* 120–127; *Mister Brau* and *Grande Gonzalez* compared, 135–136; overview, 113–116; Porta dos Fundos, 128–136
Afros and Things Related, 66–67
Afros e afins, 66–67
Agência Nacional do Cinema (ANCINE), 21, 34, 36, 38; 2017 report on pay-TV, 48
Agência Nacional do Cinema e do Audiovisual (ANCINAV), 21
Aguilera, Pedro, 85
Aïnouz, Karim, 62
Albuquerque, Mônica, 44–45
Além da Ilha, 139
Alexandrismos, 67
Algañaraz, Juliana, 110
Alice, 49
All in the Family, 43

Alvarenga, José, Jr., 148, 152, 153
Amanda, 99, 101–103
Amaral, Tata, 149
Amarelo manga, 58
"Amiguinho" (YouTube video), 129–130
Amor de 4, 61
Amor e revolução, 78
ANATEL (National Telecommunications Agency), 71
ANCINAV (National Agency of Film and the Audiovisual), 21
ANCINE, 21, 34, 36, 38; 2017 report on pay-TV, 48
Anderson, Benedict, 10
Andrade, Júlio, 50, 51
Andrade, Oswald de, 64, 153
Andrade, Patricia, 149
Angeli the Killer, 61
O ano em que meus pais saíram de férias, 150
Anões em chamas, 99, 101, 103, 105
antennas, communal, 22
Antonelli, Giovanni, 78
antropofagia, 64, 153
Appadurai, A., 90
Aqui Agora, 93
Aquino, Marçal, 148–150, 152, 153
Aragão, Helder, 59
Aragão, Nara, 58
Araújo, Joel Zito, 113–114, 119, 120–121
Araújo, Taís, 121
Araújo, Vitor, 59
Arraes, Guel, 43

202 Index

Article 3 (Audiovisual Law), 19–21
The Artist, 140
Aruanas, 143
Assédio, 139, 154–160; distribution, 154–155; screenplay, 155–159; and sexual violence, 157–159; story structure, 155–159
Assis, Cláudio, 63
Associação Brasileira do TV por Assinatura (ABTA), 27, 45
audiences, niche, 13, 73, 89–90, 144–145
Audiovisual Law, 18–19
audio-visual media and nationalism, 10–11
Audiovisual Sector Fund (FSA), 21, 33–34, 38, *39*, 42
Avenida Brasil, 94, 155
Axé, 62

Babenco, Héctor, 149
Backdoor. *See* Porta dos Fundos
Bahia, 62
Baile perfumado, 58
Baixio das bestas, 58
Balieiro, Thiago, 86
Banco Nacional de Desenvolvimento, 34
Barbosa, Jesuita, 58
Barmark, Erik, 139
Barreto, Bruno, 18, 61, 149
Barreto, Fábio, 18
basic utilization channels, 25
Batata, Rita, 87
Bauman, Zygmunt, 84
Beyond the Door, 106
Beyond the Island, 139
Bial, Pedro, 152
Bian (folksinger), 78
The Big Bang Theory, 95
Big Brother Brasil, 152
The Big Family, 43
Billig, Michael, 100
Black Fist, 67
blackness. *See* Afro-Brazilians in Brazilian media
Bloch, Adolpho, 23
Bolaño, C., 10
Bola Oito, Gilmar, 60

Bolsa Família (Family Grant), 46
Bolsonaro, Jair, 3–4, 162
Bonassi, Fernando, 148–150, 152
Borelli, Sílvia H. Simões, 10, 92–93, 95
Borges, 106, 108–110
Bossa Nova Group, 44
Box Brazil group, 61
Brant, Beto, 148, 149
Brasileiríssimos (website), 75
Brave New World, 84
Brazil Avenue, 94
Brazilian content quotas. *See* content quotas
Brazilian cultural identity: celebration of creativity, 58; comfort with ambiguity, 51–52, 57; creativity, 61; as distinct from European culture, 64–65; film, literature and music, 62; *Mister Brau*, 124–125; and Pay-TV Law, 12–13, 30; regional culture, 84; and telenovelas, 10–11, 17, 41, 113; and transnational identities, 47–48; TV Globo's role, 17, 111, 146; on YouTube, 75
Brazilian Film Company (Embrafilme), 18
Brazilian Pay-Television Association (ABTA), 27, 45
Brazilian qualified space channels, 30–32, *31*, 35, 38, *48–49*, 61
Brazilian Soccer Championship, 147
Breaking Bad, 51
Brindelli, Roberto, 53
Brittos, V. C., 10
broadband v. mobile access, 70–71
Brown, Chris, 103
Buenos Aires Web Festival, 75, 80
Burgoyne, Robert, 11
Butcher, P., 10

CABEQ. *See* Brazilian qualified space channels
cable television, 96–97
Cable TV Law, 25
Caboré Audiovisual, 68
Cabral, César, 61
Cabral, Pedro Álvares, 112
O caçador, 149
Caldas, Paulo, 63

Caldeira, Teresa, 123
Caldeirão do Huck, 98
Calloni, Antônio, 156
Camargo, Maria, 155
Campeonato Brasileiro, 147
Camurati, Carla, 18
canais brasileiros. *See* Brazilian qualified space channels
Canal Brasil, 57, 61
#CancelaNetflix, 3
Candido, Antônio, 135
Cannito, Newton, 28, 29
Canto dos Malditos Na Terra do Nunca, 77
Carandiru, 149
Carcereiros, 142
Cardoso, Fernando Henrique, 18, 21, 25
Carga pesada, 43
Carlos, Manoel, 78, 94
Carlota Joaquina, 18
Carnavais, malandros e heróis, 133
Carnaval Filmes, 57
Carnavals, Rogues, and Heroes, 133
Cartola—Música para os olhos, 58
Cartola—Music for the Eyes, 58
Carvalho, Luiz Fernando, 18, 43, 120, 149, 155
Car Wash scandal (*Lava Jato*), 2, 161–163
Casa-Grande & Senzala, 59, 124
Casé, Regina, 116–117
Casseta & Planeta, 100
Castelo Rá-Tim-Bum!, 149
Castro, João Vicente de, 106, 108, 128, 131
Castro Rocha, João Cezar de, 133–134
Cataguases Cycle, 62
Catarse (crowdfunding website), 73, 74–75
The Cattle King, 92
CATV (Community Antenna Television), 22
Caxias do Sul, 14, 79, 80, 84
center-periphery framework, 84
Central do Brasil, 18
Central Station, 18
CEQ (qualified space). *See* Brazilian qualified space channels

Chagas, Gustavo, 103–104, 129
Chapman, Matthew, 149
Charmed, 143
Chateaubriand, Assis, 6, 22
O cheiro doralo, 149
Chico Science, 65
Chico Science & Nação Zumbi, 58–60
Christian, Jean Aymar, 68, 72, 90
Ciclo de Cataguases, 62
"Cidade" (Chico Science song), 60
Cidade de Deus, 117, 119–120, 150
Cidade dos homens, 43, 116–120
CineBrasilTV, 61
Cinema Novo films, 62, 64
cinema pernambuco, 58
City of God, 117, 119–120, 150
City of Men, 43, 116–120
Civita, Roberto, 22–23
Civita, Victor, 22–23
A clínica: A farsa e os crimes de Roger Abdel-massih, 155
The Clinic: The Farse and Crimes of Dr. Roger Abdelmassih, 155
Coletivo Caboré Audiovisual, 79
College Humor (website), 98
Collor, Pedro, 1
Collor de Mello, Fernando, 1, 2, 4, 17–18, 58, 162
Comedy Central, 108
Communications, Culture, and Hegemony, 113
Community Antenna Television (CATV), 22
CONDECINE, 34, 38, 50
CONDECINE Remessa, 19
conditional access service, 32
Conspiração Filmes, 35, 50
content quotas, 48–49
Cordeiro, Erom, 55, 154
Coronation Street, 42
Coutinho, L. L., 46
Crema, Jotagá, 85
Crook, Larry, 126
crowdfunding, 73, 74–75
CSI: Nova Iguaçu, 99, 103–105
Cunha, Darlan, 115, 116–119
Curta! (qualified channel), 61

Da lama ao caos, 59
Damasceno, Enio, 59
DaMatta, Roberto, 52, 133–134
Dantas, José Guibson Delgado, 21
Dantas, Pipa, 73
data collection, 142, 145
de Brito, Vânia, 153
Decree 95.744, 23
Denninson, Stephanie, 47
Dhalia, Heitor, 149
A diarista, 148
digital distribution. *See* streaming series
Digital Intelligence Unit, 143
"Dilma: presidenta eleita do Brasil" website, 2–3
direct to home (DTH), 24, 25
DirecTV, 40
distribution licenses *(editais)*, 24
Divã, 148
Divan, 148
diversity: in casting, 87–89; in mediascape, 47; promotion of in Brazilian film, 21. *See also* Afro-Brazilians in Brazilian media
documentaries, influence on series, 63
2 filhos de Francisco, 51, 149
Dois irmãos, 155
domestic film industry, 17–18, 47
domestic violence, 101–103
Draccon, Raphael, 149
DTH (direct to home), 24, 25
A deusa ferida, 92–93, 95
D'Umbra, Fernanda, 155
Dutra, Marco, 150
Duvivier, Gregório, 98, 131

Eakin, Marshall, 12, 124
The Edge of Desire, 94
editais (distribution licenses), 24
election (1989), 1
Elite Squad, 150
Elitist Phase *(Fase Elitista)*, 7
Ellen, Jéssica, 155–156
Embodiment of Evil, 150
Embrafilme (Brazilian Film Company), 18
Em família, 78
Encarnação do demônio, 150

The End of the World, 58
Escobar, Pablo, 80, 83
Esconderijo, 67
Escosteguy, A. C., 46
O Estadão, 139
Estado mínimo (Minimal State), 18
Estado propositivo (Propositional State), 18, 21
Estado regulador (Regulatory State), 18, 21
estética sueca, 113
Esteves, Adriana, 155
Eu receberia as piores notícias dos seus lindos lábios, 149
European Union and media, 164

Fagundes, Cláudio, 61
Falcão, Clarice, 98, 130, 131
Family Grant *(Bolsa Família)*, 46
Family Ties, 94
Fanju, Aline, 106–107
Fanon, Frantz, 122
Fase Elitista (Elitist Phase), 7
Fase Populista (Populist Phase), 7–8
Febre dos ratos, 58
Feltrin, Ricardo, 140
Fernandes, João, 52
Ferreira, Lírio, 58
A Festa de menina morta, 58
Fever of Rats, 58
FGV (Fundação Getúlio Vargas), 45
FICTV competition, 85
Filhos do carnaval, 49
film industry: Brazilian content, 35–36, 38–40; domestic, 17–18; Globo Filmes, 19–21; Golden Age in Brazil, 17; investment in, 39; relationship with Hollywood, 48; *retomada*, 18
Fim do mundo, 58, 61
Flores raras, 149
Folha de São Paulo, 138, 151, 154
Fondo Filmes, 97–99, 105
A força du querer, 94
Força Tarefa, 149
Four Days in September, 18
Fox (distribution channel), 61
Fox Brasil, 50; partnership with Porta dos Fundos, 106–110

fragmentation: of audiences, with digital distribution, 138; of content, with web series, 89–90; of media, 163; of media audiences, 95; of public debate, 162
França, Louise, 59
Franco, Marielle, 162
Free Lula March, 161
Freitas, Fernanda de, 122
Freyre, Gilberto, 59, 124, 125
From Mud to Chaos, 59
FSA (Fundo Setorial do Audiovisual), 21, 33–34, 38, *39,* 42
FSA PRODAV, 58
Fundação Getúlio Vargas (FGV), 45
Fundo Setorial do Audiovisual (FSA), 21, 33–34, 38, *39,* 42
Furtado, Jorge, 121, 125

Garcia, Xando, 53
Garib, Adriano, 53
Garin, Laila, 89
Giannecchini, Daina, 85, 89
Gibson, Isadora, 59, 64
Gil, Gilberto, 21
Globo: contrasted with Netflix, 151, 159; dominance of, 40, 48; telenovelas, 165–166. *See also* streaming series
Globo Cabo, 24
Globo Filmes, 19–21, 34–35
Globo Play, 14–15, 138, 145
Globosat, 24
Globo series, 44
Globo Standard of Quality, 8, 92, 111
Globo TV, 23–25
Goes, Tony, 138
Goiás, 62
Golden Age of Brazilian film, 17
Gomes, Marcelo, 62, 63
Gomes, Michel, 88, 89
The Good Doctor, 142–143, 154
Grande família, 43, 118–119
Grande Gonzalez, 106, 108, 130–136
Gray, Herman, 128
Grijó, Wesley Pereira, 114
Guedes, Hermila, 155
Gurgel, Alexandra, 67

Haddad, Fernando, 3
Hall, Stuart, 120, 134, 135
Hamburger, Cao, 149, 150
Hamburger, Esther, 6, 9, 10–11, 162
Harassment, 139, 154–160
Hastings, Reed, 139–140
Hatoum, Milton, 155
HBO Latin America, 49
HBO subscriber model, 96
Heavy Load, 43
Heise, Tatiana Signorelli, 47, 57
Helinho (o Pequeno Príncipe), 63
Hiding Place, 67
Hollywood: influence in Brazil, 110–111; U.S. studios in Brazil, 19–20
Hostage, 106–107
The Housekeeper, 148
Huck's Cauldron, 98
Hunger Games, 140
Hunt, Darnell M., 127
The Hunter, 149
Huxley, Aldous, 84

Ianina, Júlia, 52, 86
I'd Receive the Worst News from Your Beautiful Lips, 149
Ikeda, Marcelo, 18, 21
Ilha de Ferro, 143
Images from the Day (Imagens do dia), 6
imagined community, Brazil as. *See* Brazilian cultural identity
independent production companies: contrasted with network television, 99–101; Hollywood's influence on, 20; Pay-TV Law, 36, 38, 42, 44, 48. *See also* Conspiração Filmes; O2 Filmes; Porta dos Fundos
individual/person binary, 133–134
In Family, 78
Infante, Rafael, 98, 131
Information and Communication Technologies (TIC) Report 2018, 70
Inmates, 142
Instagram web series, 79–80, 82
intellectual property rights, 33
International Academy of Cinema, 51
Internet access, 66, 69–72, 140–141

Internet series: *3%*, 84–90; audience contrasted with telenovela audience, 68; increasing access to Internet, 69–72; *Marcos*, 79–84; *Septo*, 73–79; YouTube, 66–69
O invasor, 148
Iron Island, 143

Joffily, José, 61
Johnson, Randal, 111, 126
Jornada Lula livre, 161
jornalismo de guerra (journalism as warfare), 2
Jornal Nacional, 1
José, Leonardo, 153

Kantar Ibope Media, 46
Kehl, M. R., 10
Kibe Loco (website), 97–98, 103
The Killers, 148–149
Killing Eve, 143
Koshikumo, Cássio, 88
Kotscho, Carolina, 149

Lacerda, Hilton, 57–58, 61–62
Laços de famílias, 94
Lama dos dias, 57–65
La Pastina, A. C., 10, 41
Lava Jato (Car Wash scandal), 2, 161–163
Law 8.685/93, 18–19
Law 8.977/95, 25
Law 12.485/11. *See* Pay-TV Law (2011)
Leão, Débora (Negrita MC), 59
Lei do Audiovisual, 18–19
Lei do Cabo, 25
LGBTQ+ audience, 74, 78
Libardi, Dani, 85
Lieff, Daniel, 50
Lima, Letícia, 98, 101, 106–107
Line B-PRODAV (ANCINE), 34
Lines of Action (ANCINE), 34, 38
Linha direta, 118–119
Lipsztein, Gustavo, 50
"Little Friend" (YouTube video), 129–130
Little People in Flames, 99, 101, 103, 105
The Little Prince's Rap against Greasy Souls, 63

Lobato, Ramon, 147
Lobby, 106
Lobianco, Luis, 106, 108, 130
local content, under pay-TV laws, 30–32
Lopes, Thati, 108
López, Ana M., 10
Lost, 153
Lotz, Amanda D.: on broadcast networks, 137; on Internet-distributed television, 87; on Network-Era advertising, 28; on Post-Network Era, 5–6; on subscriber-supported television, 45; on tech-driven media v. legacy media, 143–145; on U. S. media landscape, 166; *We Now Disrupt This Broadcast*, 96–97
Love and Revolution, 78
Luisa & os Alquimistas, 78
Luiz, Geyson, 59
Lula da Silva, Luiz Inácio, 1–3, 18, 21, 45–46; Car Wash scandal, 161–163
Lunas, Marcelo, 63
Luzano, Rafael, 88

Malu mulher, 43
Malu Woman, 43
Mandrake, 49
Mango Yellow, 58
mangrove beats, 58–60, 64, 65
manguebeats, 58–60, 64, 65
Mantovani, Braúlio, 149, 150
Marcos: An Almost Original Web Series,, 14, 68, 79–84
Marinho, Roberto, 1, 7
Marins, José Mojica, 150
Martín-Barbero, Jesús, 113
Massarolo, J. C., 45, 164
The Masters and the Slaves, 124
Os matadores, 148–149
Mato Grosso do Sul, 62
Matriz Street, 42–43
Mauro, Humberto, 47, 62
Mauro Filho, Lúcia, 118–119
Mautner, Amora, 155
Mbembe, Achille, 122–123
The Mechanism (O mecanismo), 2–3, 161–163
Meirelles, Fernando, 43, 119–120, 150

Mello, Selton, 161
Melo Neto, João Cabral, 63
Mendonça Filho, Kleber, 62
Mercês, Thiago das, 59
Mesel, Kátia, 63
Mesquita, D., 45, 145–146, 164
Mesquita, João, 143
#metoo movement, 155, 159
Miami Web Fest, 80
Miller, Toby, 69, 71
A Million Little Things, 143
Minimal State *(Estado mínimo)*, 18
Ministry of Communication, 23
Miranda, Luís, 124
Mister Brau, 120–127, 135–136
MMDS (multichannel multipoint distribution), 25
Montes, Raphael, 149
Morais, K. S. de, 34
Morelli, Paulo, 117
Motta, Zezé, 88, 89
Mulher de fases, 49
Müller, Tainá, 78
multichannel multipoint distribution (MMDS), 25
Murta, C. M. G., 141–142
Muylaert, Ana, 47

Nakamura, Ivan, 88
Narcos, 68, 80
Natal, Rio Grande do Norte, 14, 73, 79
National Agency of Film and the Audiovisual (ANCINAV), 21
National Bank of Development, 34
National Film Agency (ANCINE), 21, 34, 36, 38, 48
nationalism, language, and media, 10–11
National Reconstruction Party (PRN), 1
National Telecommunications Agency (ANATEL), 71
A Negação do Brasil: O negro na telenovela brasileira, 113
The Negotiation of Brazil: The Afro-Brazilian and the Brazilian Telenovela, 113
Negrita MC (Débora Leão), 59
"Negro" (YouTube video), 128–129
Nercessian, Stepan, 54

Neri, Nátaly, 66–67
Net Brasil, 24
"netcasting," 73
Net Claro, 140
Netflix: boycott of, 3; contrasted with TV Globo, 87–88, 151, 159; influence on political sphere, 161; *The Mechanism*, 2–3; and series produced in Brazil, 85
Netflix Brasil, 139–140
Netflix Nations, 147
Neto, Felipe, 66
Net Serviços, 24
Netto, Leonardo, 156
Network-Era television, 5, 7, 16, 28, 75, 91, 138
Neves, Aécio, 2
niche audiences, 13, 73, 89–90, 144–145
Nina, 149
nine o'clock telenovelas, 94
1984, 84
Os normais, 148
The Normal Ones, 148
novelas das nove, 94
Nudeliman, Sabrina, 35
Nunes, Whindersson, 66

O2 Filmes, 35, 119, 154
"O cão sem plumas" (poem by Melo Neto), 63
Oliveira, Marcus, 118
Oliveira, Vaneza, 88, 89
1 Against All, 50–57, 62
1 room, 68, 79–80, 83
Ônibus 174, 107
Open TV, 68
Orozco, Guillermo, 69, 71
Ortiz, R., 10
Orwell, George, 84
"O sistema," 161–163
The Other Side of Paradise, 94
O outro lado do paraíso, 94
over-the-top (OTT) content, 13
OZ, 96

Pacto Filmes, 57
Padilha, José, 2, 3, 61, 80, 107, 150
padrão Globo de qualidade, 8

Index

Parafernalha, 66
Paramaker studios, 66
Paraná, 62
The Party of the Dead Girl, 58
pay-television, 22–29; Brazilian content, 13; distribution, 26, 26–27; financial investors, 25–26; market strategies, 25; penetration rates, 35, 45–46, 140–141; quotas, 13; statistics, 164; subscriber diversity, 46; subscription costs, 35; viewership statistics, 46–47
Pay-Television: 20 Years of Evolution, 22
pay-television series: *1 contra todos*, 50–57; diversity in programming, 47–50; *Lama dos dias*, 57–65; overview of series, 42–47; quotas, 42, 47–50
Pay-TV Law (2011): barriers to access, eliminating, 32–34; and independent production, 44, 165; investment in local production, 38–39; and local content, 34–38; and media expansion, 30; and Post-Network Era, 41; and promotion of Brazilian culture, 30; quotas, 13–14, 30–32; and series, 163; television immediately prior to, 22–27; urban dominance v. regional diversification, 40
Perfumed Ball, 58
Pernambuco, 58, 62, 63, 65
Pfeiffer, Daniela, 35
Pontual, Adelina, 63
Populist Phase *(Fase Populista)*, 7–8
Porchat, Fábio, 97, 130, 131
Porta afora, 106
Portable, 106
Porta dos Fundos, 14; and Afro-Brazilians, 128–136; *Amanda*, 101–103; *Borges*, 108–110; contrasted with TV Globo, 110–112; *CSI: Nova Iguaçu*, 103–105; expansion of content portfolio, 104–106; formation and early days, 97–101; partnership with Fox Brasil, 106–110; and pay-television, 106; production quality, 110; as YouTube success, 97
Porta dos Fundos: Lifetime Contract, 106
Portaria, 106
Portátil, 106
Portela, Karoline Grubert Bezerra, 110

Porto, Mauro, 11, 162
Porto, Viviane, 88, 89
Portugal, Rafael, 108
Possani, Paula, 155
Possebon, Samuel, 22, 24, 27
Post-Network Era, 5–6, 16–17, 28, 29
presidential elections, 1–5
prestige programming, 43–44
print media, 10–11
Priolli, Gabriel, 10, 92–93, 95
PRN (National Reconstruction Party), 1
Programa Brasil de Todas as Telas, 58
O programa do Ratinho, 93
Programa Nacional de Desestatização, 18
Program for Brazil on All Screens, 58
Program for National Privatization, 18
Propositional State *(Estado Propositivo)*, 18, 21, 45–46
Provisional Measure 2.228-1, 19
Provisional Measure 151/90, 18
PT (Workers' Party), 1–3
Punho Negro, 67

qualified space. *See* Brazilian qualified space channels
O quatrilho, 18
The Quatrilho, 18
O que é isso, companheiro?, 18
quotas: Brazilian content, 128; Brazilian qualified space channels, 30–32, 35–36, 37, 48–49; and diverse Brazilian audiences, 61; future possibilities, 164; and pay-television series, 42, 47–50; Porta dos Fundos, 110; quota requirements, 57; quota system, 107

racial democracy, Brazil as, 121–122, 124–126, 129–130
racism, 117–120. *See also* Afro-Brazilians in Brazilian media
Ramalho, Dennison, 149–150
Ramil, Karina, 108
Ramos, Lázaro, 121
Rangel, Manuel, 42
O rap do Pequeno Príncipe contra as almas sebosas, 63
Reaching for the Moon, 149

Reborn, 92
Recife, 58–61, 63–65
Recife de dentro pra fora, 63
Recife from Inside Out, 63
Record (broadcast network), 137
Rede Record (broadcast network), 4, 93, 98
"Redução" (YouTube video), 128, 129
Refém, 106–107
regional media production v. urban axis domination: distribution, 40, 73–74, 79; and diverse audiences, 62, 139; Natal and Caxias do Sul, 14; Recife, 58; and socially relevant topics, 7, 11, 67–68
Regulatory State *(Estado regulador)*, 18, 21
O Rei do Gado, 92
Renascer, 18, 92
retomada, of Brazilian film, 18, 47
Reymond, Cauã, 149
Rihanna, 103
Rio de Janeiro and São Paulo axis. *See* regional media production
Rio Grande do Norte, 73–74, 79
Rio Grande do Sul, 79
Rocha, Glauber, 47, 62
Rocha, Pedro, 139
Rodrigues, Gárdia, 21
Rodrigues, José Geraldo, 87
Rohas, Juliana, 149–150
Rosas-Montero, T. C., 123
Rousseff, Dilma, 2–4, 162
Rua da Matriz, 42–43

Sacramento, Igor, 149
Salles, Walter, 18
Samydarsh: Os artistas de rua, 63
Samydarsh: The Street Artists, 63
Santos, Sílvio, 23
Santos, Suzy dos, 19–21
São Paulo and Rio de Janeiro axis. *See* regional media production
Sá Pessoa, Gabriela, 151
satellite service, 24
Saturday Night Live, 104
Sauma, George, 122

Sayes, Julie, 149
SBF, Ian, 97, 101, 108, 130
SBT (Sistema Brasileiro de Televisão), 23, 93, 137, 140
Schaeffer, Eduardo, 143
Schmidt, Paulo Roberto, 44
Schroder, Carlos Henrique, 141
Schwarz, Roberto, 7
Schwertner, Suzana, 120
Scourge of Beasts, 58
Seattle Web Fest, 80
Septo, 14, 68, 73–79
Septum, 14, 68, 73–79
Sertanejo, 62
serviço de acesso condicionado, 32
Serviço Especial de Televisão (TVA), 23, 25
SETA (Union of Pay-Television Companies), 27
Severo, Diogo, 80
Sex in the City, 96
sexuality, changing attitudes, 73–74
sexual violence, 101–103, 157–159
Shaw, Lisa, 47
Shippados, 143
Show do Kibe, 98
Sifuentes, 41
Silva, Douglas, 115, 116–119
Silva, G. R., 20
Silveira, Breno, 50, 51, 58, 149
Sindicato de Empresas de TV por Assinatura (SETA), 27
Sistema Brasileiro de Televisão (SBF), 23, 93, 137, 140
Slings and Arrows, 43
"small screens era." *See* Post-Network Era
smart phones, 71
The Smell from the Sewage Drain, 149
Smith, Michael D., 72, 137, 138, 145
Soares, Amauri, 151
socioeconomic inequality, 64, 69–71
Sodré, Muniz, 114
O som do amor, 67
Som e fúria, 43
Sons of Carnival, 49
The Sopranos, 96
The Sound of Love, 67

Sousa, Adam Henrique Freire, 34, 40, 114, 163
Special Service Subscription Television (TVA), 23, 25
Spiegel, Lynn, 6
Spiller, Letícia, 117–118
Stam, Robert, 64
A Starry Sky, 149
Starvos, Thomas, 50
Stranger Things, 153
Straubhaar, Joseph, 11, 41, 44
Streaming, Sharing, Stealing: Big Data and the Future of Entertainment, 137
streaming series: *Assédio*, 154–160; Globo and series, 139–148; Globo Play, 141–148; Netflix Brasil, 139–140; overview, 137–139; *Supermax*, 148–154
subscriber-supported platform, 45, 147
subscription video-on-demand (SVOD), 164
Subúrbia, 127
super Brazilian channels. *See* Brazilian qualified space channels
Supermax, 142; distribution, 150–151; as horror-reality hybrid, 152–153; reception, 151–152; writing, 148–150
SVOD (subscription video-on-demand), 164
Swedish aesthetic, 113

Tabet, Antônio, 97–98, 103–104, 107, 108, 128, 131
Talma, Simona, 77
Tanaka, Luana, 88
Tá no Ar: A TV na TV, 100
Task-Force, 149
Tattoo, 58
Tatuagem, 58
Tay, Jinna, 6
Tchôca, Matheus, 59
TCU (Tribunal de Contas), 163
Tecnologias de Informação e Comunicação (TIC), 70
Telang, Rahul, 72, 137, 138, 145
Tela Quente, 142, 146, 154
Telecine Play, 147
Telecom Americas, 40

telenovelas: Afro-Brazilian characters, 114; and audiences, 43–44, 68; and Brazilian self-concept, 113; and declining audience share, 93–96; and lesbian relationships, 78; nine o'clock telenovelas, 94; and TV Globo's dominance, 48, 91–92, 138; and web series, 78–79; writing, 44–45
teleteatros, 7, 43
television: access, 43–44; barriers to access, 32–33; cultural influence of, 11; domestic content, 42; economic barriers, 44; introduced in Brazil, 6–7; linear contrasted with non-linear, 144–145; series, 36–37, 37, 61; writing, 44
"The System," 161–163
3%, 14, 68, 84–90, 139
Tibiriçá, Eduardo, 44
TIC (Information and Communication Technologies) Report 2018, 70
Time Warner, 40
Toda forma de amor, 61
Totoro, Gabriel, 103–106, 131
The Trespasser, 148
Tribunal de Contas (TCU), 163
triple-play packages, 33
Tropa de Elite, 61, 150
Tropicália movement, 62
True Detective, 153
Turner, Graeme, 6
TVA (Special Service Subscription Television), 23, 25
TV Excelsior, 7
TV Globo: advertising revenue, 9–10; challenges to dominance of, 12–13; changing influence of post-Network Era, 17; contrasted with Netflix, 87–88; contrasted with pay-television, 95–96; contrasted with Porta dos Fundos, 110–112; decline in audience share, 91–93, 95–96; dominance of, 4–5, 9, 11, 75, 95–96; link to military dictatorship, 7; and political coverage, 1, 2; political influence of, 3–4; and racism, 117–120; series, 7–8, 42–43; series contrasted with *telenovelas*, 8–9, *9*; telenovelas, 7–10, 78–79, 94

TV Manchete, 23
TV por Assinatura, 27
TV por assinatura: 20 anos de evolução, 22
TV Tupi, 6, 7, 23
2 Sons of Francisco, 51, 149
Two Brothers, 155

Uemura, Daniel, 88
Um céu de estrelas, 149
1 contra todos, 50–57, 62
1 quarto, 68, 79–80, 83
Unidade de Inteligência Digital, 143
Union of Pay-Television Companies (SETA), 27
United States: comparison of audiences, 94–95; *CSI: Miami, CSI: NY*, 103; and end of mass audience era, 96; Hollywood influence in Brazil, 110–111; model for TV Globo, 7

Van Veen, Ricky, 98
Variety, 141
Veja, 1
Viacom, 110

videocassette recorders, 93
Vieira, A. G., 141–142
Vieira, João, Jr., 58
Viladarga, Vicente, 155
Viral, 106
Vogue, Edson, 59
Volpatto, Elisa, 156

Walking Dead, 153
Wallach, Joe, 24
Watching Race: Television and the Struggle for "Blackness," 128
Webédia, 66
web series and telenovelas, 78–79
We Now Disrupt This Broadcast, 96
Werner e os mortos, 61
whiteness in Brazil, 113, 119
Wierson, Arick, 4
Woman of Phases, 49
Workers' Party (PT), 1–3
writer's room model, 149–150

The Year My Parents Went on Vacation, 150
YouTube, 66–69, 80, 82, 85–86, 110

ELI LEE CARTER is associate professor of Brazilian literature, film, and television at the University of Virginia. He is the author of *Reimagining Brazilian Television: Luiz Fernando Carvalho's Contemporary Vision*.

REFRAMING MEDIA, TECHNOLOGY, AND CULTURE IN LATIN/O AMERICA

Edited by Héctor Fernández L'Hoeste and Juan Carlos Rodríguez

Reframing Media, Technology, and Culture in Latin/o America explores how Latin American and Latino audiovisual (film, television, digital), musical (radio, recordings, live performances, dancing), and graphic (comics, photography, advertising) cultural practices reframe and reconfigure social, economic, and political discourses at a local, national, and global level. In addition, it looks at how information networks reshape public and private policies, and the enactment of new identities in civil society. The series also covers how different technologies have allowed and continue to allow for the construction of new ethnic spaces. It not only contemplates the interaction between new and old technologies but also how the development of brand-new technologies redefines cultural production.

Telling Migrant Stories: Latin American Diaspora in Documentary Film, edited by Esteban E. Loustaunau and Lauren E. Shaw (2018; paperback edition, 2021)

Mestizo Modernity: Race, Technology, and the Body in Postrevolutionary Mexico, by David S. Dalton (2018; first paperback edition, 2021)

The Insubordination of Photography: Documentary Practices under Chile's Dictatorship, by Ángeles Donoso Macaya (2020; first paperback edition, 2023)

Digital Humanities in Latin America, edited by Héctor Fernández L'Hoeste and Juan Carlos Rodríguez (2020; first paperback edition, 2023)

Pablo Escobar and Colombian Narcoculture, by Aldona Bialowas Pobutsky (2020; first paperback edition, 2025)

The New Brazilian Mediascape: Television Production in the Digital Streaming Age, by Eli Lee Carter (2020; first paperback edition, 2025)

Univision, Telemundo, and the Rise of Spanish-Language Television in the United States, by Craig Allen (2020; first paperback edition, 2023)

Cuba's Digital Revolution: Citizen Innovation and State Policy, edited by Ted A. Henken and Sara Garcia Santamaria (2021; first paperback edition, 2022)

Afro-Latinx Digital Connections, edited by Eduard Arriaga and Andrés Villar (2021)

The Lost Cinema of Mexico: From Lucha Libre to Cine Familiar and Other Churros, edited by Olivia Cosentino and Brian Price (2022)

Neo-Authoritarian Masculinity in Brazilian Crime Film, by Jeremy Lehnen (2022)

The Rise of Central American Film in the Twenty-First Century, edited by Mauricio Espinoza and Jared List (2023)

Internet, Humor, and Nation in Latin America, edited by Héctor Fernández L'Hoeste and Juan Poblete (2024)

Tropical Time Machines: Science Fiction in the Contemporary Hispanic Caribbean, by Emily A. Maguire (2024)

Digital Satire in Latin America: Online Video Humor as Hybrid Alternative Media, by Paul Alonso (2024)
Periodicals in Latin America: Interdisciplinary Approaches to Serialized Print Culture, edited by Maria Chiara D'Argenio and Claire Lindsay (2025)

www.ingramcontent.com/pod-product-compliance
Lightning Source LLC
Chambersburg PA
CBHW031813220426
43662CB00007B/620